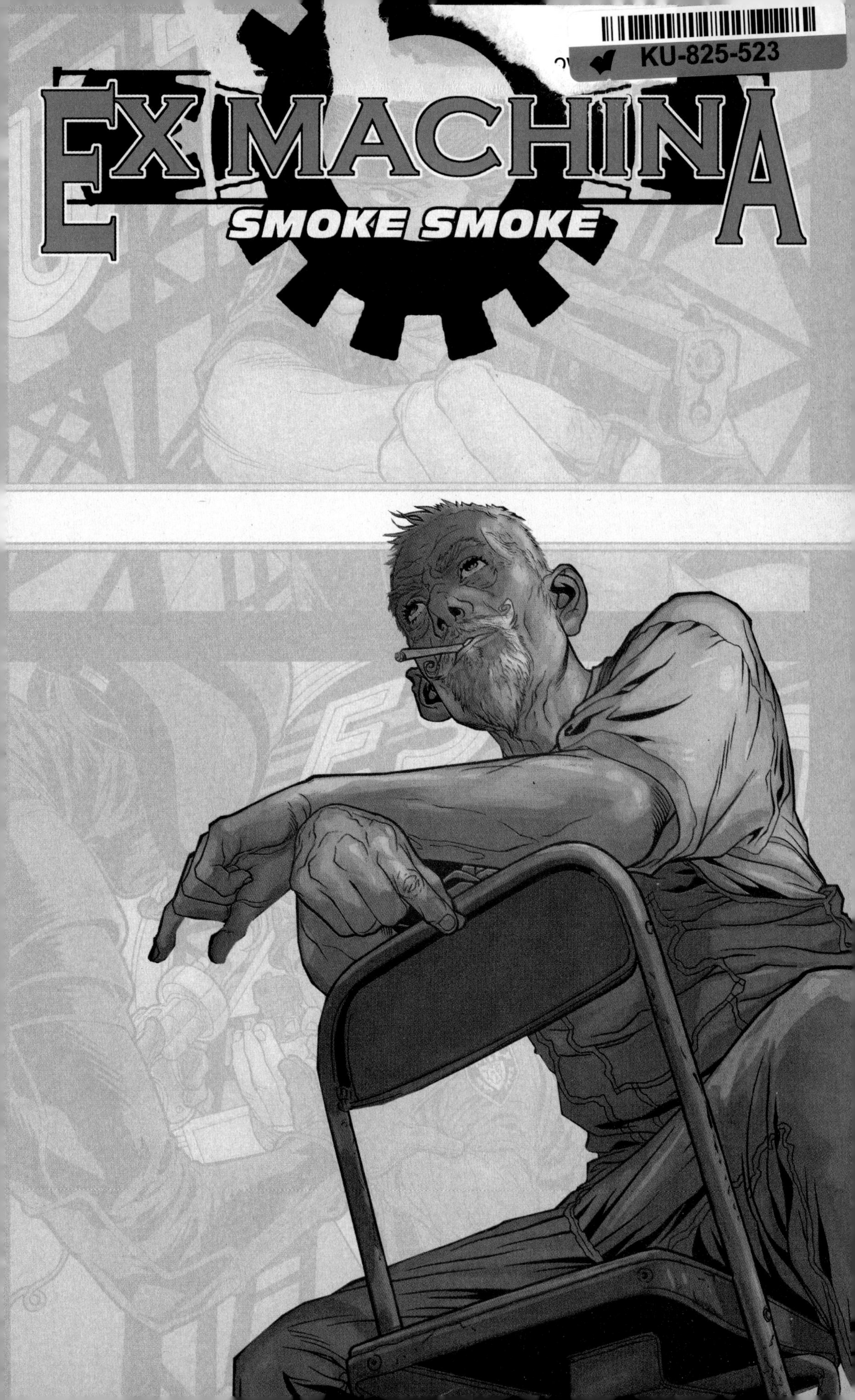
EX MACHINA
SMOKE SMOKE

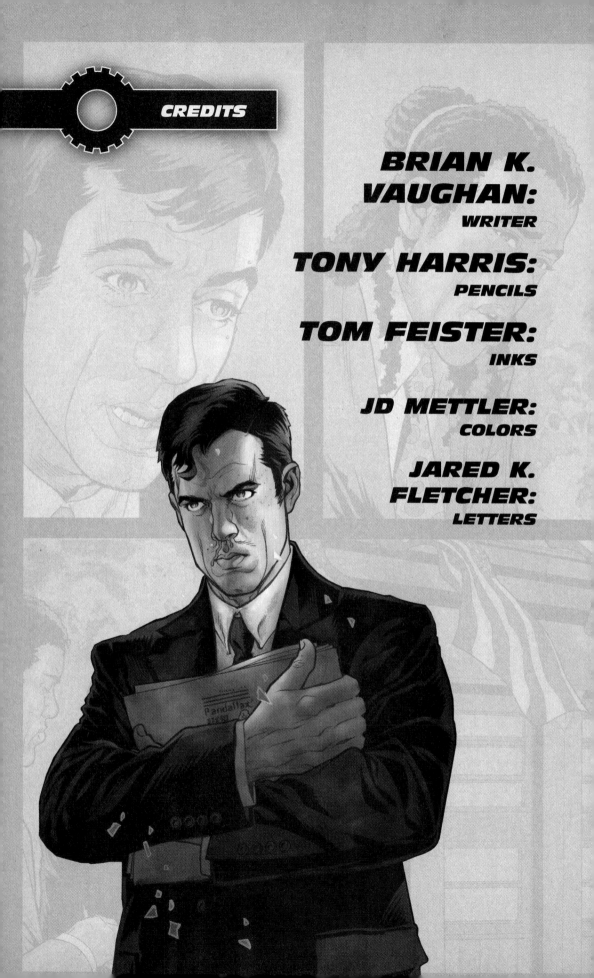

CREDITS

BRIAN K. VAUGHAN:
WRITER

TONY HARRIS:
PENCILS

TOM FEISTER:
INKS

JD METTLER:
COLORS

JARED K. FLETCHER:
LETTERS

EX MACHINA: SMOKE SMOKE. Published by
WildStorm Productions, an imprint of DC Comics.
888 Prospect St. #240, La Jolla, CA 92037. Cover,
compilation copyright © 2007 Brian K. Vaughan
and Tony Harris. All Rights Reserved.
EX MACHINA is ™ Brian K. Vaughan and Tony
Harris. Originally published in single magazine
form as EX MACHINA #21-25 © 2006, 2007
Brian K. Vaughan and Tony Harris.

Chapter 1

Smoke Smoke

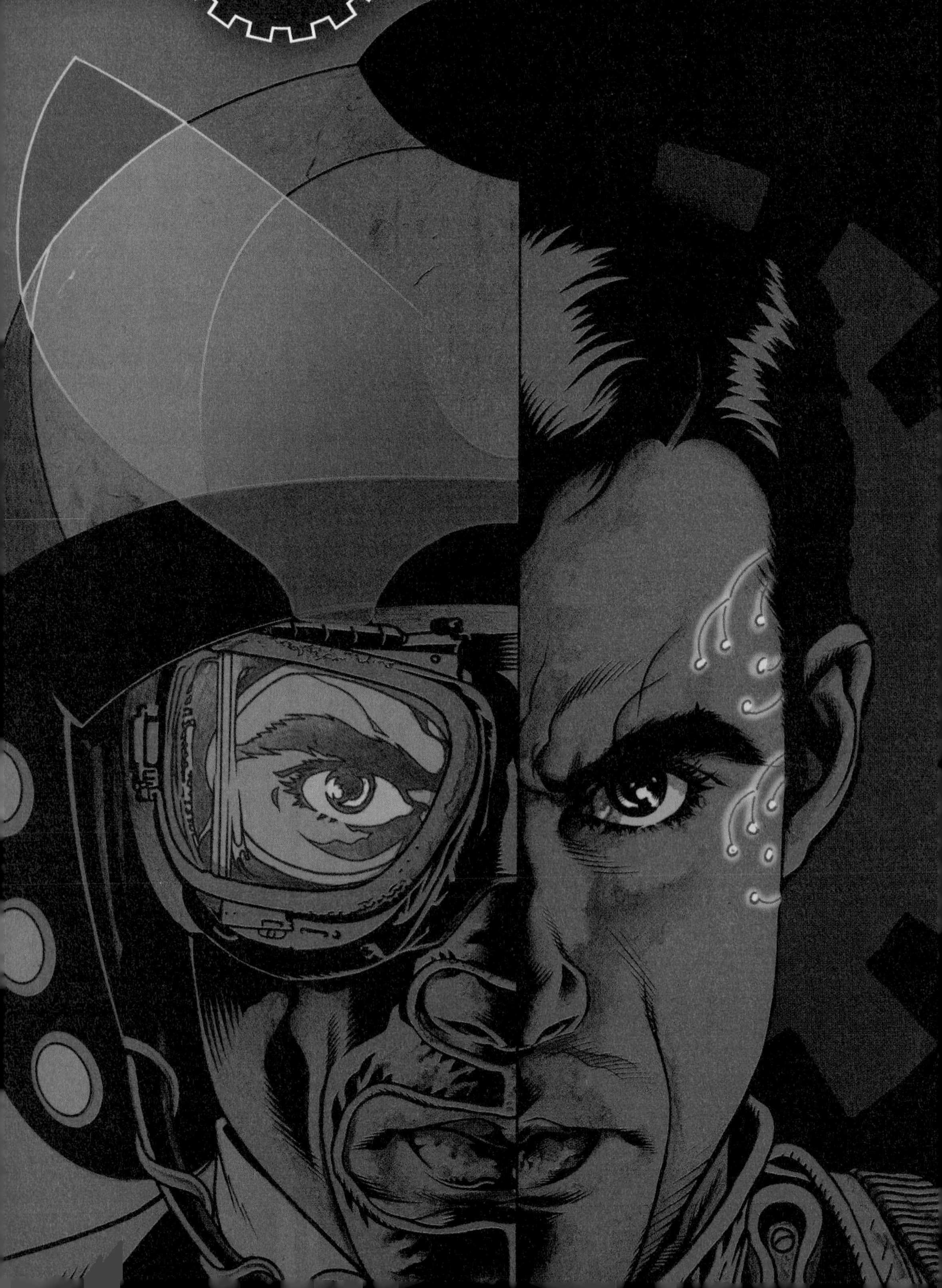

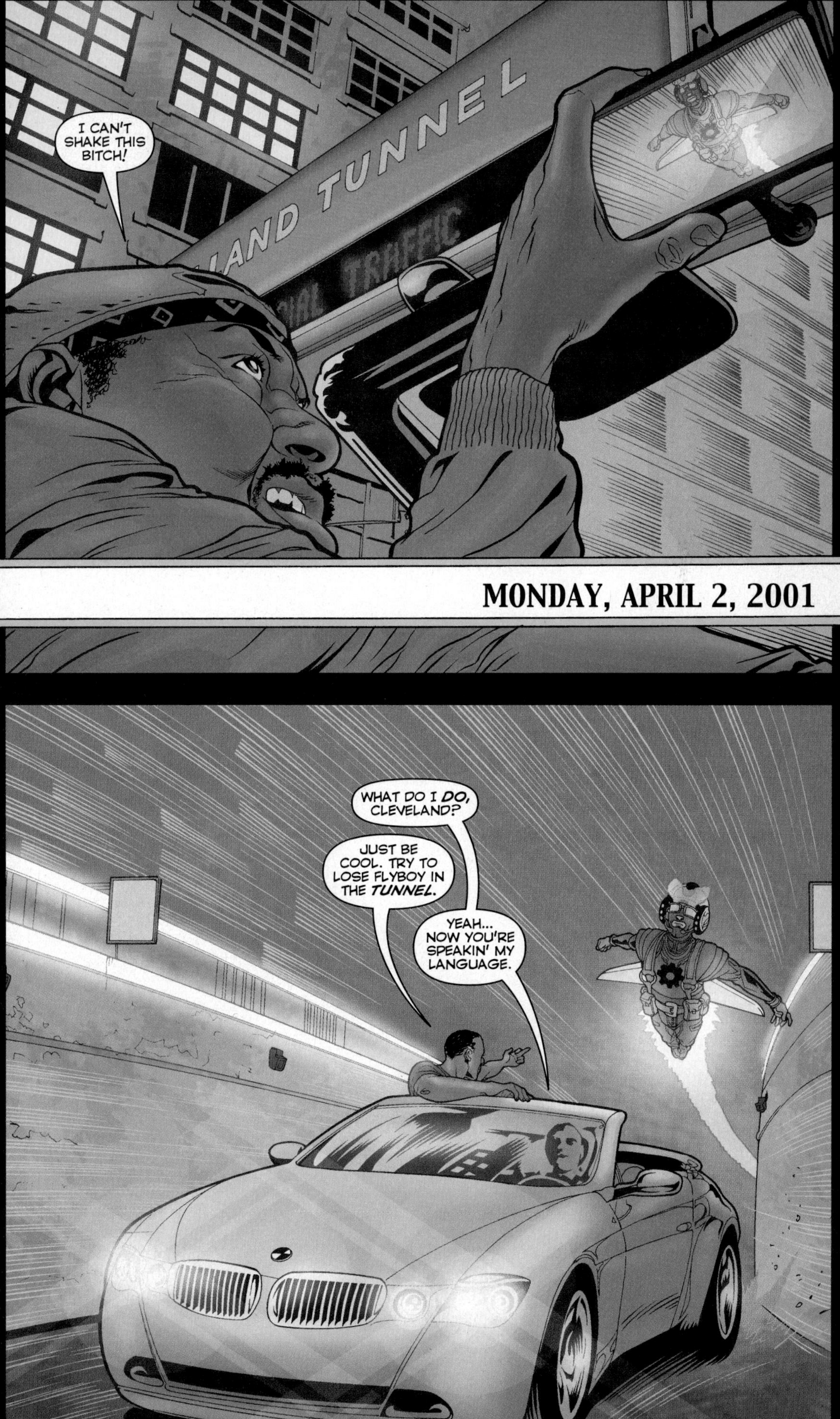
I CAN'T SHAKE THIS BITCH!
LAND TUNNEL
MONDAY, APRIL 2, 2001
WHAT DO I *DO*, CLEVELAND?
JUST BE COOL. TRY TO LOSE FLYBOY IN THE *TUNNEL*.
YEAH... NOW YOU'RE SPEAKIN' MY LANGUAGE.

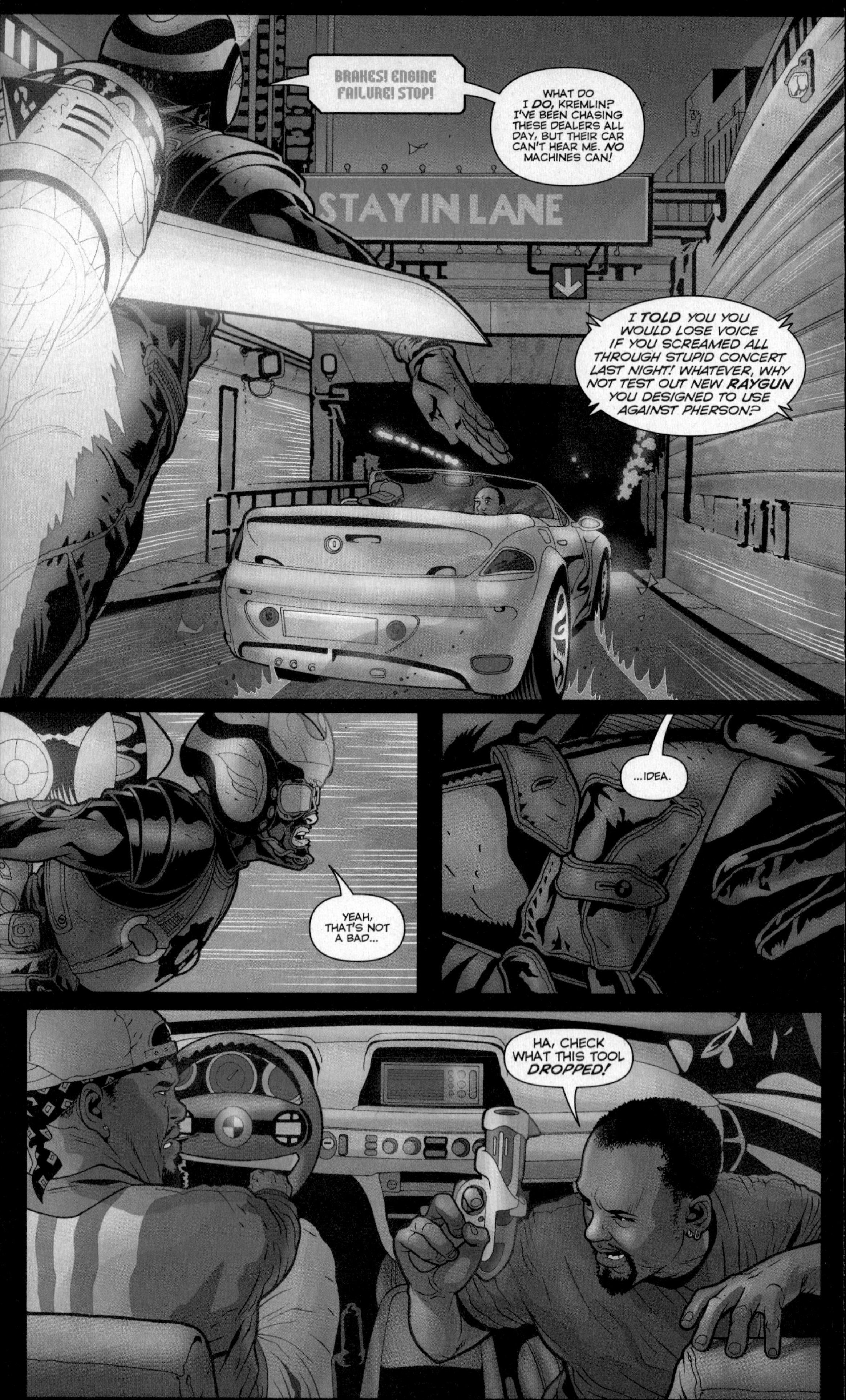
BRAKES! ENGINE FAILURE! STOP!
WHAT DO I *DO*, KREMLIN? I'VE BEEN CHASING THESE DEALERS ALL DAY, BUT THEIR CAR CAN'T HEAR ME. *NO* MACHINES CAN!
STAY IN LANE
I *TOLD* YOU YOU WOULD LOSE VOICE IF YOU SCREAMED ALL THROUGH STUPID CONCERT LAST NIGHT! WHATEVER, WHY NOT TEST OUT NEW *RAYGUN* YOU DESIGNED TO USE AGAINST PHERSON?
YEAH, THAT'S NOT A BAD...
...IDEA.
HA, CHECK WHAT THIS TOOL *DROPPED!*

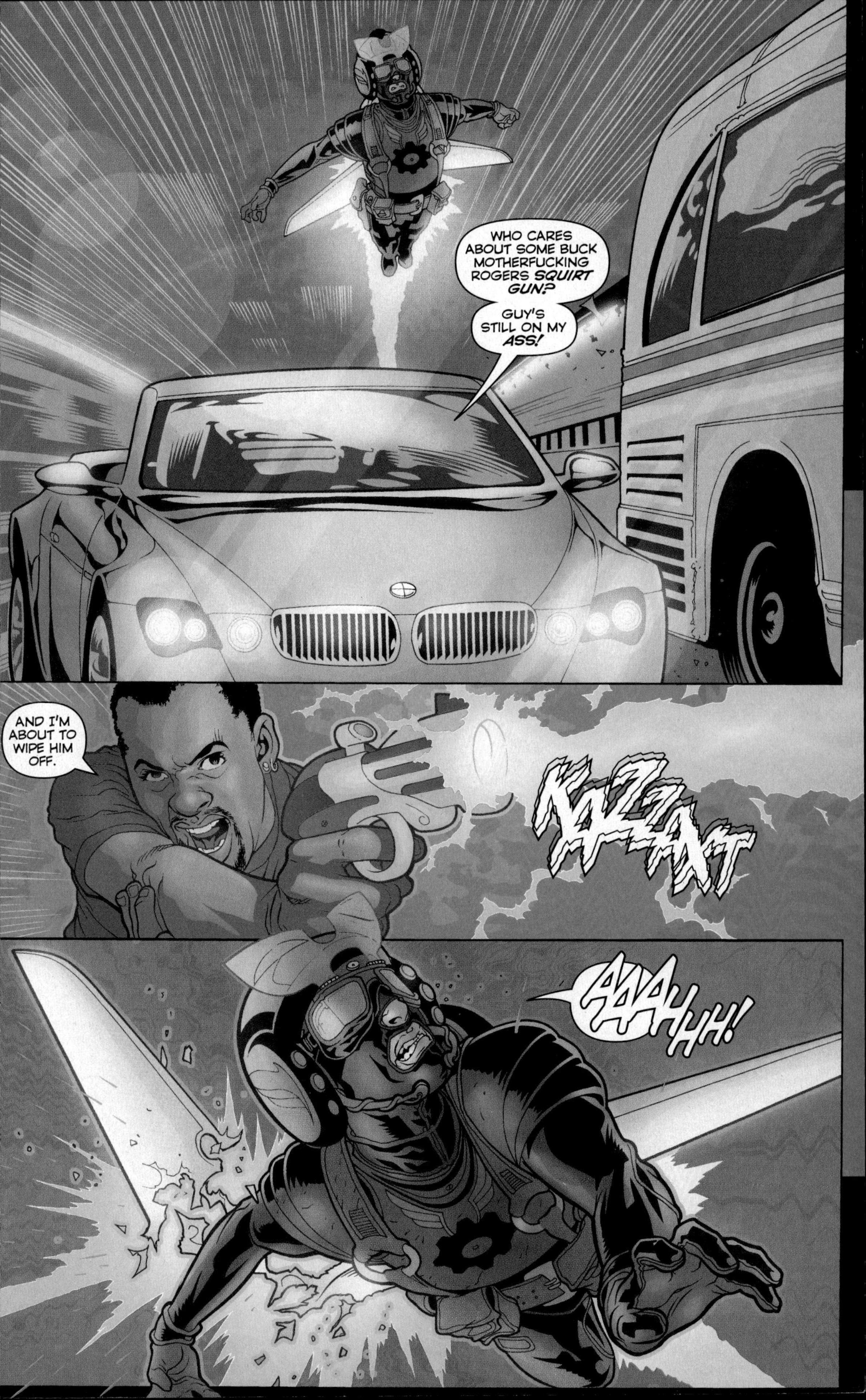
WHO CARES ABOUT SOME BUCK MOTHERFUCKING ROGERS *SQUIRT GUN?*
GUY'S STILL ON MY *ASS!*
AND I'M ABOUT TO WIPE HIM OFF.
KAZZAT
AAAAHHH!

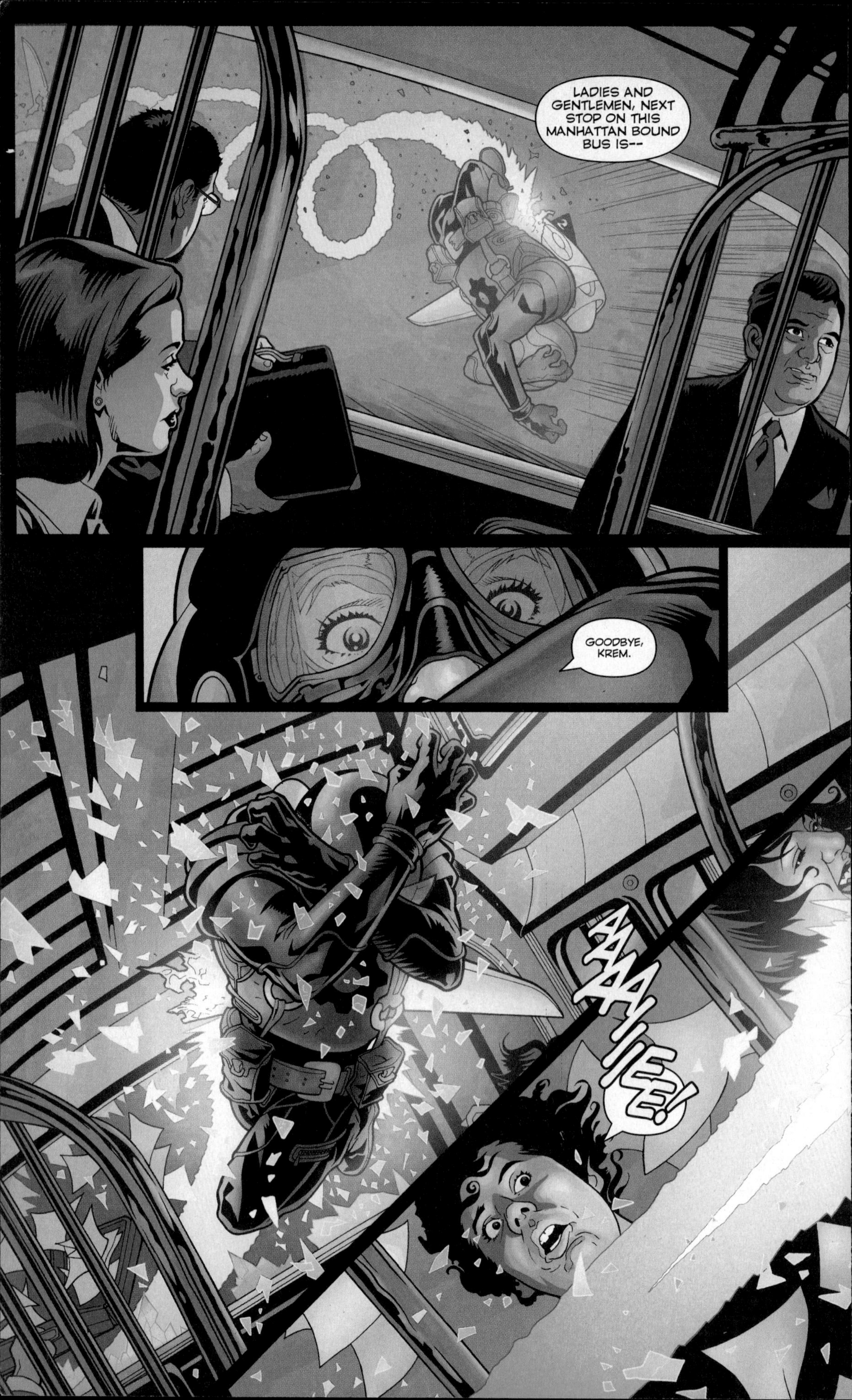
LADIES AND GENTLEMEN, NEXT STOP ON THIS MANHATTAN BOUND BUS IS--
GOODBYE, KREM.
AAAAAIIEE!

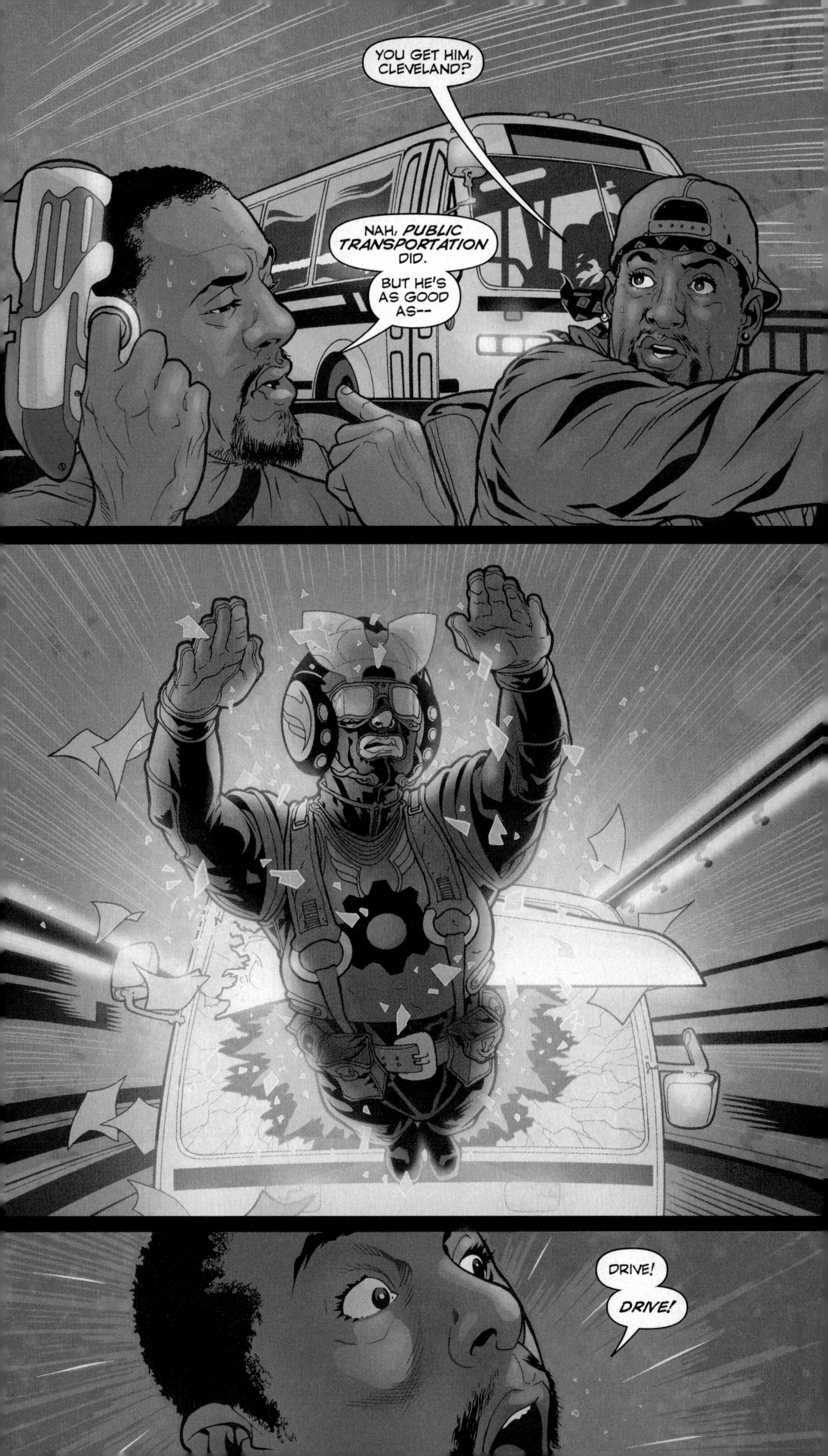
YOU GET HIM, CLEVELAND?
NAH, *PUBLIC TRANSPORTATION* DID.
BUT HE'S AS GOOD AS--
DRIVE!
DRIVE!

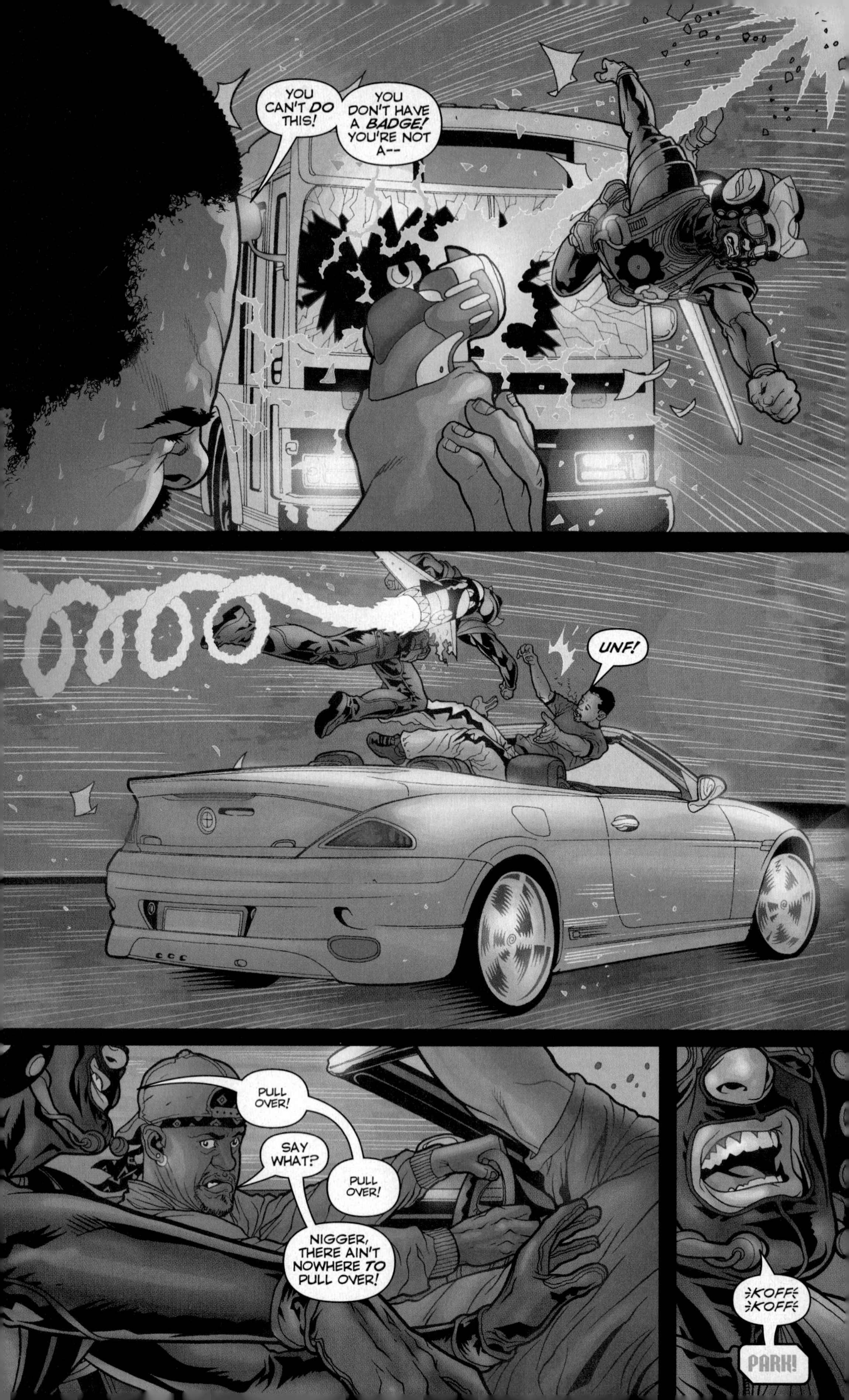
YOU CAN'T *DO* THIS!
YOU DON'T HAVE A *BADGE!* YOU'RE NOT A--
UNF!
PULL OVER!
SAY WHAT?
PULL OVER!
NIGGER, THERE AIN'T NOWHERE *TO* PULL OVER!
KOFF KOFF
PARK!

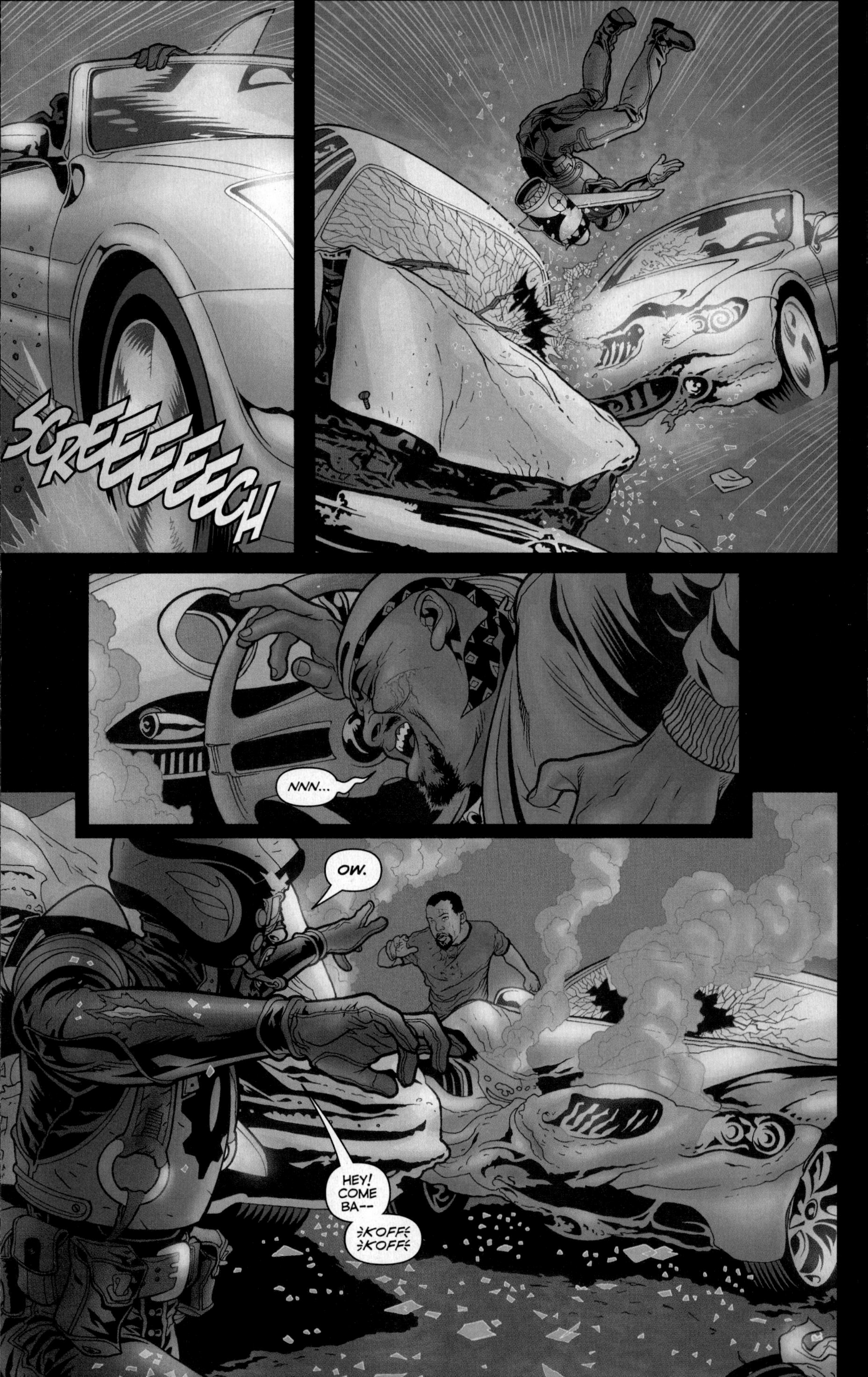
SCREEEEEEECH
NNN...
OW.
HEY! COME BA--
KOFF KOFF

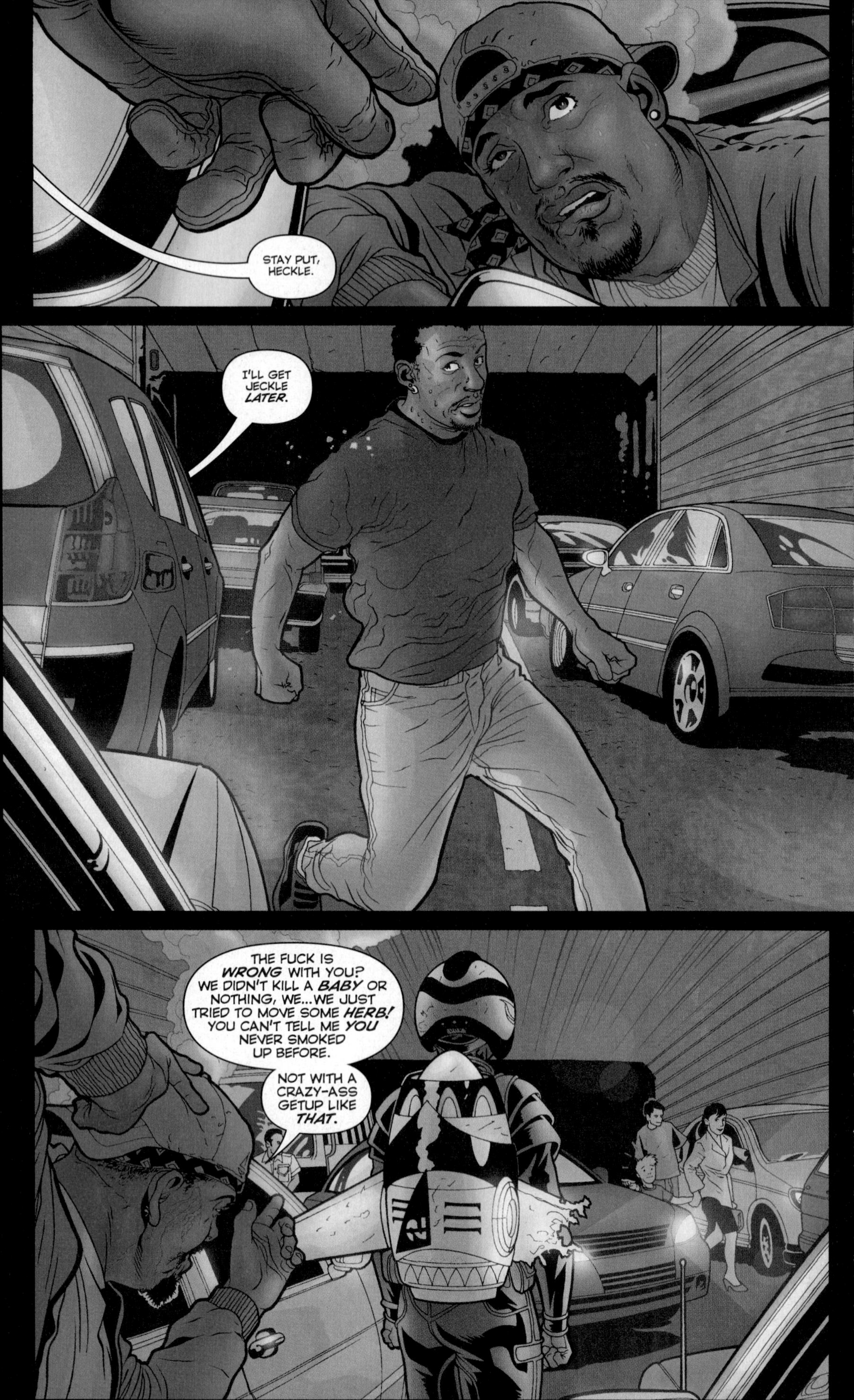
STAY PUT, HECKLE.
I'LL GET JECKLE LATER.
THE FUCK IS WRONG WITH YOU? WE DIDN'T KILL A BABY OR NOTHING, WE...WE JUST TRIED TO MOVE SOME HERB! YOU CAN'T TELL ME YOU NEVER SMOKED UP BEFORE.
NOT WITH A CRAZY-ASS GETUP LIKE THAT.

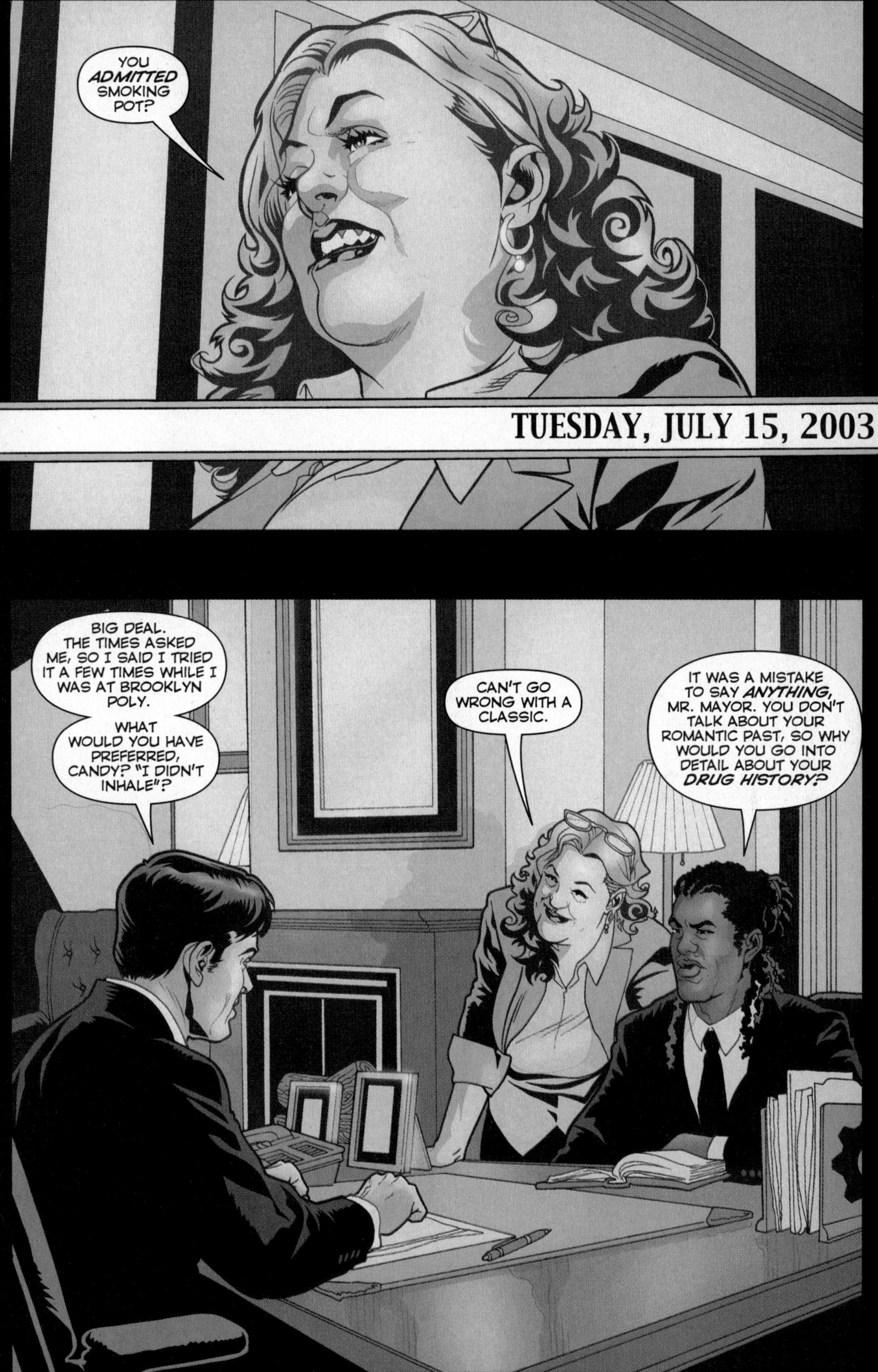
YOU ADMITTED SMOKING POT?
TUESDAY, JULY 15, 2003
BIG DEAL. THE TIMES ASKED ME, SO I SAID I TRIED IT A FEW TIMES WHILE I WAS AT BROOKLYN POLY.
WHAT WOULD YOU HAVE PREFERRED, CANDY? "I DIDN'T INHALE"?
CAN'T GO WRONG WITH A CLASSIC.
IT WAS A MISTAKE TO SAY ANYTHING, MR. MAYOR. YOU DON'T TALK ABOUT YOUR ROMANTIC PAST, SO WHY WOULD YOU GO INTO DETAIL ABOUT YOUR DRUG HISTORY?

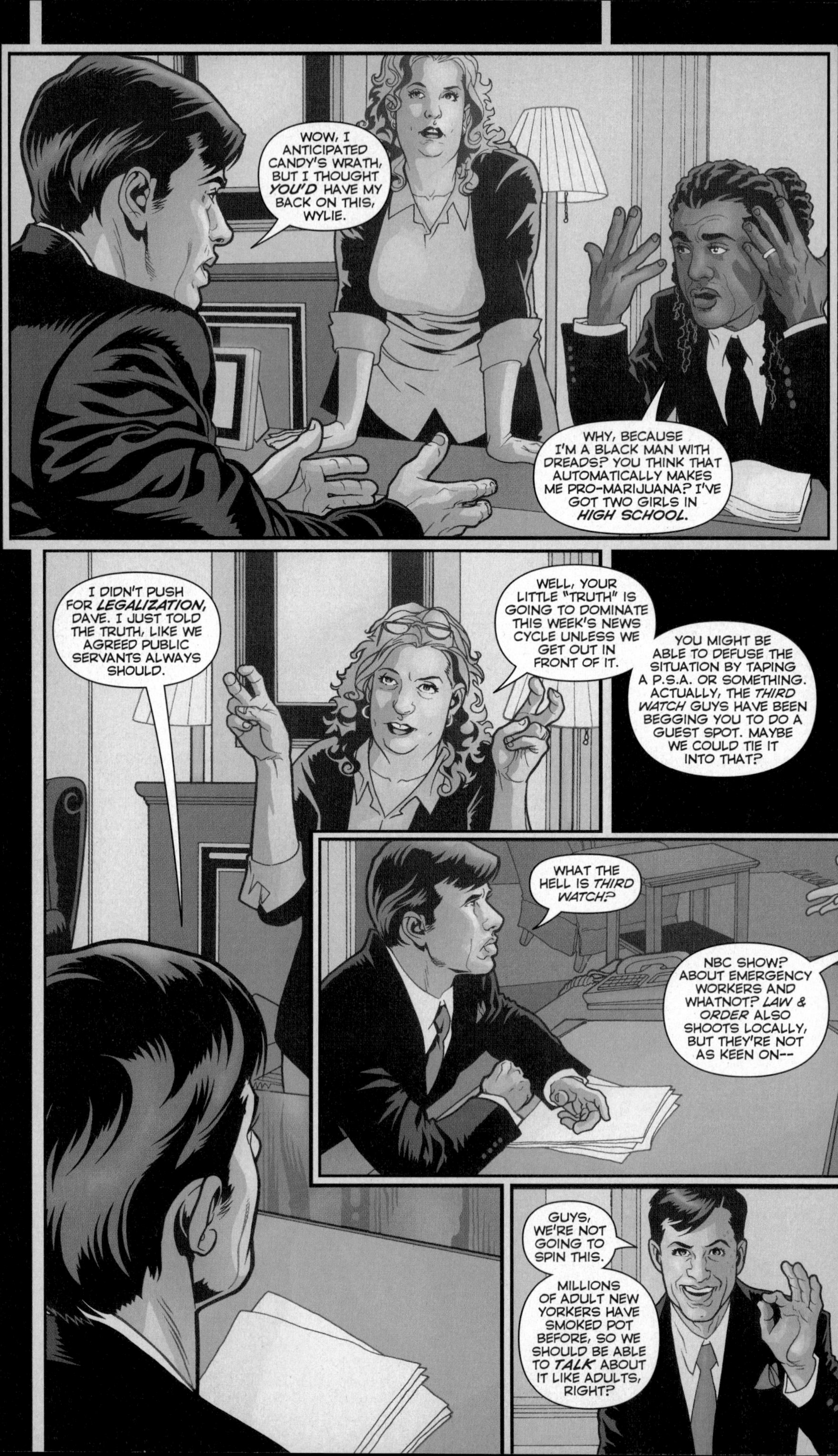
WOW, I ANTICIPATED CANDY'S WRATH, BUT I THOUGHT *YOU'D* HAVE MY BACK ON THIS, WYLIE.
WHY, BECAUSE I'M A BLACK MAN WITH DREADS? YOU THINK THAT AUTOMATICALLY MAKES ME PRO-MARIJUANA? I'VE GOT TWO GIRLS IN ***HIGH SCHOOL.***
I DIDN'T PUSH FOR ***LEGALIZATION,*** DAVE. I JUST TOLD THE TRUTH, LIKE WE AGREED PUBLIC SERVANTS ALWAYS SHOULD.
WELL, YOUR LITTLE "TRUTH" IS GOING TO DOMINATE THIS WEEK'S NEWS CYCLE UNLESS WE GET OUT IN FRONT OF IT.
YOU MIGHT BE ABLE TO DEFUSE THE SITUATION BY TAPING A P.S.A. OR SOMETHING. ACTUALLY, THE *THIRD WATCH* GUYS HAVE BEEN BEGGING YOU TO DO A GUEST SPOT. MAYBE WE COULD TIE IT INTO THAT?
WHAT THE HELL IS *THIRD WATCH?*
NBC SHOW? ABOUT EMERGENCY WORKERS AND WHATNOT? *LAW & ORDER* ALSO SHOOTS LOCALLY, BUT THEY'RE NOT AS KEEN ON--
GUYS, WE'RE NOT GOING TO SPIN THIS.
MILLIONS OF ADULT NEW YORKERS HAVE SMOKED POT BEFORE, SO WE SHOULD BE ABLE TO *TALK* ABOUT IT LIKE ADULTS, RIGHT?

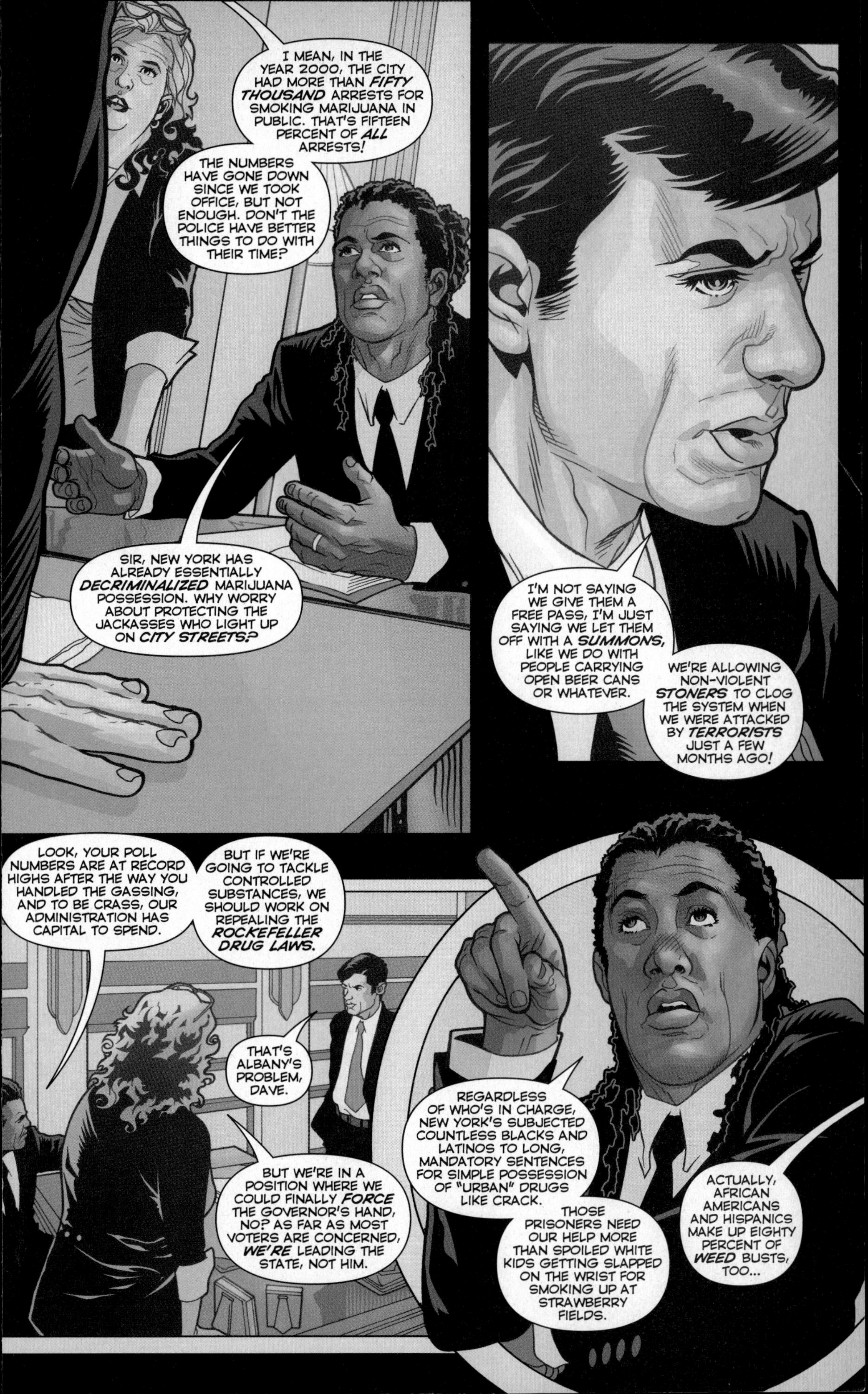
I MEAN, IN THE YEAR 2000, THE CITY HAD MORE THAN FIFTY THOUSAND ARRESTS FOR SMOKING MARIJUANA IN PUBLIC. THAT'S FIFTEEN PERCENT OF ALL ARRESTS!
THE NUMBERS HAVE GONE DOWN SINCE WE TOOK OFFICE, BUT NOT ENOUGH. DON'T THE POLICE HAVE BETTER THINGS TO DO WITH THEIR TIME?
SIR, NEW YORK HAS ALREADY ESSENTIALLY DECRIMINALIZED MARIJUANA POSSESSION. WHY WORRY ABOUT PROTECTING THE JACKASSES WHO LIGHT UP ON CITY STREETS?
I'M NOT SAYING WE GIVE THEM A FREE PASS, I'M JUST SAYING WE LET THEM OFF WITH A SUMMONS, LIKE WE DO WITH PEOPLE CARRYING OPEN BEER CANS OR WHATEVER.
WE'RE ALLOWING NON-VIOLENT STONERS TO CLOG THE SYSTEM WHEN WE WERE ATTACKED BY TERRORISTS JUST A FEW MONTHS AGO!
LOOK, YOUR POLL NUMBERS ARE AT RECORD HIGHS AFTER THE WAY YOU HANDLED THE GASSING, AND TO BE CRASS, OUR ADMINISTRATION HAS CAPITAL TO SPEND.
BUT IF WE'RE GOING TO TACKLE CONTROLLED SUBSTANCES, WE SHOULD WORK ON REPEALING THE ROCKEFELLER DRUG LAWS.
THAT'S ALBANY'S PROBLEM, DAVE.
BUT WE'RE IN A POSITION WHERE WE COULD FINALLY FORCE THE GOVERNOR'S HAND, NO? AS FAR AS MOST VOTERS ARE CONCERNED, WE'RE LEADING THE STATE, NOT HIM.
REGARDLESS OF WHO'S IN CHARGE, NEW YORK'S SUBJECTED COUNTLESS BLACKS AND LATINOS TO LONG, MANDATORY SENTENCES FOR SIMPLE POSSESSION OF "URBAN" DRUGS LIKE CRACK.
THOSE PRISONERS NEED OUR HELP MORE THAN SPOILED WHITE KIDS GETTING SLAPPED ON THE WRIST FOR SMOKING UP AT STRAWBERRY FIELDS.
ACTUALLY, AFRICAN AMERICANS AND HISPANICS MAKE UP EIGHTY PERCENT OF WEED BUSTS, TOO...

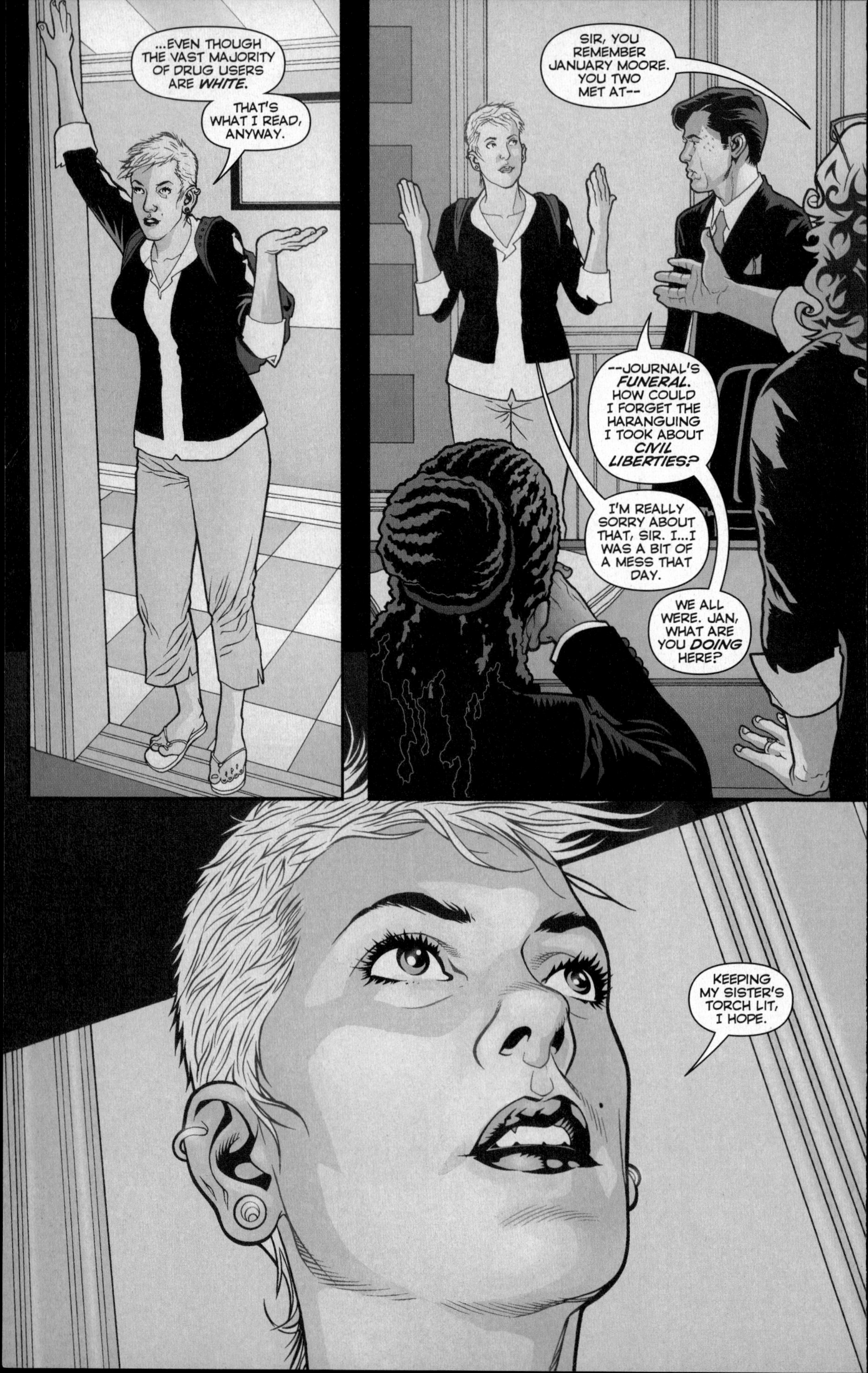
...EVEN THOUGH THE VAST MAJORITY OF DRUG USERS ARE *WHITE*.
THAT'S WHAT I READ, ANYWAY.
SIR, YOU REMEMBER JANUARY MOORE. YOU TWO MET AT--
--JOURNAL'S *FUNERAL*. HOW COULD I FORGET THE HARANGUING I TOOK ABOUT *CIVIL LIBERTIES?*
I'M REALLY SORRY ABOUT THAT, SIR. I...I WAS A BIT OF A MESS THAT DAY.
WE ALL WERE. JAN, WHAT ARE YOU *DOING* HERE?
KEEPING MY SISTER'S TORCH LIT, I HOPE.

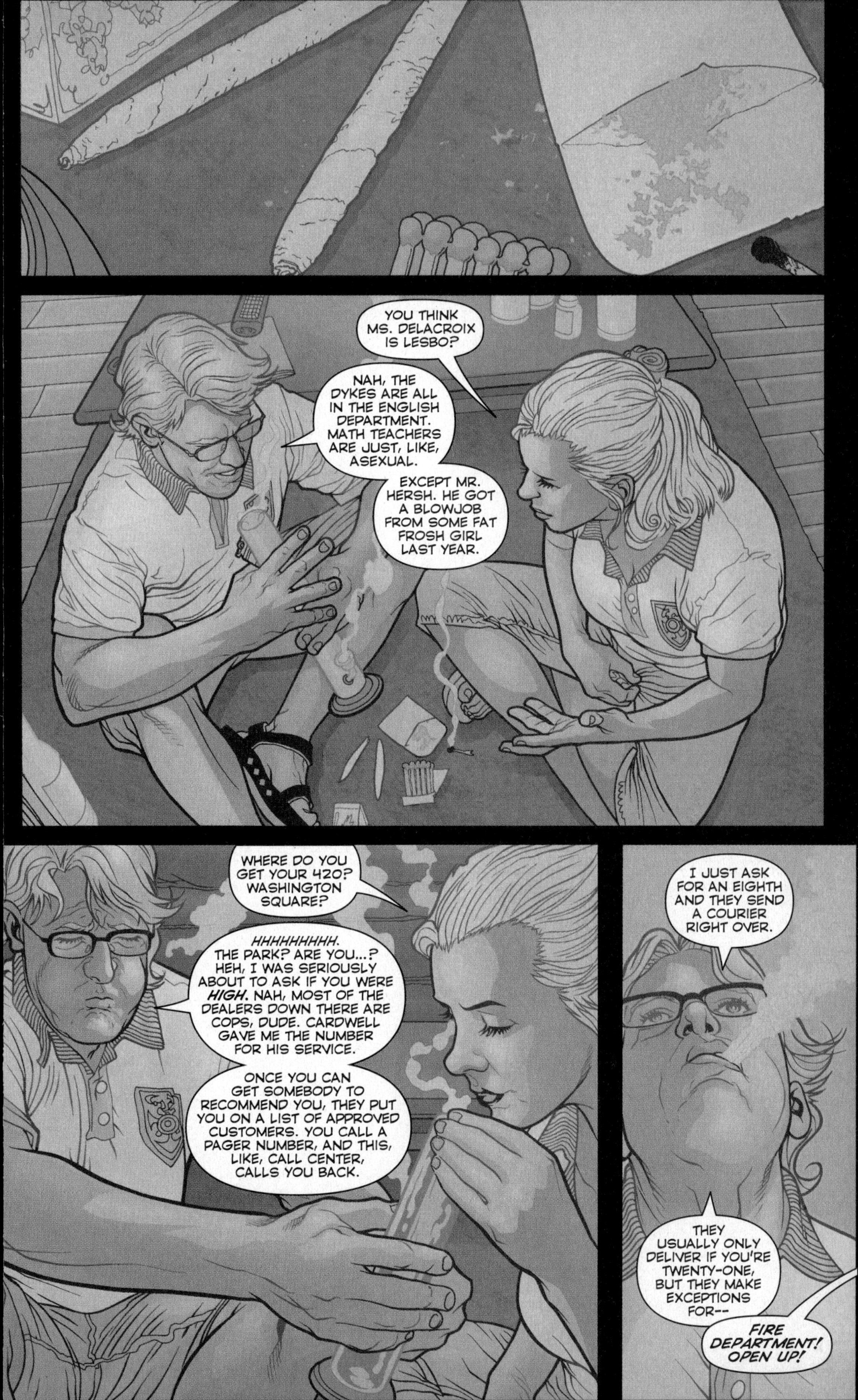
YOU THINK MS. DELACROIX IS LESBO?
NAH, THE DYKES ARE ALL IN THE ENGLISH DEPARTMENT. MATH TEACHERS ARE JUST, LIKE, ASEXUAL.
EXCEPT MR. HERSH. HE GOT A BLOWJOB FROM SOME FAT FROSH GIRL LAST YEAR.
WHERE DO YOU GET YOUR 420? WASHINGTON SQUARE?
HHHHHHHHH. THE PARK? ARE YOU...? HEH, I WAS SERIOUSLY ABOUT TO ASK IF YOU WERE ***HIGH***. NAH, MOST OF THE DEALERS DOWN THERE ARE COPS, DUDE. CARDWELL GAVE ME THE NUMBER FOR HIS SERVICE.
ONCE YOU CAN GET SOMEBODY TO RECOMMEND YOU, THEY PUT YOU ON A LIST OF APPROVED CUSTOMERS. YOU CALL A PAGER NUMBER, AND THIS, LIKE, CALL CENTER, CALLS YOU BACK.
I JUST ASK FOR AN EIGHTH AND THEY SEND A COURIER RIGHT OVER.
THEY USUALLY ONLY DELIVER IF YOU'RE TWENTY-ONE, BUT THEY MAKE EXCEPTIONS FOR--
FIRE DEPARTMENT! OPEN UP!

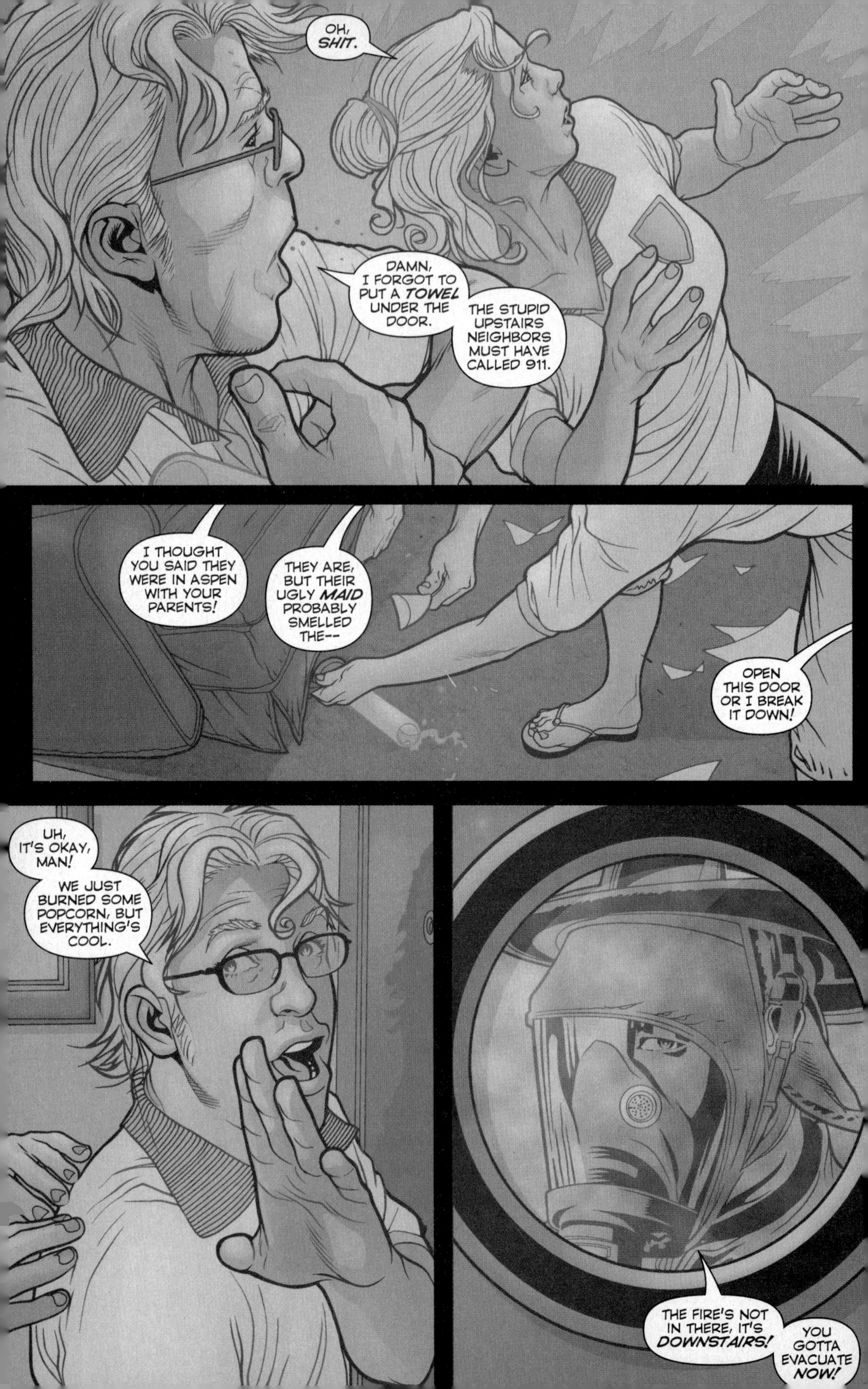
OH, SHIT.
DAMN, I FORGOT TO PUT A TOWEL UNDER THE DOOR.
THE STUPID UPSTAIRS NEIGHBORS MUST HAVE CALLED 911.
I THOUGHT YOU SAID THEY WERE IN ASPEN WITH YOUR PARENTS!
THEY ARE, BUT THEIR UGLY MAID PROBABLY SMELLED THE--
OPEN THIS DOOR OR I BREAK IT DOWN!
UH, IT'S OKAY, MAN!
WE JUST BURNED SOME POPCORN, BUT EVERYTHING'S COOL.
THE FIRE'S NOT IN THERE, IT'S DOWNSTAIRS!
YOU GOTTA EVACUATE NOW!

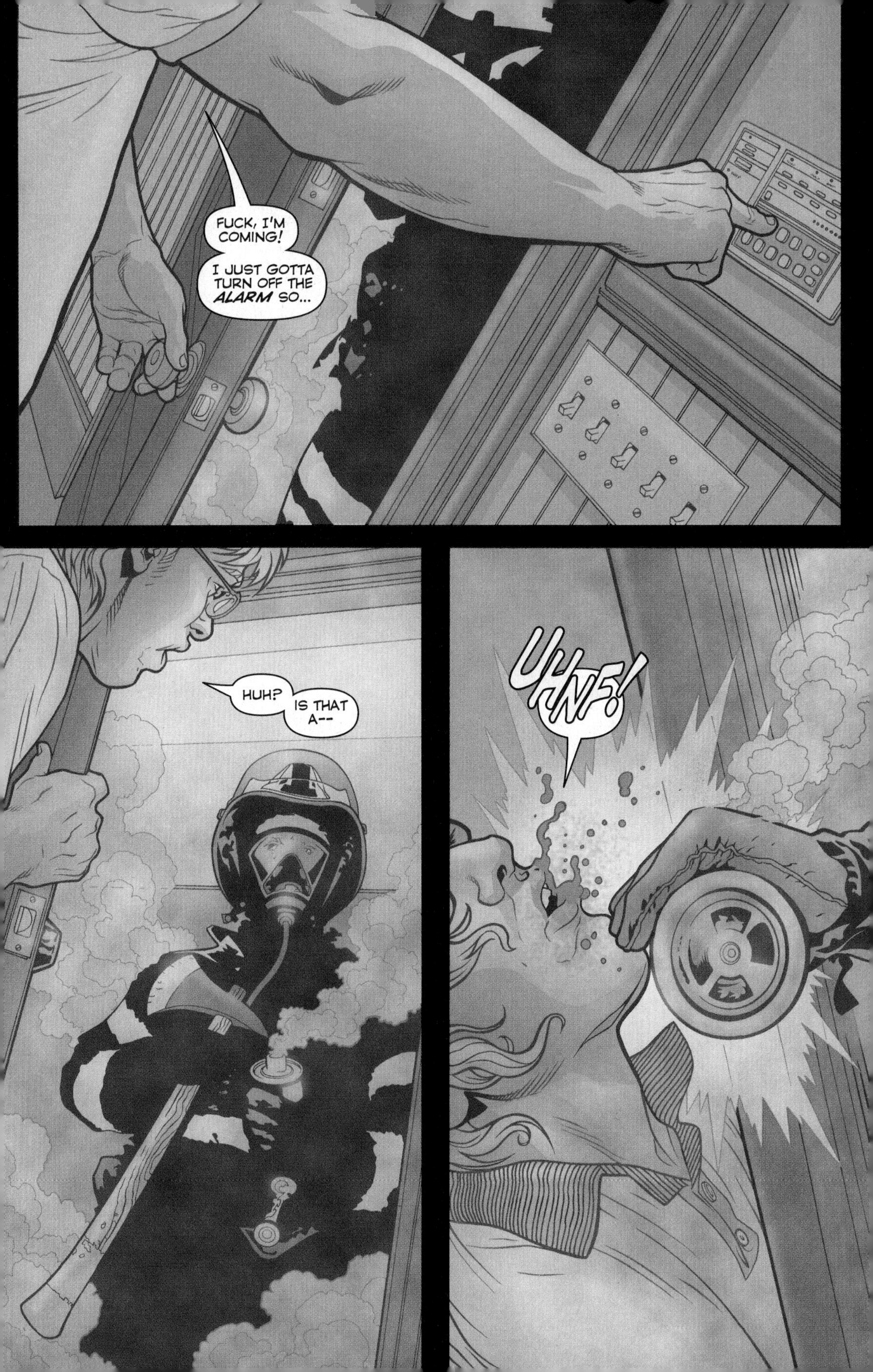
FUCK, I'M COMING!
I JUST GOTTA TURN OFF THE ALARM SO...
HUH?
IS THAT A--
UHNF!

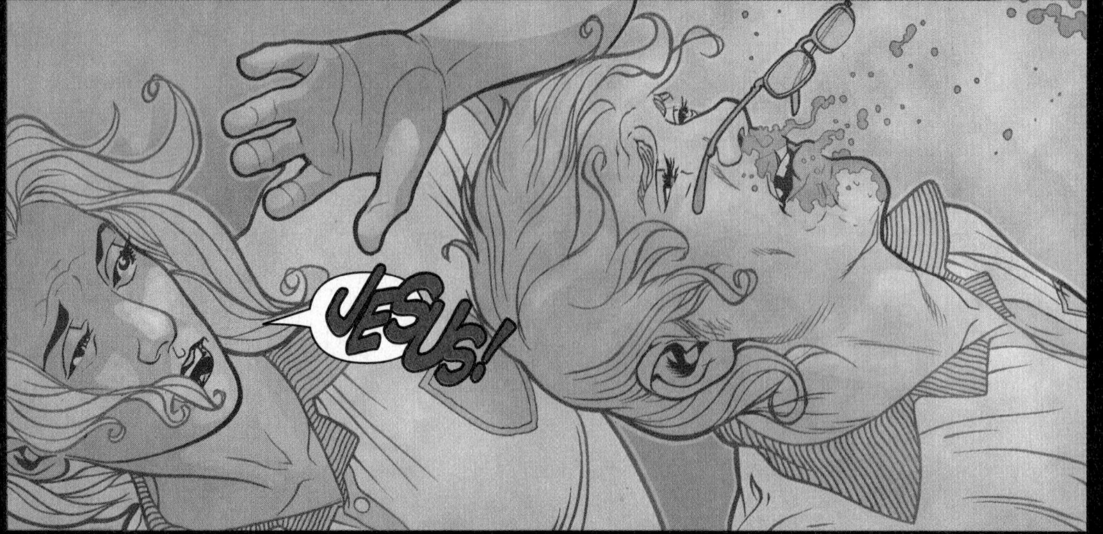
JESUS!

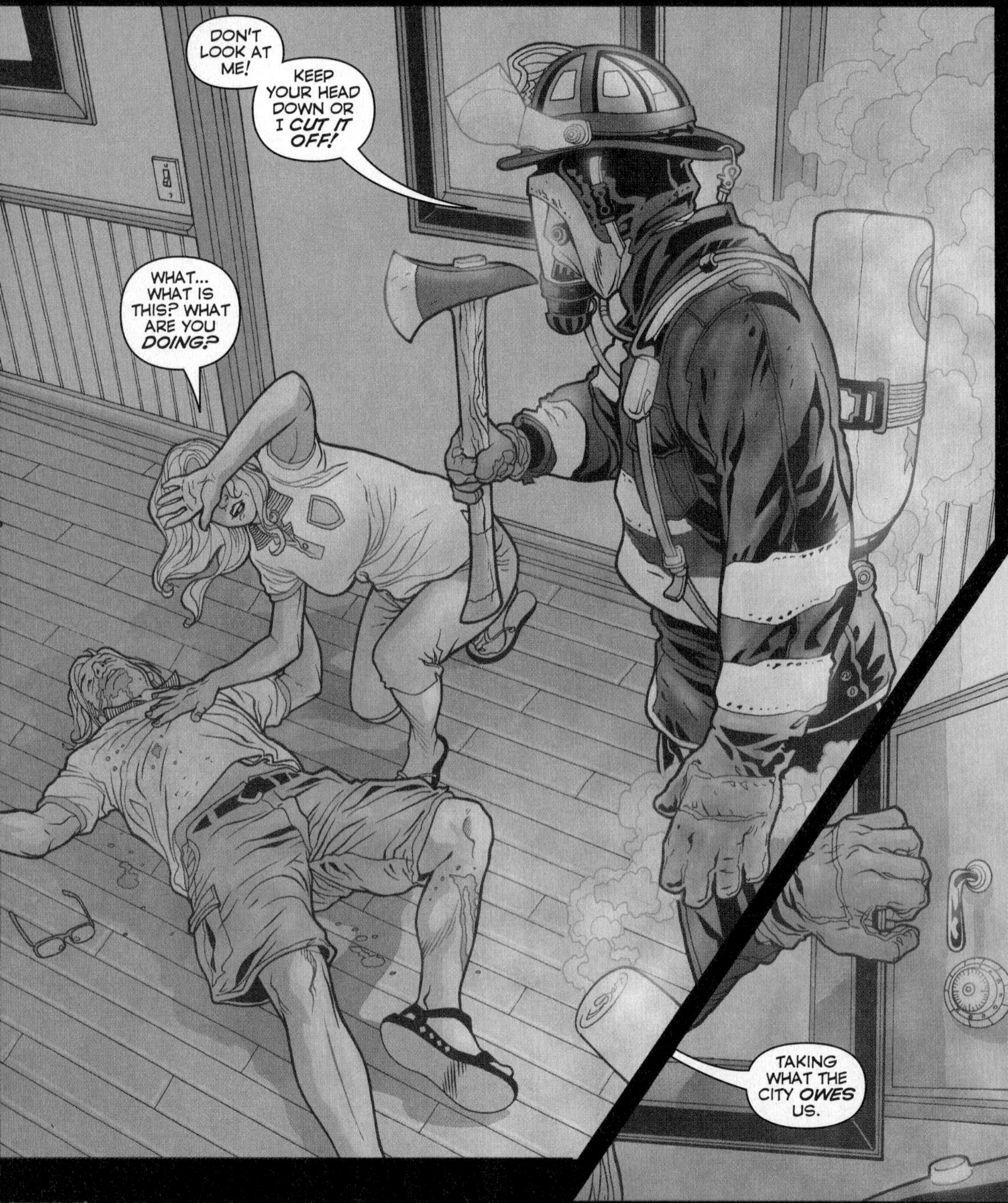
DON'T LOOK AT ME!
KEEP YOUR HEAD DOWN OR I *CUT IT OFF!*
WHAT... WHAT IS THIS? WHAT ARE YOU *DOING?*
TAKING WHAT THE CITY *OWES* US.

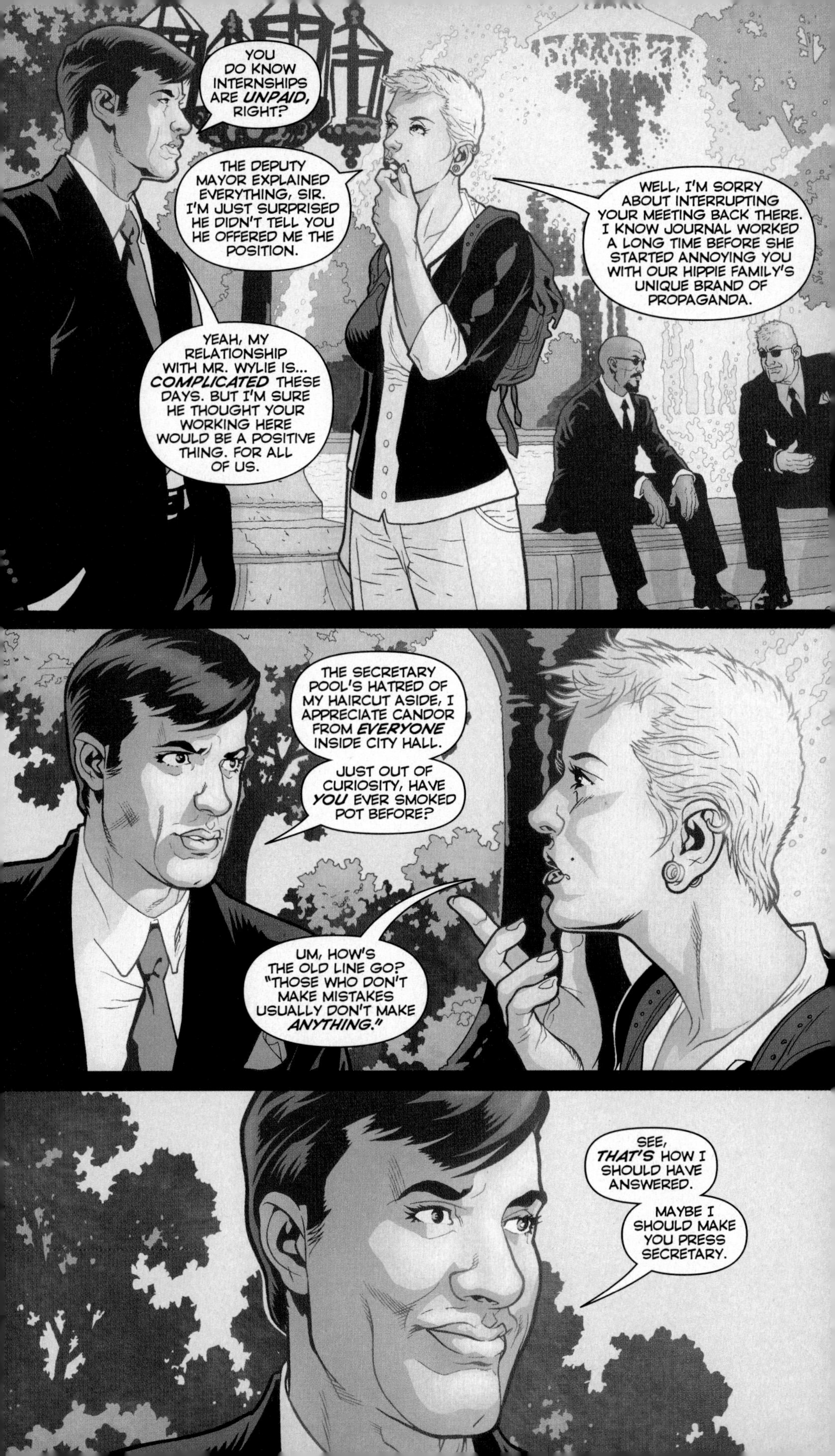
YOU DO KNOW INTERNSHIPS ARE UNPAID, RIGHT?
THE DEPUTY MAYOR EXPLAINED EVERYTHING, SIR. I'M JUST SURPRISED HE DIDN'T TELL YOU HE OFFERED ME THE POSITION.
WELL, I'M SORRY ABOUT INTERRUPTING YOUR MEETING BACK THERE. I KNOW JOURNAL WORKED A LONG TIME BEFORE SHE STARTED ANNOYING YOU WITH OUR HIPPIE FAMILY'S UNIQUE BRAND OF PROPAGANDA.
YEAH, MY RELATIONSHIP WITH MR. WYLIE IS... COMPLICATED THESE DAYS. BUT I'M SURE HE THOUGHT YOUR WORKING HERE WOULD BE A POSITIVE THING. FOR ALL OF US.
THE SECRETARY POOL'S HATRED OF MY HAIRCUT ASIDE, I APPRECIATE CANDOR FROM EVERYONE INSIDE CITY HALL.
JUST OUT OF CURIOSITY, HAVE YOU EVER SMOKED POT BEFORE?
UM, HOW'S THE OLD LINE GO? "THOSE WHO DON'T MAKE MISTAKES USUALLY DON'T MAKE ANYTHING."
SEE, THAT'S HOW I SHOULD HAVE ANSWERED.
MAYBE I SHOULD MAKE YOU PRESS SECRETARY.

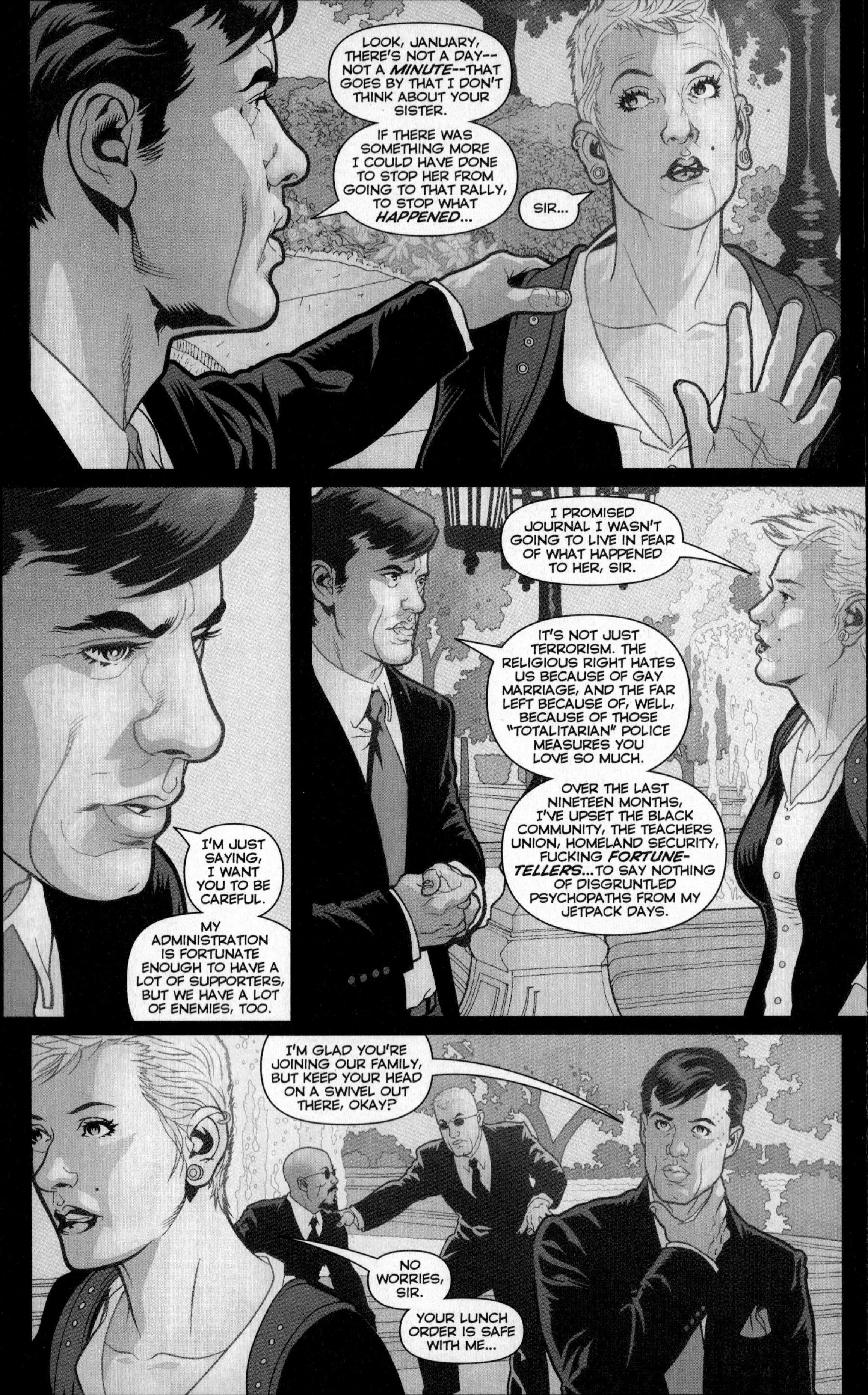

LOOK, JANUARY, THERE'S NOT A DAY-- NOT A *MINUTE*--THAT GOES BY THAT I DON'T THINK ABOUT YOUR SISTER.
IF THERE WAS SOMETHING MORE I COULD HAVE DONE TO STOP HER FROM GOING TO THAT RALLY, TO STOP WHAT *HAPPENED*...
SIR...
I'M JUST SAYING, I WANT YOU TO BE CAREFUL.
MY ADMINISTRATION IS FORTUNATE ENOUGH TO HAVE A LOT OF SUPPORTERS, BUT WE HAVE A LOT OF ENEMIES, TOO.
I PROMISED JOURNAL I WASN'T GOING TO LIVE IN FEAR OF WHAT HAPPENED TO HER, SIR.
IT'S NOT JUST TERRORISM. THE RELIGIOUS RIGHT HATES US BECAUSE OF GAY MARRIAGE, AND THE FAR LEFT BECAUSE OF, WELL, BECAUSE OF THOSE "TOTALITARIAN" POLICE MEASURES YOU LOVE SO MUCH.
OVER THE LAST NINETEEN MONTHS, I'VE UPSET THE BLACK COMMUNITY, THE TEACHERS UNION, HOMELAND SECURITY, FUCKING *FORTUNE-TELLERS*...TO SAY NOTHING OF DISGRUNTLED PSYCHOPATHS FROM MY JETPACK DAYS.
I'M GLAD YOU'RE JOINING OUR FAMILY, BUT KEEP YOUR HEAD ON A SWIVEL OUT THERE, OKAY?
NO WORRIES, SIR.
YOUR LUNCH ORDER IS SAFE WITH ME...

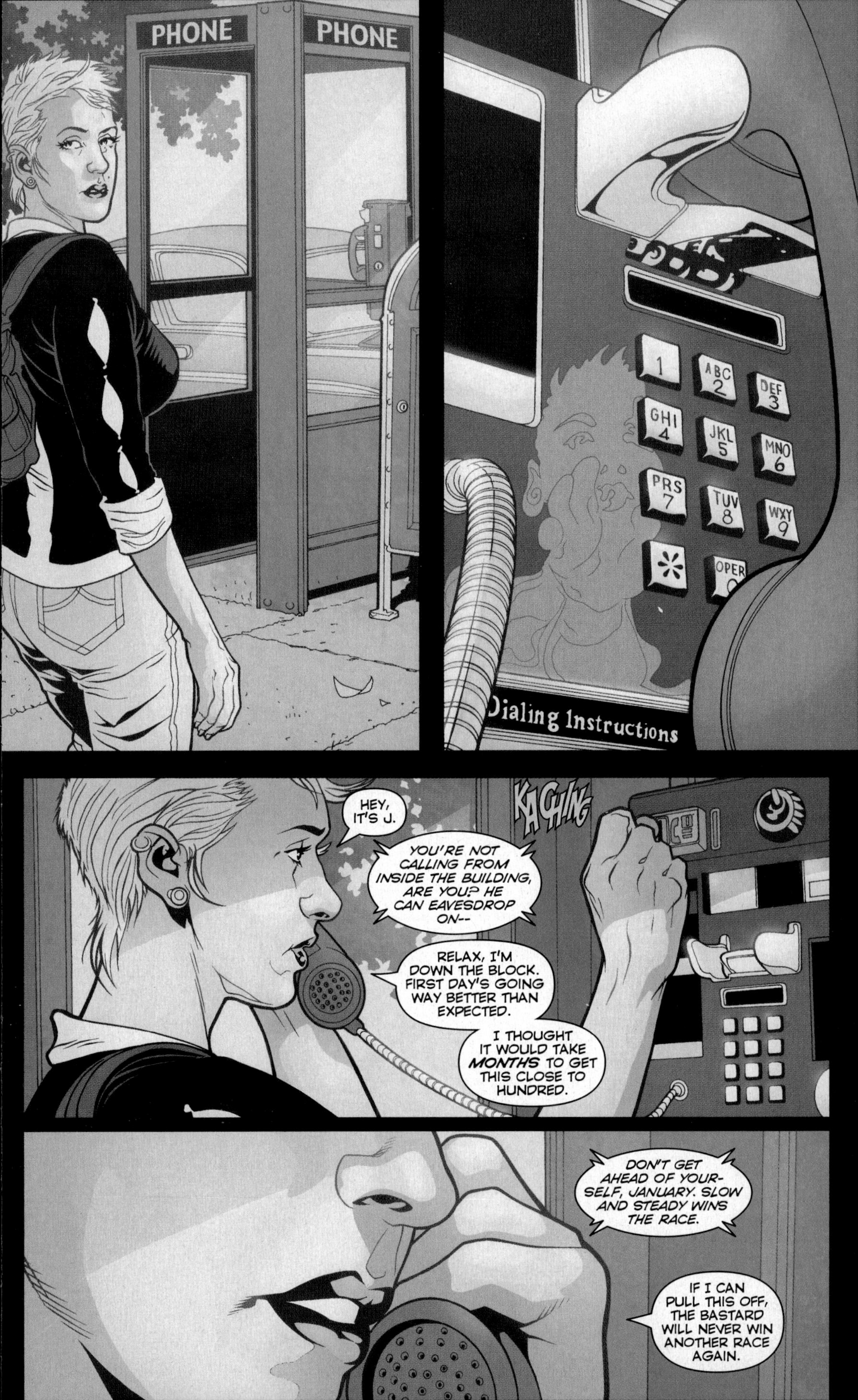
PHONE
PHONE
1
ABC 2
DEF 3
GHI 4
JKL 5
MNO 6
PRS 7
TUV 8
WXY 9
OPER 0
Dialing Instructions
KACHING
HEY, IT'S J.
YOU'RE NOT CALLING FROM INSIDE THE BUILDING, ARE YOU? HE CAN EAVESDROP ON--
RELAX, I'M DOWN THE BLOCK. FIRST DAY'S GOING WAY BETTER THAN EXPECTED.
I THOUGHT IT WOULD TAKE MONTHS TO GET THIS CLOSE TO HUNDRED.
DON'T GET AHEAD OF YOURSELF, JANUARY. SLOW AND STEADY WINS THE RACE.
IF I CAN PULL THIS OFF, THE BASTARD WILL NEVER WIN ANOTHER RACE AGAIN.

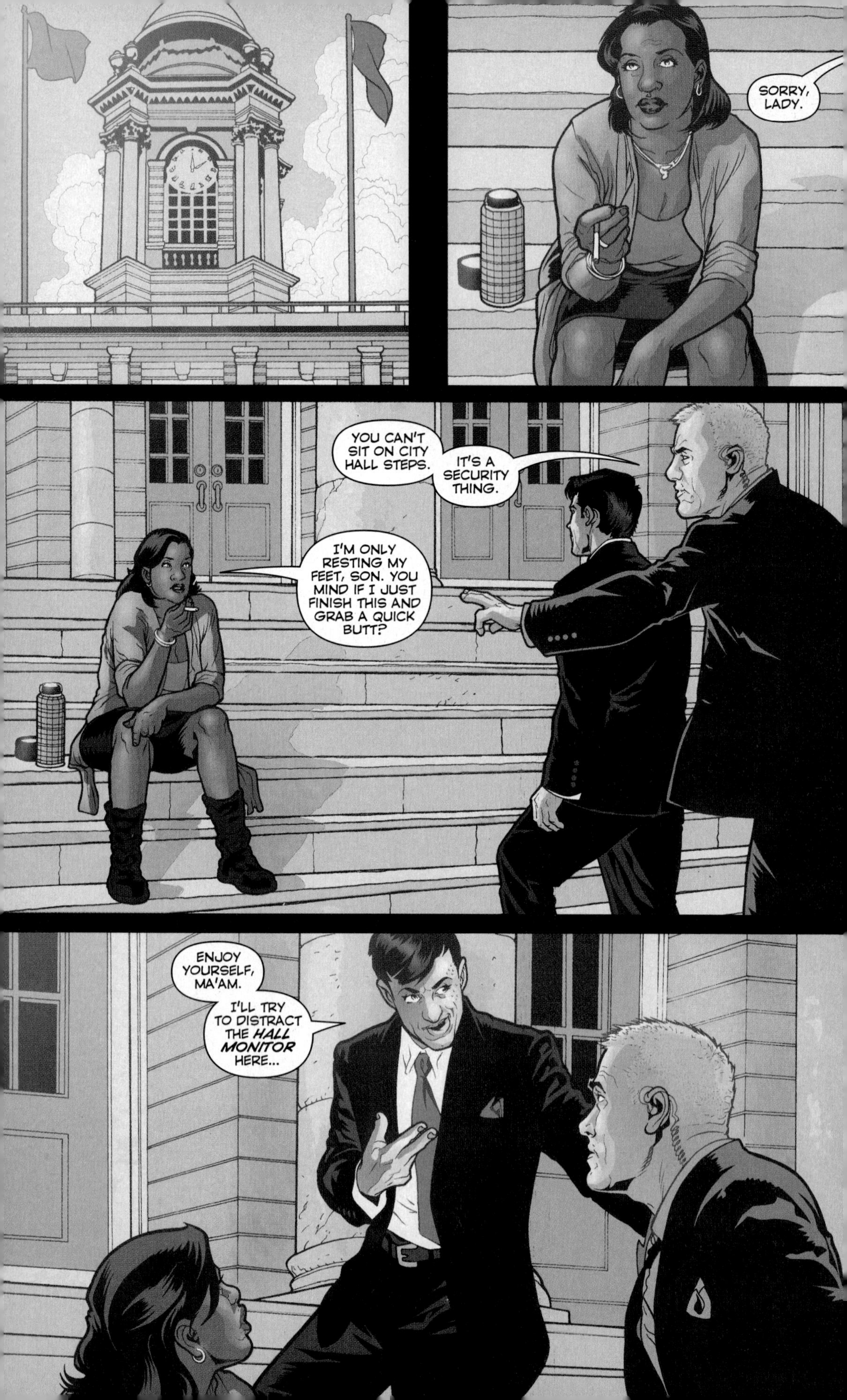
SORRY, LADY.
YOU CAN'T SIT ON CITY HALL STEPS.
IT'S A SECURITY THING.
I'M ONLY RESTING MY FEET, SON. YOU MIND IF I JUST FINISH THIS AND GRAB A QUICK BUTT?
ENJOY YOURSELF, MA'AM.
I'LL TRY TO DISTRACT THE *HALL MONITOR* HERE...

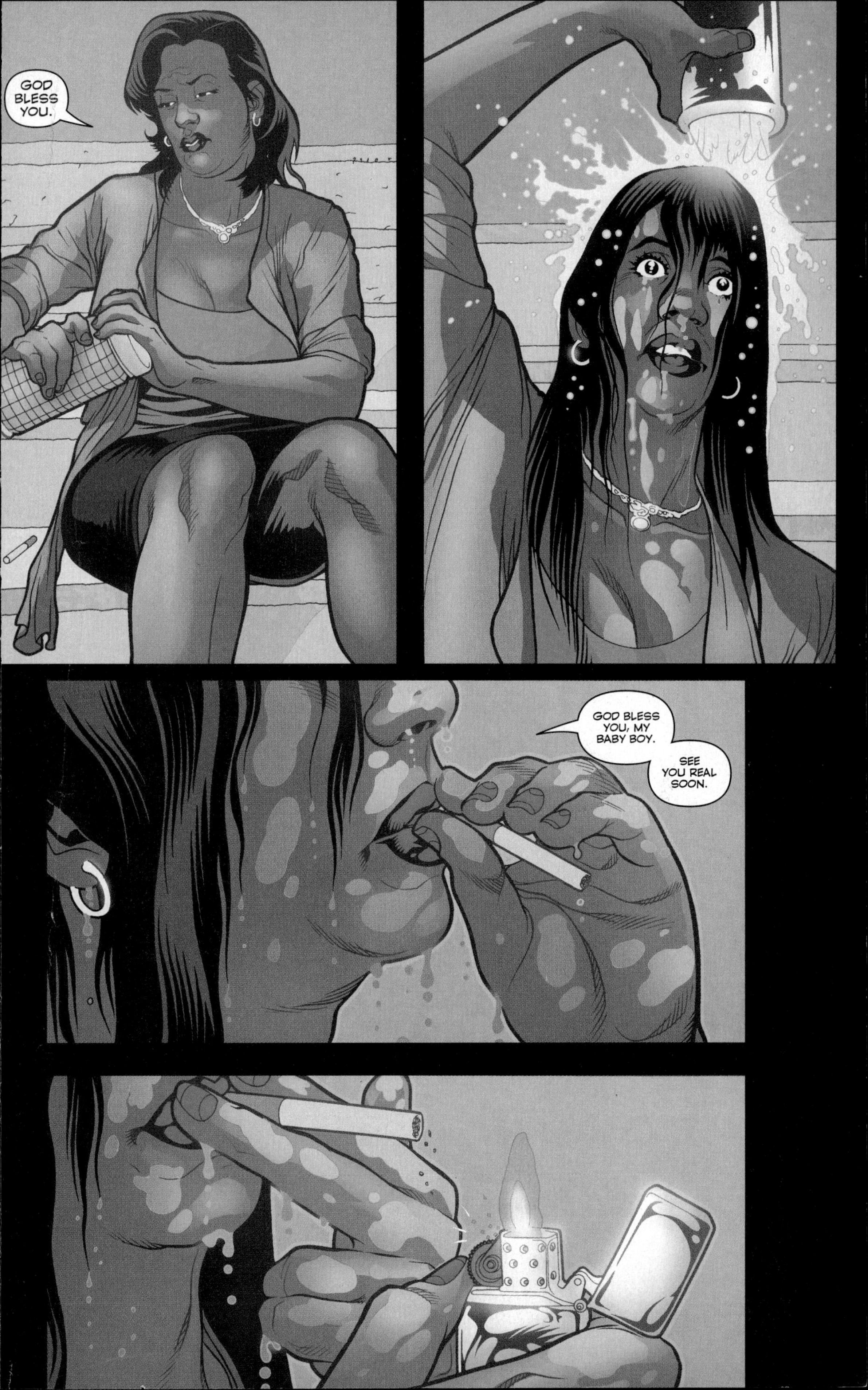
GOD BLESS YOU.
GOD BLESS YOU, MY BABY BOY.
SEE YOU REAL SOON.

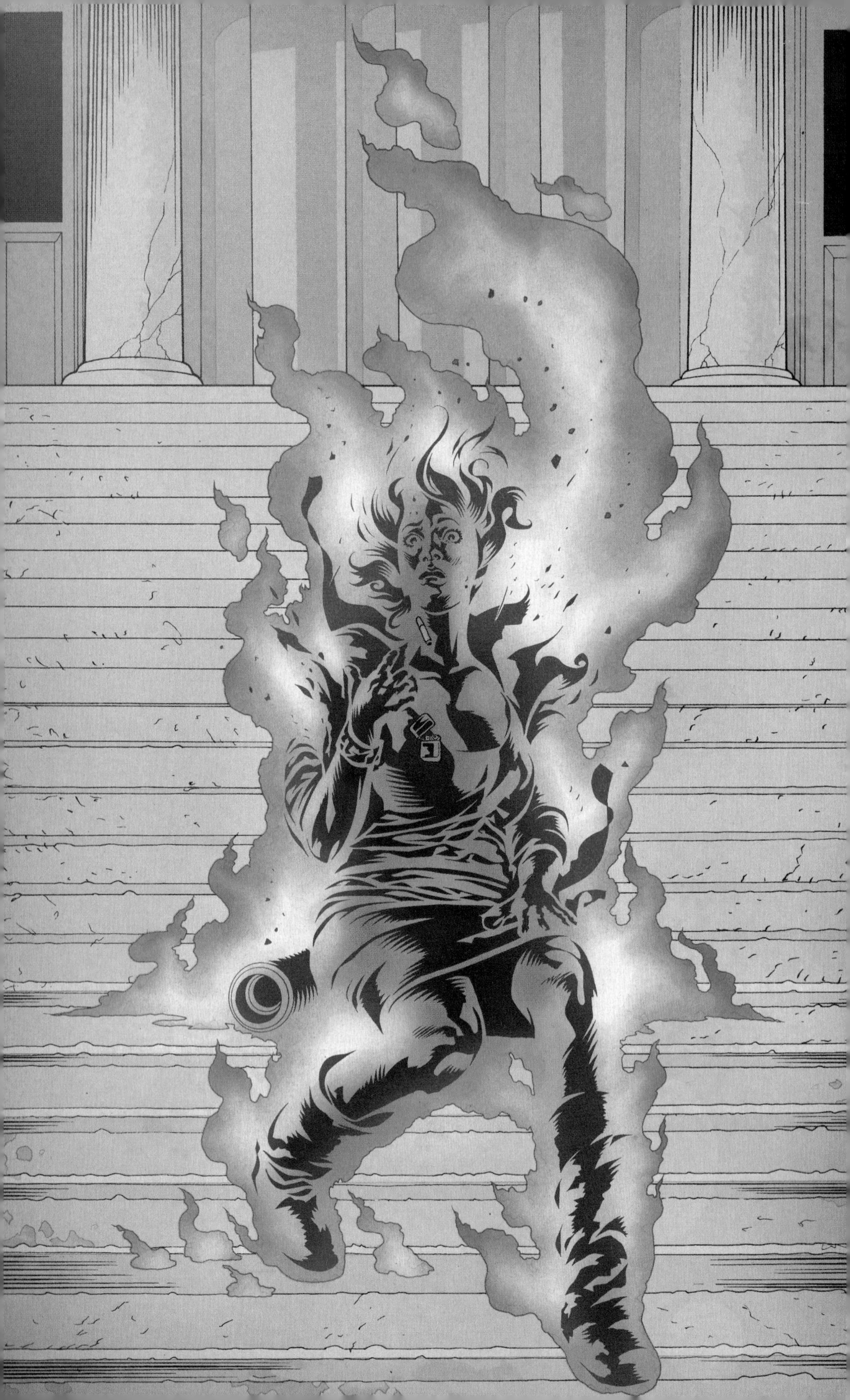

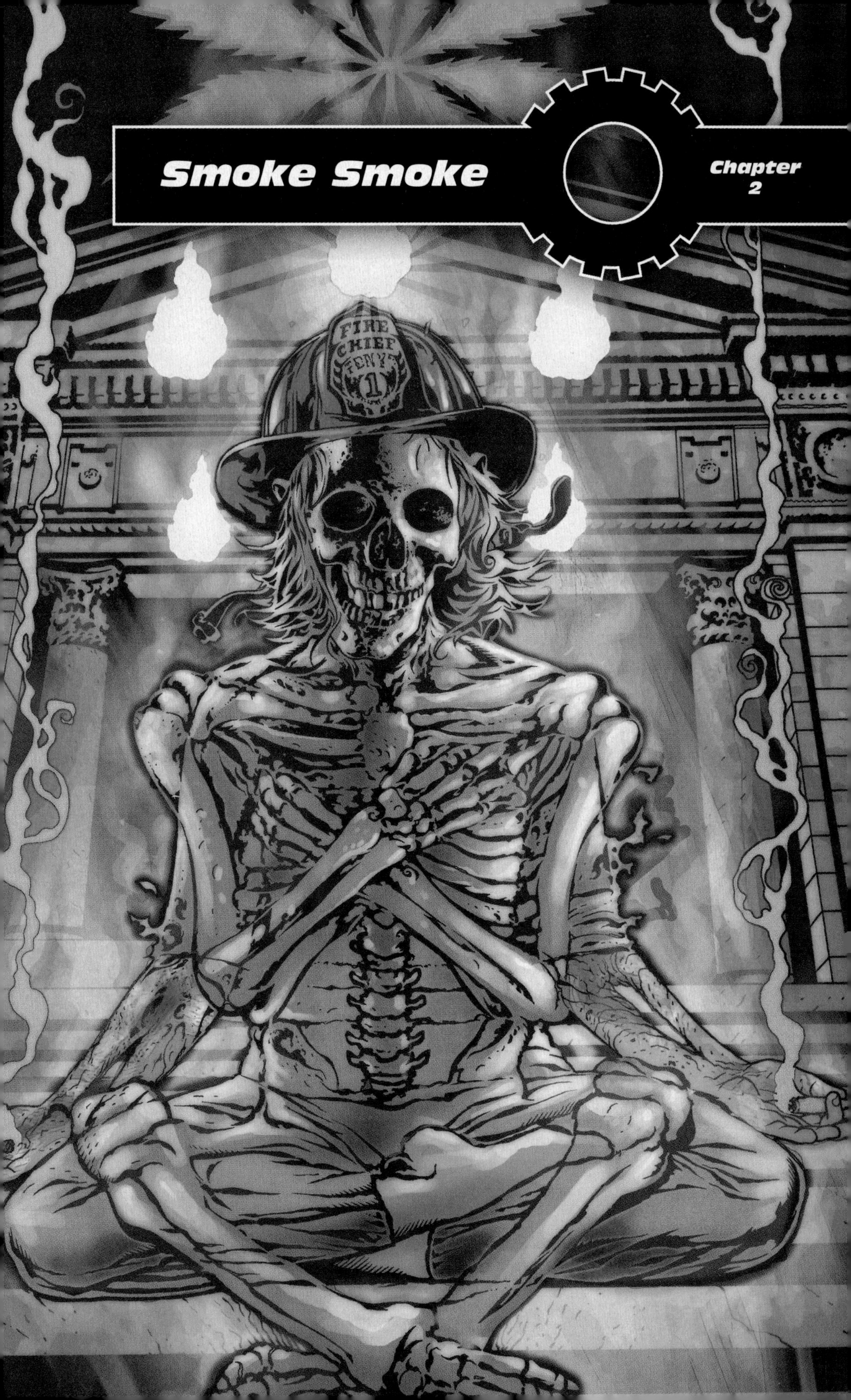
Smoke Smoke
Chapter 2
FIRE CHIEF
FDNY
1

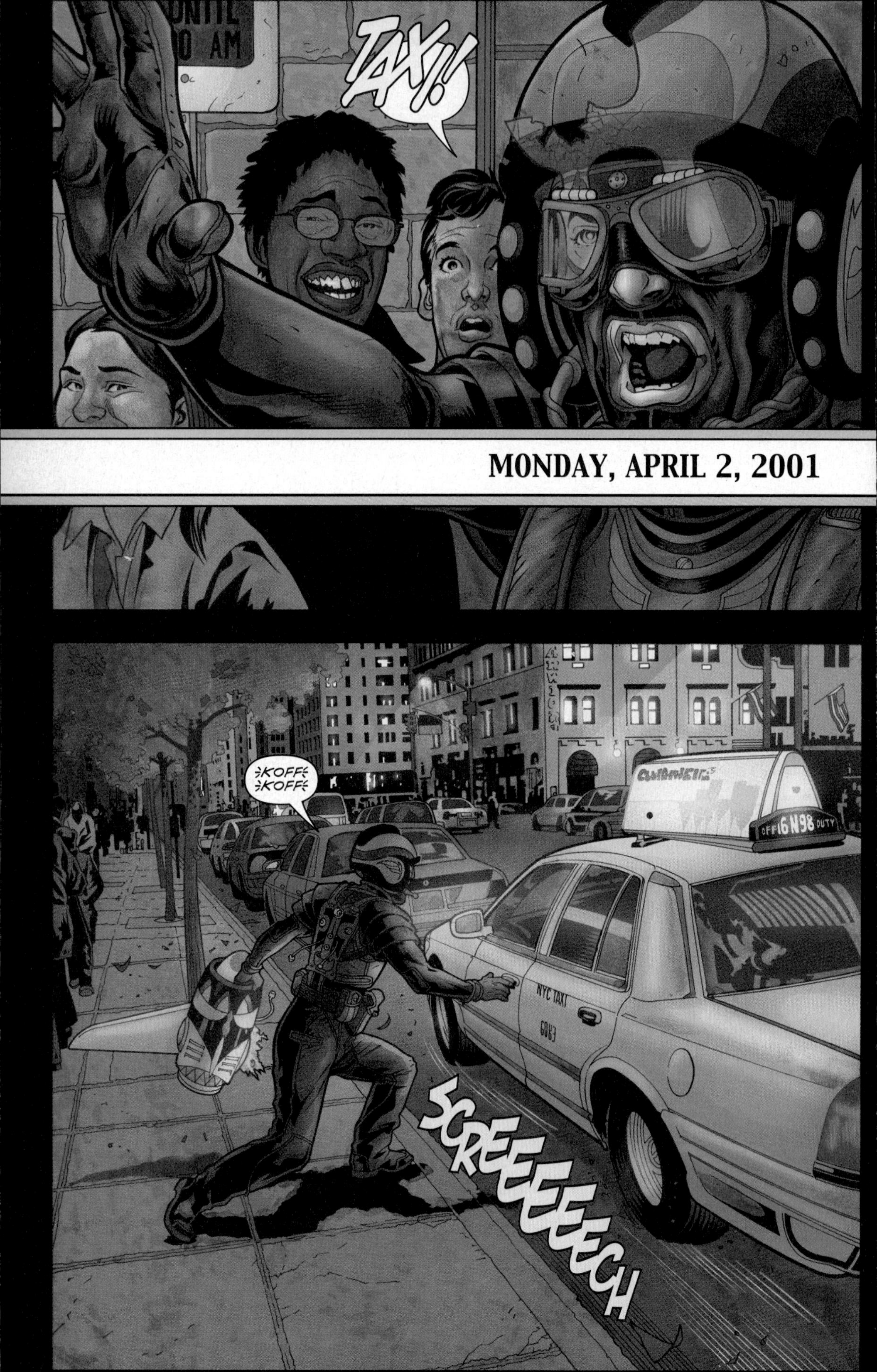
TAXI!!
MONDAY, APRIL 2, 2001
KOFF KOFF
SCREEEEEEECH
NYC TAXI

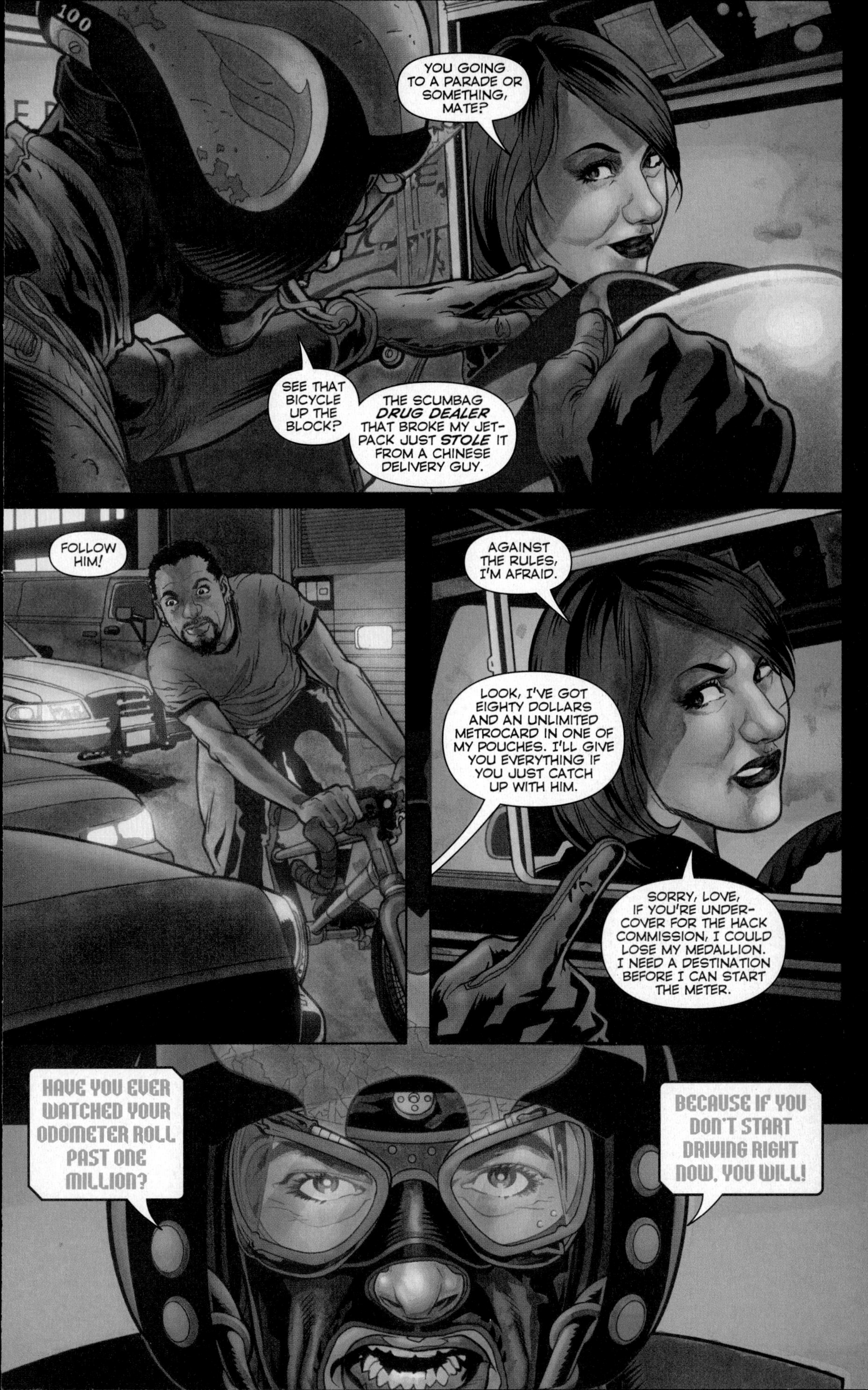
YOU GOING TO A PARADE OR SOMETHING, MATE?
SEE THAT BICYCLE UP THE BLOCK?
THE SCUMBAG DRUG DEALER THAT BROKE MY JET-PACK JUST STOLE IT FROM A CHINESE DELIVERY GUY.
FOLLOW HIM!
AGAINST THE RULES, I'M AFRAID.
LOOK, I'VE GOT EIGHTY DOLLARS AND AN UNLIMITED METROCARD IN ONE OF MY POUCHES. I'LL GIVE YOU EVERYTHING IF YOU JUST CATCH UP WITH HIM.
SORRY, LOVE, IF YOU'RE UNDER-COVER FOR THE HACK COMMISSION, I COULD LOSE MY MEDALLION. I NEED A DESTINATION BEFORE I CAN START THE METER.
HAVE YOU EVER WATCHED YOUR ODOMETER ROLL PAST ONE MILLION?
BECAUSE IF YOU DON'T START DRIVING RIGHT NOW, YOU WILL!

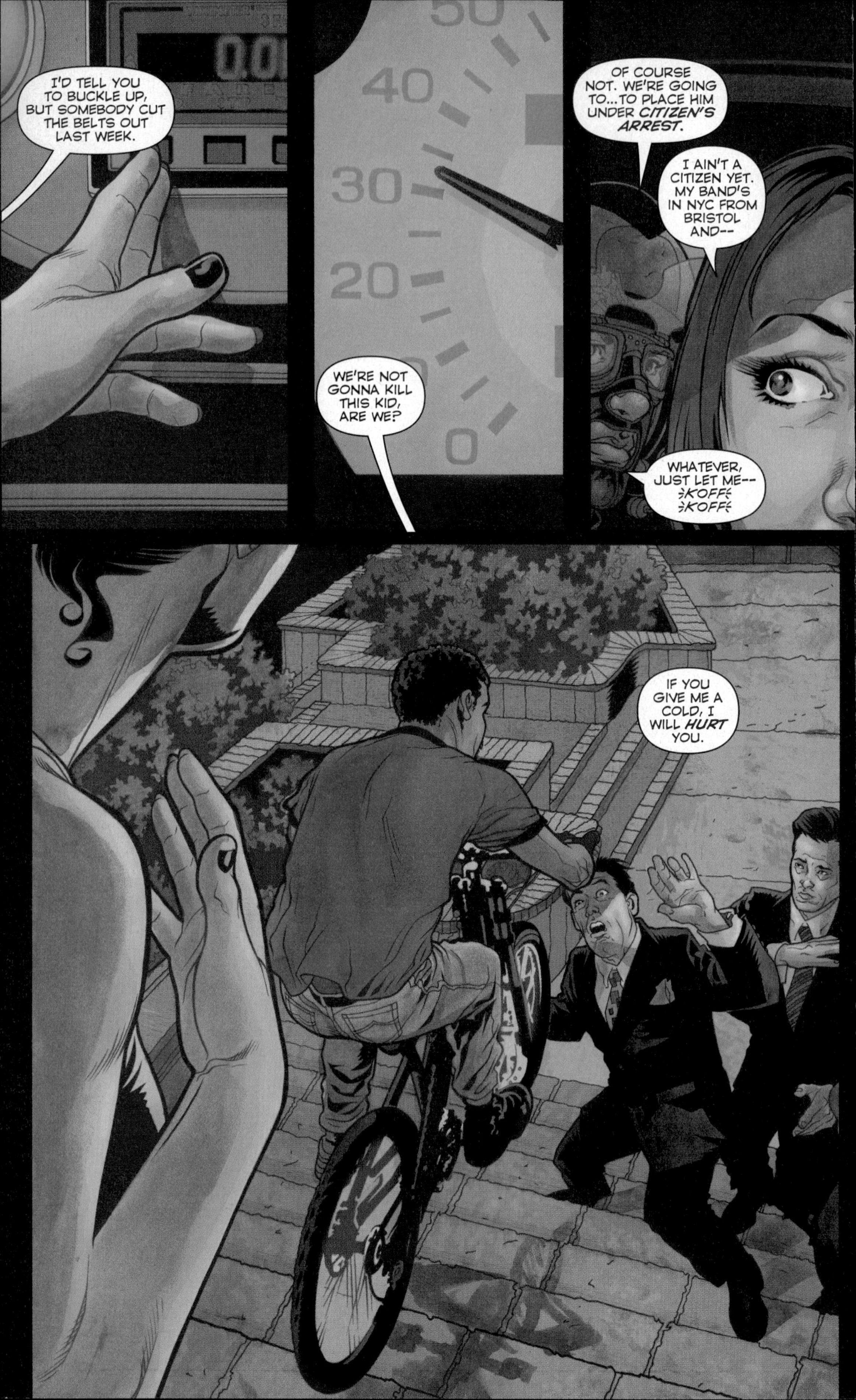
I'D TELL YOU TO BUCKLE UP, BUT SOMEBODY CUT THE BELTS OUT LAST WEEK.
WE'RE NOT GONNA KILL THIS KID, ARE WE?
OF COURSE NOT. WE'RE GOING TO...TO PLACE HIM UNDER *CITIZEN'S ARREST*.
I AIN'T A CITIZEN YET. MY BAND'S IN NYC FROM BRISTOL AND--
WHATEVER, JUST LET ME-- *KOFF* *KOFF*
IF YOU GIVE ME A COLD, I WILL *HURT* YOU.

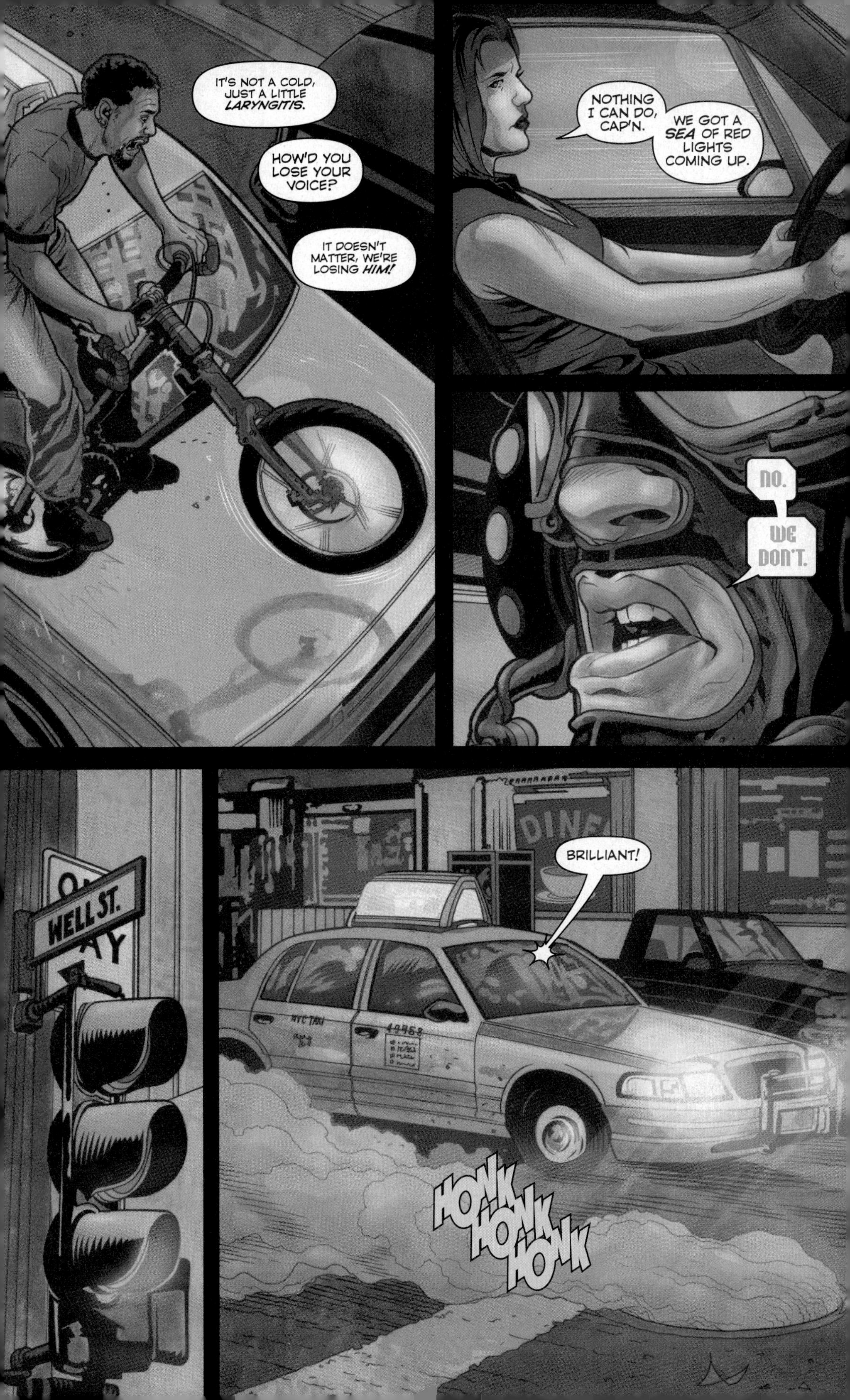
IT'S NOT A COLD, JUST A LITTLE LARYNGITIS.
HOW'D YOU LOSE YOUR VOICE?
IT DOESN'T MATTER, WE'RE LOSING HIM!
NOTHING I CAN DO, CAP'N.
WE GOT A SEA OF RED LIGHTS COMING UP.
NO.
WE DON'T.
WELL ST.
BRILLIANT!
HONK HONK HONK

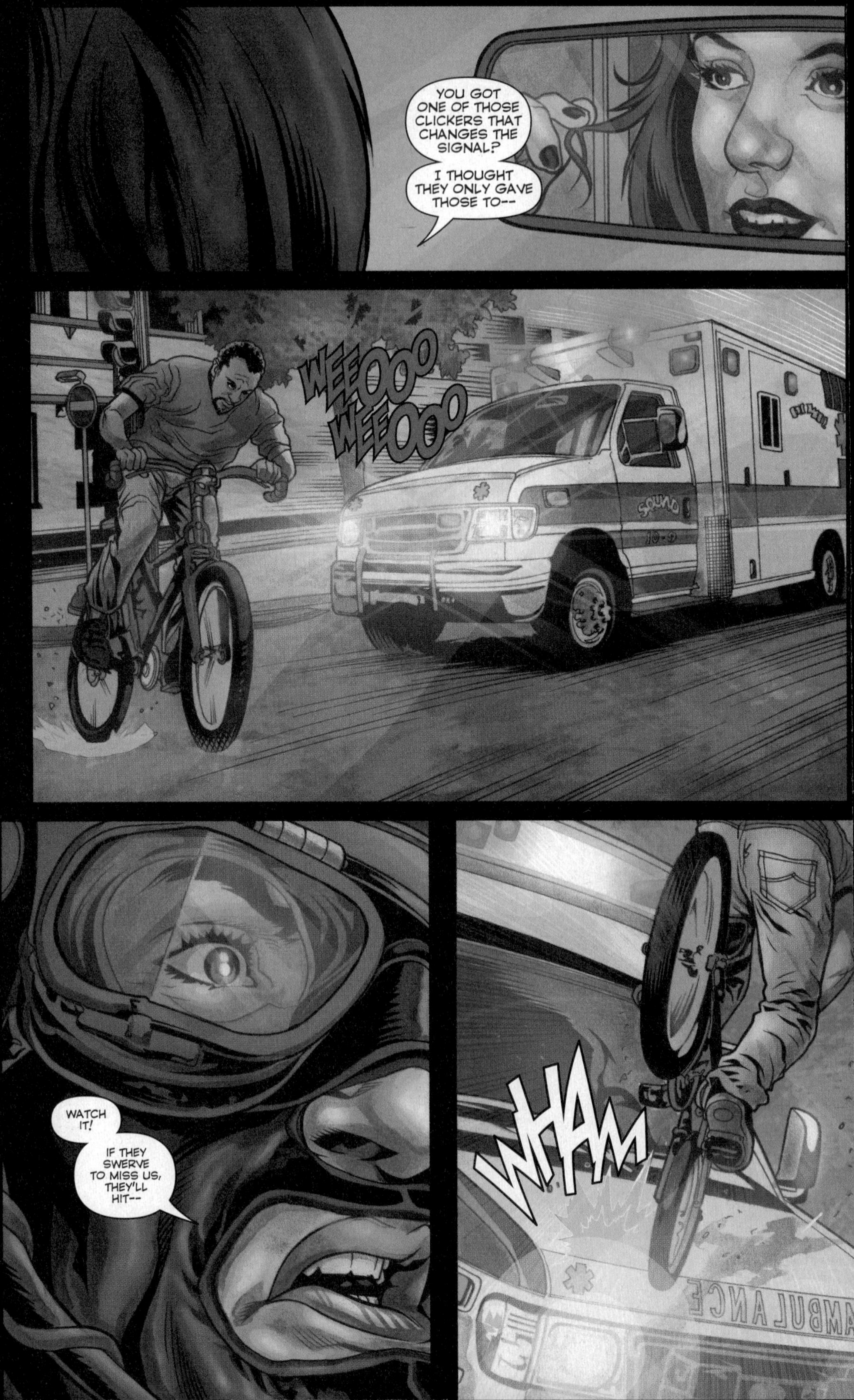
YOU GOT ONE OF THOSE CLICKERS THAT CHANGES THE SIGNAL?
I THOUGHT THEY ONLY GAVE THOSE TO--
WEEOOO WEEOOO
WATCH IT!
IF THEY SWERVE TO MISS US, THEY'LL HIT--
WHAM
AMBULANCE

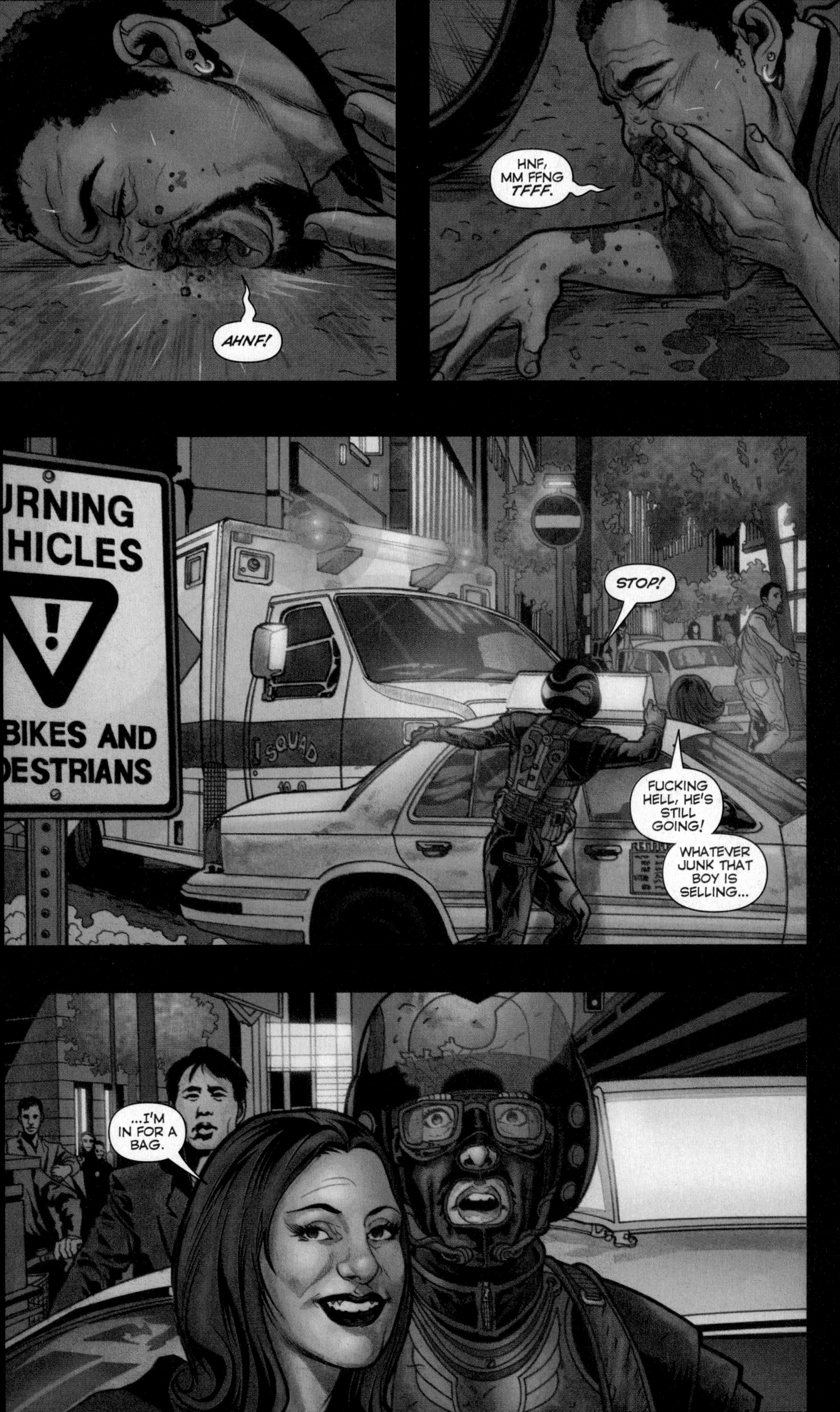
AHNF!
HNF, MM FFNG TFFF.
URNING
HICLES
BIKES AND
DESTRIANS
SQUAD
STOP!
FUCKING HELL, HE'S STILL GOING!
WHATEVER JUNK THAT BOY IS SELLING...
...I'M IN FOR A BAG.

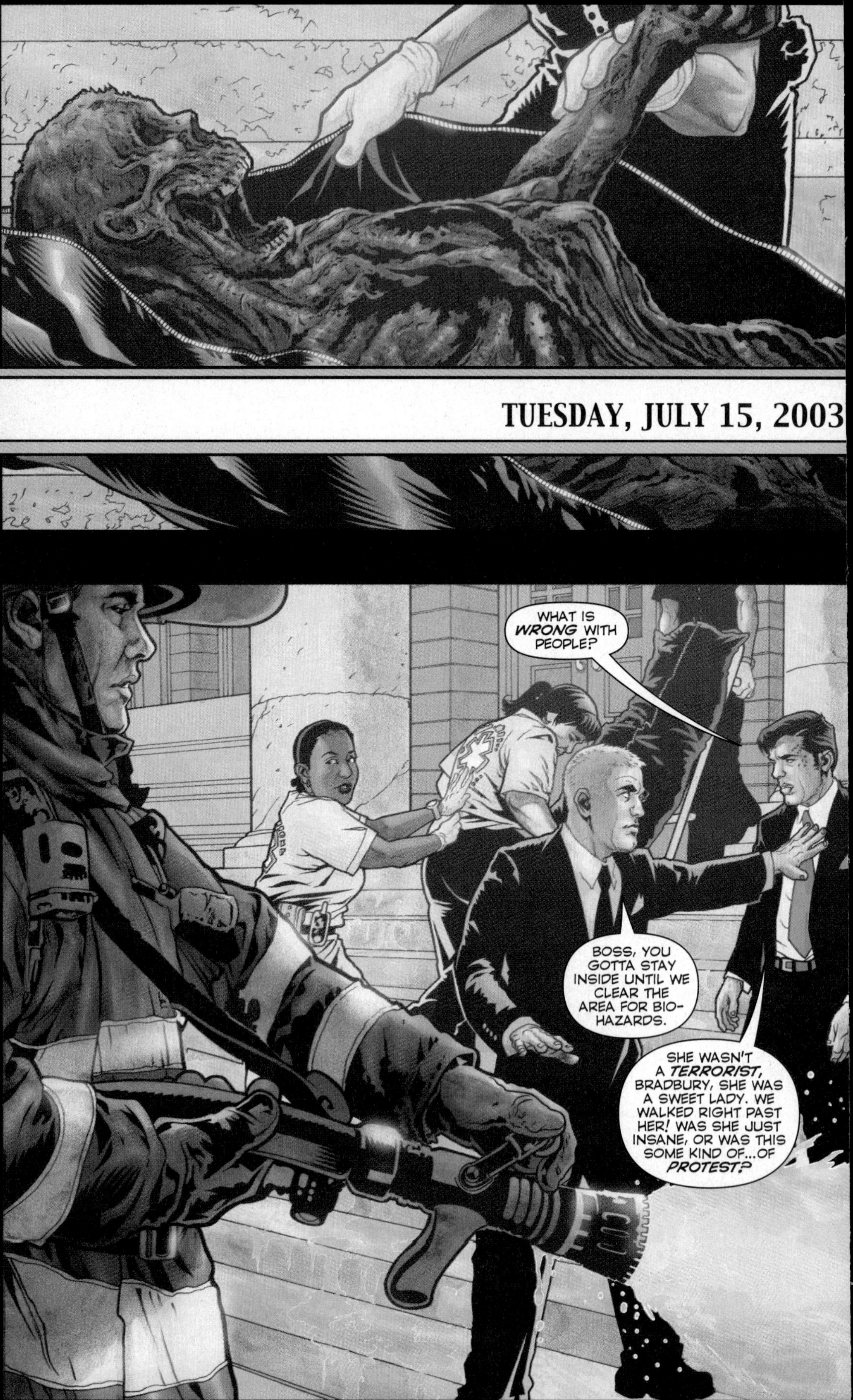
TUESDAY, JULY 15, 2003
WHAT IS WRONG WITH PEOPLE?
BOSS, YOU GOTTA STAY INSIDE UNTIL WE CLEAR THE AREA FOR BIO-HAZARDS.
SHE WASN'T A TERRORIST, BRADBURY, SHE WAS A SWEET LADY. WE WALKED RIGHT PAST HER! WAS SHE JUST INSANE, OR WAS THIS SOME KIND OF...OF PROTEST?

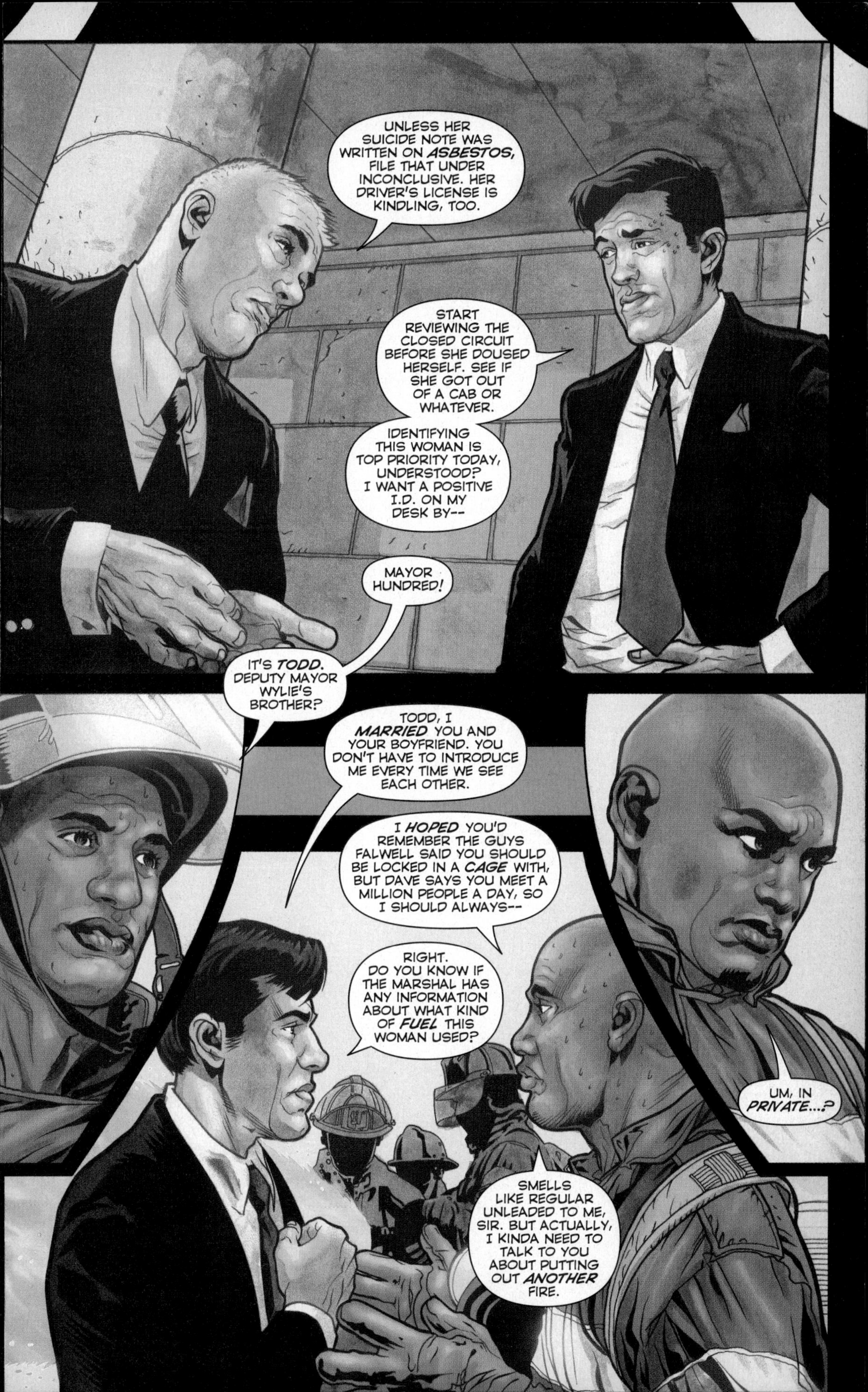
UNLESS HER SUICIDE NOTE WAS WRITTEN ON *ASBESTOS,* FILE THAT UNDER INCONCLUSIVE. HER DRIVER'S LICENSE IS KINDLING, TOO.
START REVIEWING THE CLOSED CIRCUIT BEFORE SHE DOUSED HERSELF. SEE IF SHE GOT OUT OF A CAB OR WHATEVER.
IDENTIFYING THIS WOMAN IS TOP PRIORITY TODAY, UNDERSTOOD? I WANT A POSITIVE I.D. ON MY DESK BY--
MAYOR HUNDRED!
IT'S *TODD.* DEPUTY MAYOR WYLIE'S BROTHER?
TODD, I ***MARRIED*** YOU AND YOUR BOYFRIEND. YOU DON'T HAVE TO INTRODUCE ME EVERY TIME WE SEE EACH OTHER.
I *HOPED* YOU'D REMEMBER THE GUYS FALWELL SAID YOU SHOULD BE LOCKED IN A *CAGE* WITH, BUT DAVE SAYS YOU MEET A MILLION PEOPLE A DAY, SO I SHOULD ALWAYS--
RIGHT. DO YOU KNOW IF THE MARSHAL HAS ANY INFORMATION ABOUT WHAT KIND OF *FUEL* THIS WOMAN USED?
UM, IN *PRIVATE...?*
SMELLS LIKE REGULAR UNLEADED TO ME, SIR. BUT ACTUALLY, I KINDA NEED TO TALK TO YOU ABOUT PUTTING OUT ***ANOTHER*** FIRE.

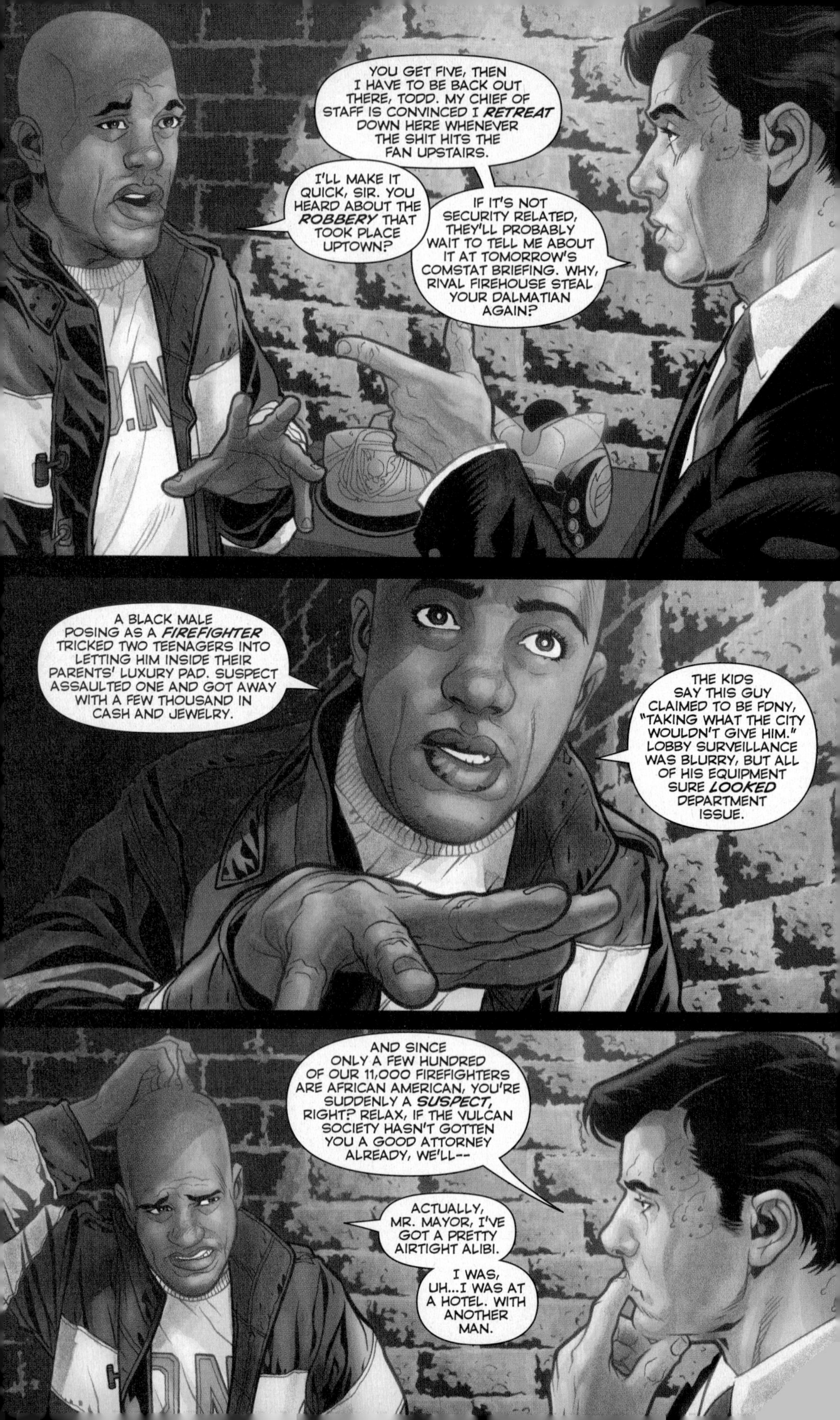

YOU GET FIVE, THEN I HAVE TO BE BACK OUT THERE, TODD. MY CHIEF OF STAFF IS CONVINCED I *RETREAT* DOWN HERE WHENEVER THE SHIT HITS THE FAN UPSTAIRS.
I'LL MAKE IT QUICK, SIR. YOU HEARD ABOUT THE *ROBBERY* THAT TOOK PLACE UPTOWN?
IF IT'S NOT SECURITY RELATED, THEY'LL PROBABLY WAIT TO TELL ME ABOUT IT AT TOMORROW'S COMSTAT BRIEFING. WHY, RIVAL FIREHOUSE STEAL YOUR DALMATIAN AGAIN?
A BLACK MALE POSING AS A *FIREFIGHTER* TRICKED TWO TEENAGERS INTO LETTING HIM INSIDE THEIR PARENTS' LUXURY PAD. SUSPECT ASSAULTED ONE AND GOT AWAY WITH A FEW THOUSAND IN CASH AND JEWELRY.
THE KIDS SAY THIS GUY CLAIMED TO BE FDNY, "TAKING WHAT THE CITY WOULDN'T GIVE HIM." LOBBY SURVEILLANCE WAS BLURRY, BUT ALL OF HIS EQUIPMENT SURE *LOOKED* DEPARTMENT ISSUE.
AND SINCE ONLY A FEW HUNDRED OF OUR 11,000 FIREFIGHTERS ARE AFRICAN AMERICAN, YOU'RE SUDDENLY A *SUSPECT,* RIGHT? RELAX, IF THE VULCAN SOCIETY HASN'T GOTTEN YOU A GOOD ATTORNEY ALREADY, WE'LL--
ACTUALLY, MR. MAYOR, I'VE GOT A PRETTY AIRTIGHT ALIBI.
I WAS, UH...I WAS AT A HOTEL. WITH ANOTHER MAN.

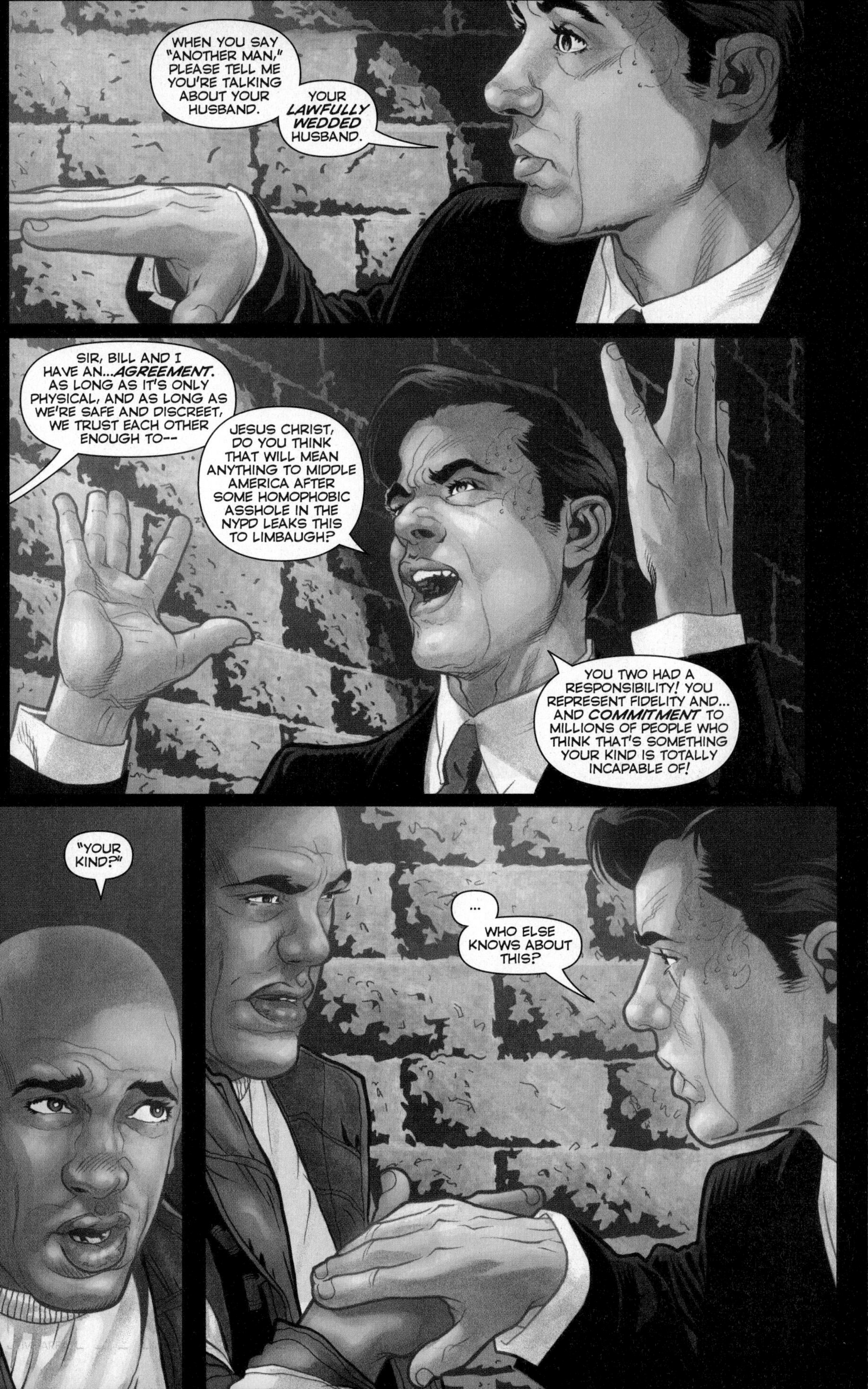
WHEN YOU SAY "ANOTHER MAN," PLEASE TELL ME YOU'RE TALKING ABOUT YOUR HUSBAND.
YOUR LAWFULLY WEDDED HUSBAND.
SIR, BILL AND I HAVE AN...AGREEMENT. AS LONG AS IT'S ONLY PHYSICAL, AND AS LONG AS WE'RE SAFE AND DISCREET, WE TRUST EACH OTHER ENOUGH TO--
JESUS CHRIST, DO YOU THINK THAT WILL MEAN ANYTHING TO MIDDLE AMERICA AFTER SOME HOMOPHOBIC ASSHOLE IN THE NYPD LEAKS THIS TO LIMBAUGH?
YOU TWO HAD A RESPONSIBILITY! YOU REPRESENT FIDELITY AND... AND COMMITMENT TO MILLIONS OF PEOPLE WHO THINK THAT'S SOMETHING YOUR KIND IS TOTALLY INCAPABLE OF!
"YOUR KIND?"
...
WHO ELSE KNOWS ABOUT THIS?

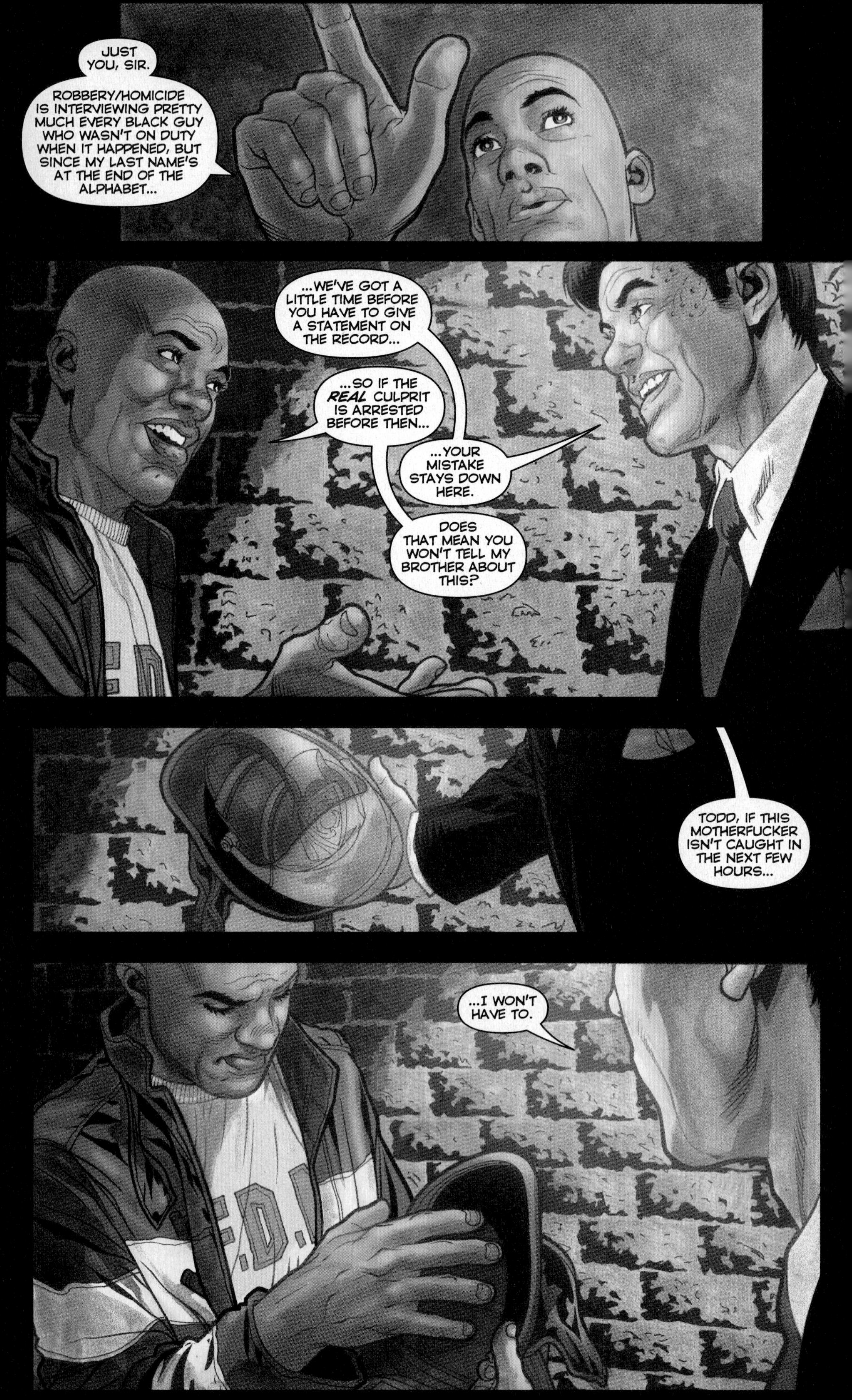
JUST YOU, SIR.
ROBBERY/HOMICIDE IS INTERVIEWING PRETTY MUCH EVERY BLACK GUY WHO WASN'T ON DUTY WHEN IT HAPPENED, BUT SINCE MY LAST NAME'S AT THE END OF THE ALPHABET...
...WE'VE GOT A LITTLE TIME BEFORE YOU HAVE TO GIVE A STATEMENT ON THE RECORD...
...SO IF THE REAL CULPRIT IS ARRESTED BEFORE THEN...
...YOUR MISTAKE STAYS DOWN HERE.
DOES THAT MEAN YOU WON'T TELL MY BROTHER ABOUT THIS?
TODD, IF THIS MOTHERFUCKER ISN'T CAUGHT IN THE NEXT FEW HOURS...
...I WON'T HAVE TO.

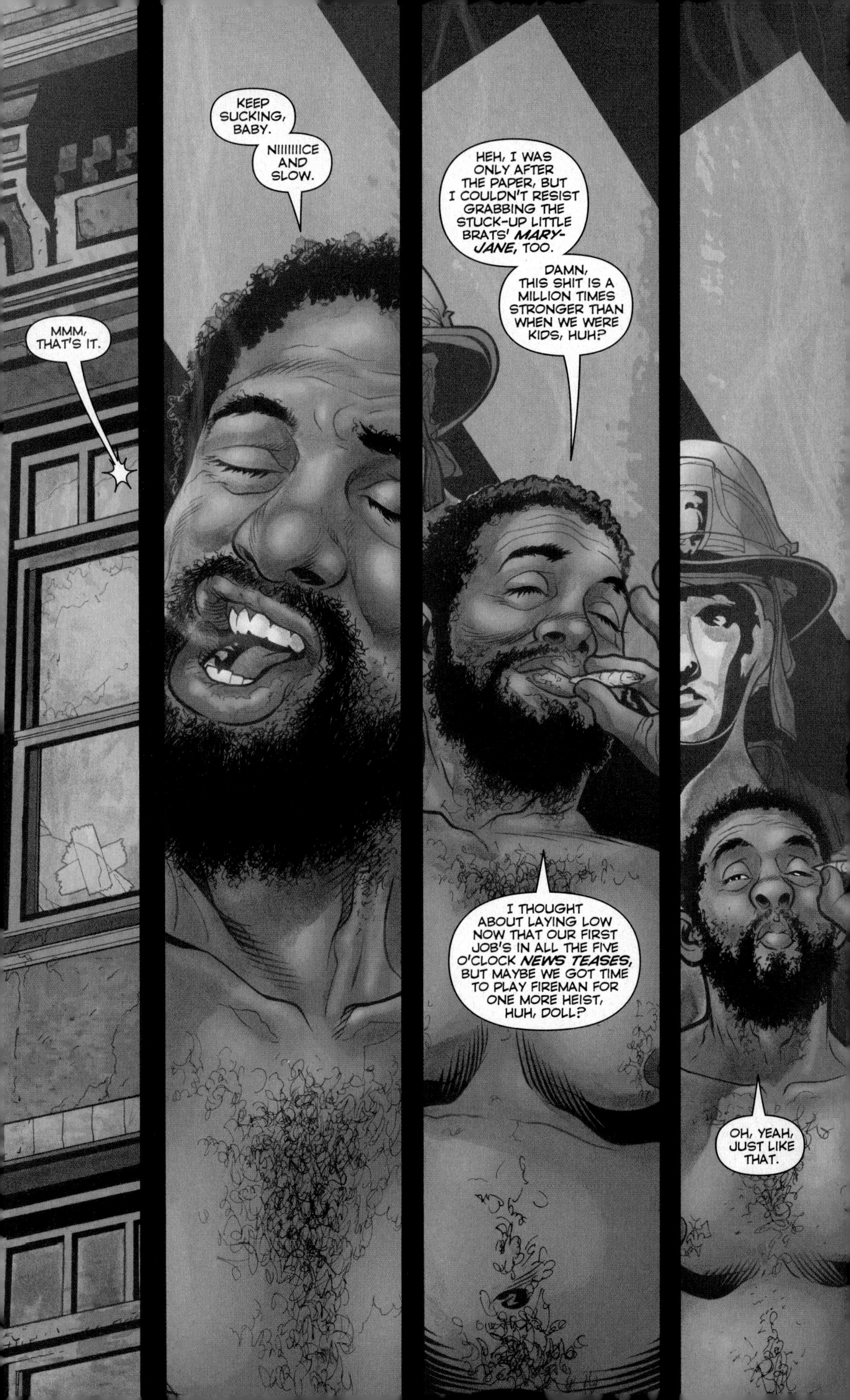
MMM, THAT'S IT.
KEEP SUCKING, BABY.
NIIIIIICE AND SLOW.
HEH, I WAS ONLY AFTER THE PAPER, BUT I COULDN'T RESIST GRABBING THE STUCK-UP LITTLE BRATS' *MARY-JANE,* TOO.
DAMN, THIS SHIT IS A MILLION TIMES STRONGER THAN WHEN WE WERE KIDS, HUH?
I THOUGHT ABOUT LAYING LOW NOW THAT OUR FIRST JOB'S IN ALL THE FIVE O'CLOCK *NEWS TEASES,* BUT MAYBE WE GOT TIME TO PLAY FIREMAN FOR ONE MORE HEIST, HUH, DOLL?
OH, YEAH, JUST LIKE THAT.

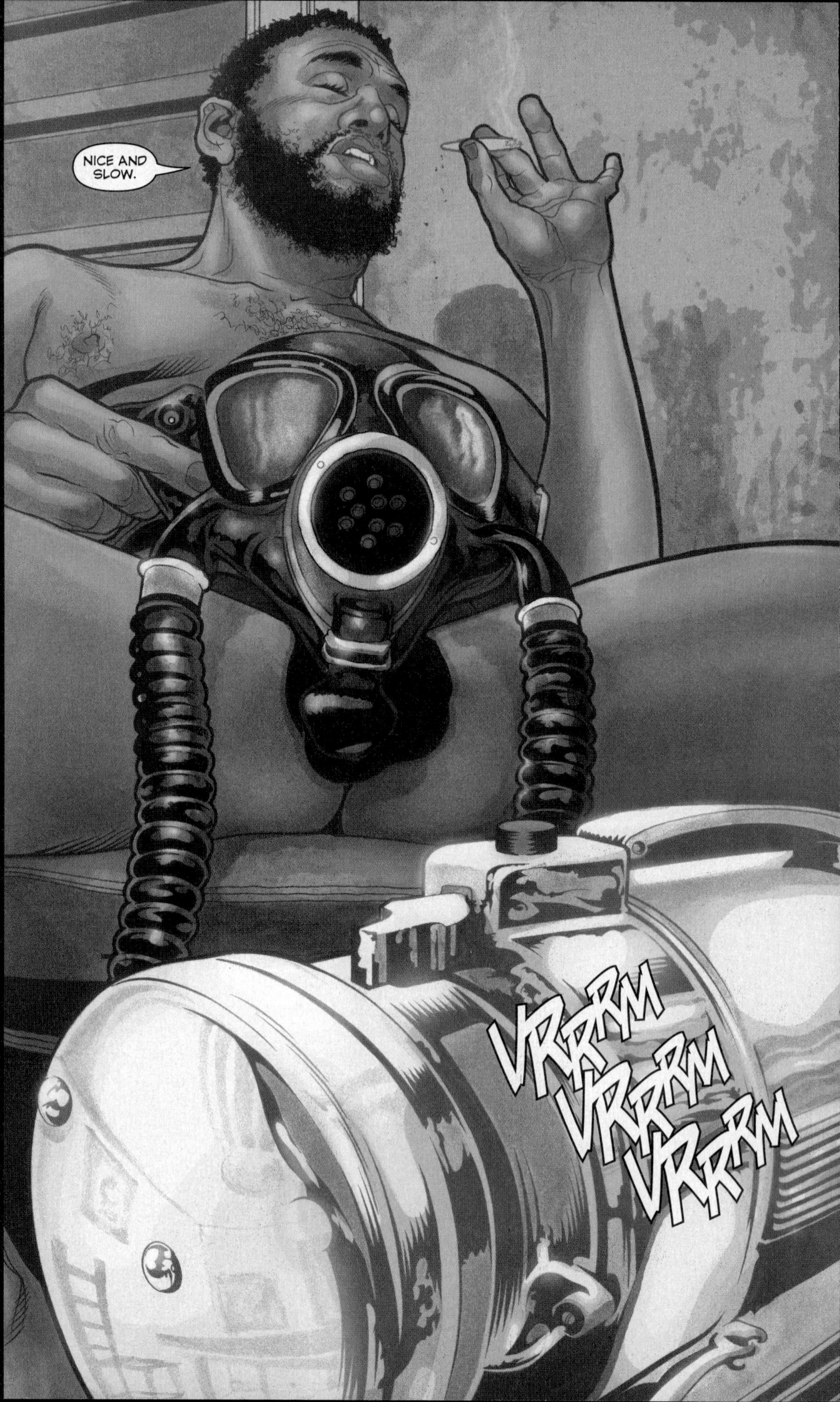
NICE AND SLOW.
VRRRM
VRRRM
VRRRM

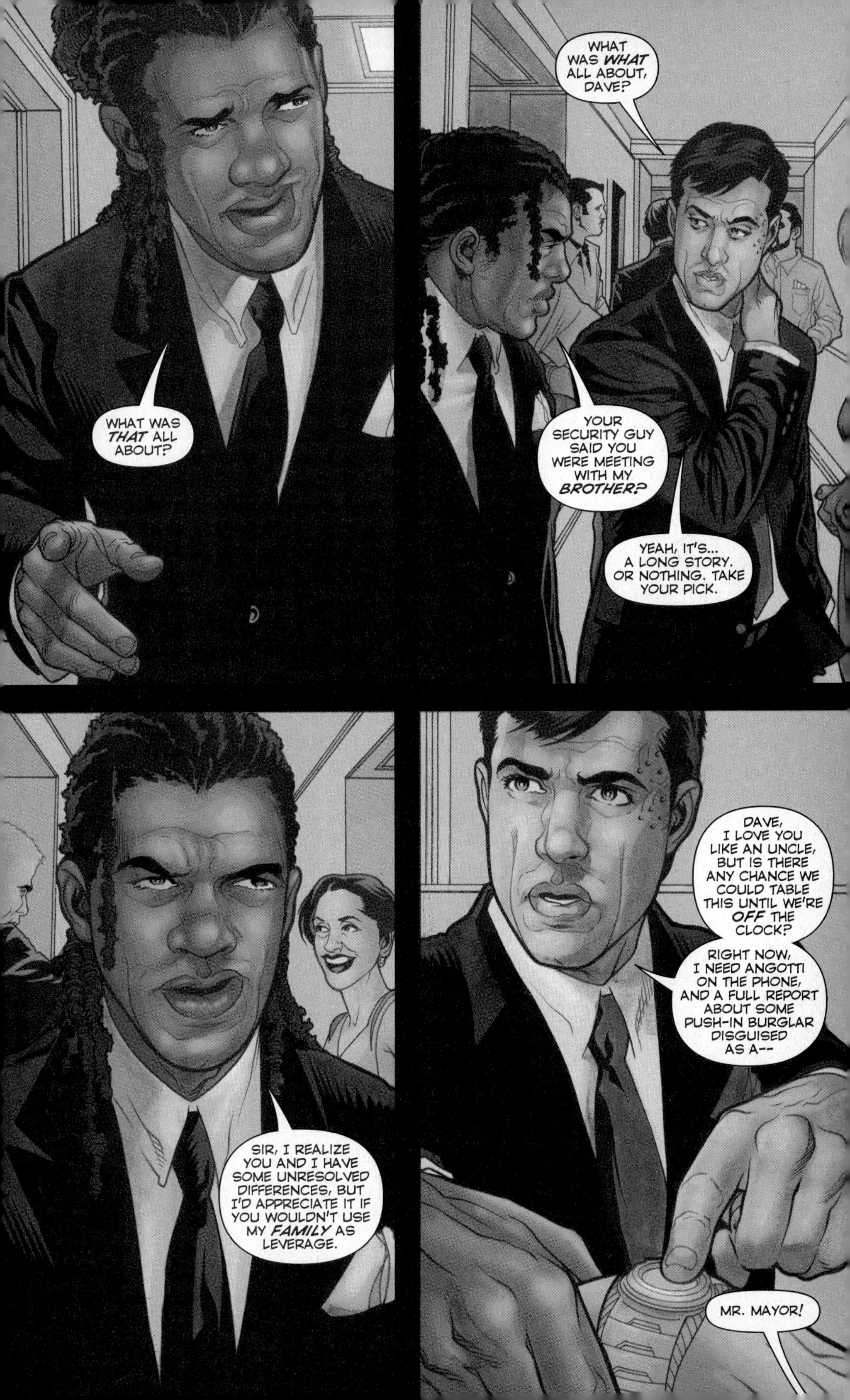
WHAT WAS *THAT* ALL ABOUT?
WHAT WAS *WHAT* ALL ABOUT, DAVE?
YOUR SECURITY GUY SAID YOU WERE MEETING WITH MY *BROTHER?*
YEAH, IT'S... A LONG STORY. OR NOTHING. TAKE YOUR PICK.
SIR, I REALIZE YOU AND I HAVE SOME UNRESOLVED DIFFERENCES, BUT I'D APPRECIATE IT IF YOU WOULDN'T USE MY *FAMILY* AS LEVERAGE.
DAVE, I LOVE YOU LIKE AN UNCLE, BUT IS THERE ANY CHANCE WE COULD TABLE THIS UNTIL WE'RE *OFF* THE CLOCK?
RIGHT NOW, I NEED ANGOTTI ON THE PHONE, AND A FULL REPORT ABOUT SOME PUSH-IN BURGLAR DISGUISED AS A--
MR. MAYOR!

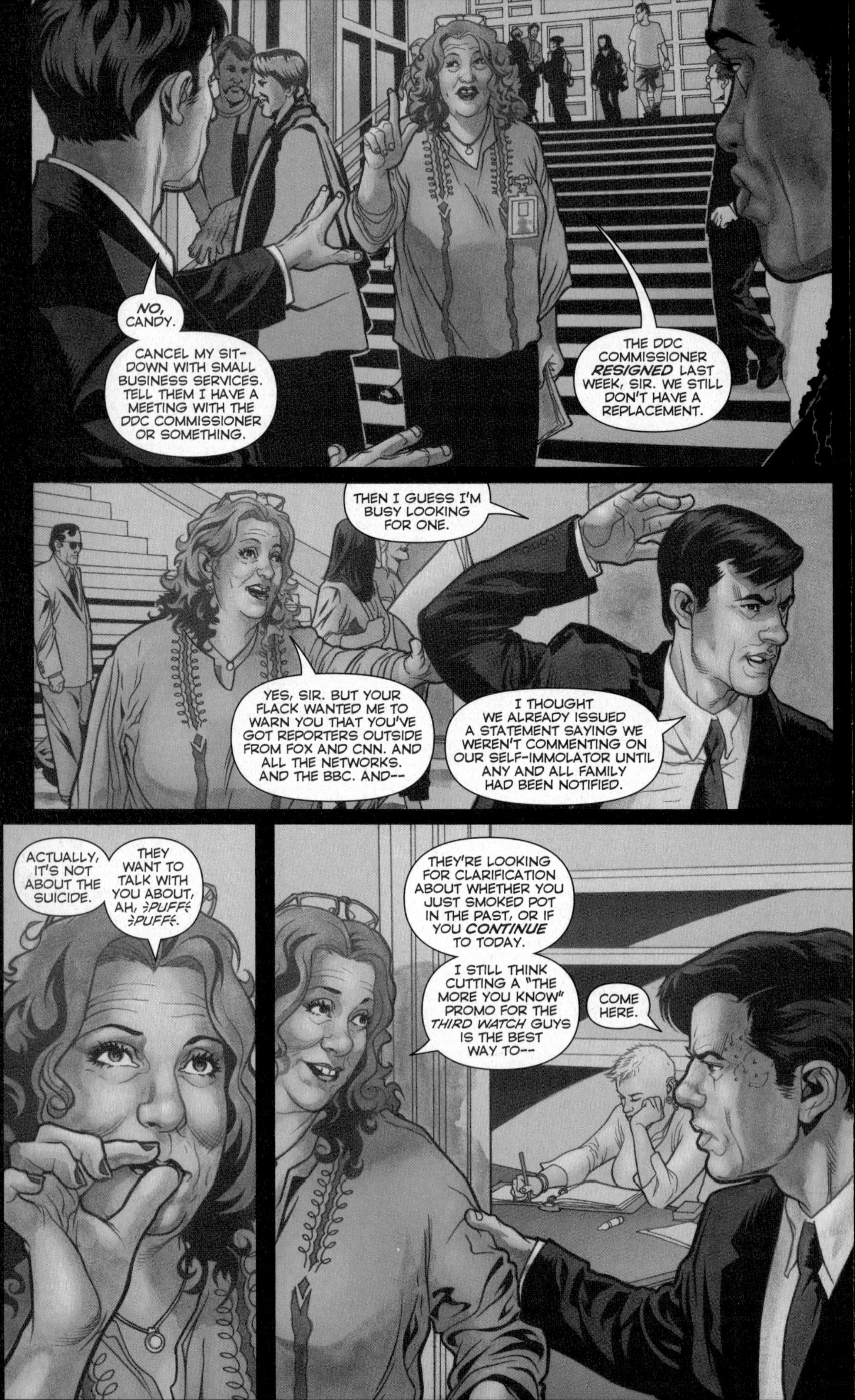
NO, CANDY.
CANCEL MY SIT-DOWN WITH SMALL BUSINESS SERVICES. TELL THEM I HAVE A MEETING WITH THE DDC COMMISSIONER OR SOMETHING.
THE DDC COMMISSIONER RESIGNED LAST WEEK, SIR. WE STILL DON'T HAVE A REPLACEMENT.
THEN I GUESS I'M BUSY LOOKING FOR ONE.
YES, SIR. BUT YOUR FLACK WANTED ME TO WARN YOU THAT YOU'VE GOT REPORTERS OUTSIDE FROM FOX AND CNN. AND ALL THE NETWORKS. AND THE BBC. AND--
I THOUGHT WE ALREADY ISSUED A STATEMENT SAYING WE WEREN'T COMMENTING ON OUR SELF-IMMOLATOR UNTIL ANY AND ALL FAMILY HAD BEEN NOTIFIED.
ACTUALLY, IT'S NOT ABOUT THE SUICIDE.
THEY WANT TO TALK WITH YOU ABOUT, AH, PUFF PUFF.
THEY'RE LOOKING FOR CLARIFICATION ABOUT WHETHER YOU JUST SMOKED POT IN THE PAST, OR IF YOU CONTINUE TO TODAY.
I STILL THINK CUTTING A "THE MORE YOU KNOW" PROMO FOR THE THIRD WATCH GUYS IS THE BEST WAY TO--
COME HERE.

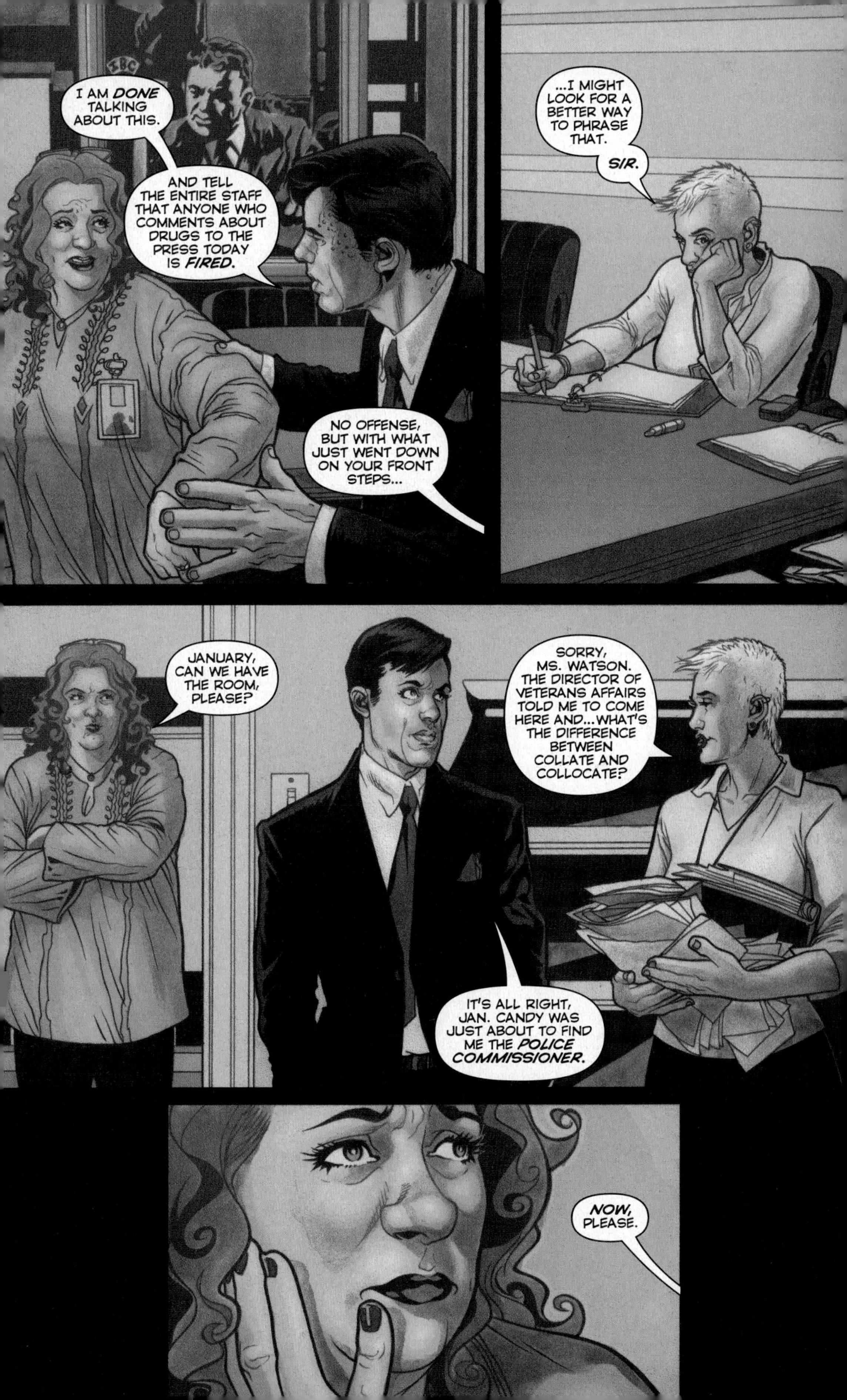
I AM DONE TALKING ABOUT THIS.
AND TELL THE ENTIRE STAFF THAT ANYONE WHO COMMENTS ABOUT DRUGS TO THE PRESS TODAY IS FIRED.
NO OFFENSE, BUT WITH WHAT JUST WENT DOWN ON YOUR FRONT STEPS...
...I MIGHT LOOK FOR A BETTER WAY TO PHRASE THAT.
SIR.
JANUARY, CAN WE HAVE THE ROOM, PLEASE?
SORRY, MS. WATSON. THE DIRECTOR OF VETERANS AFFAIRS TOLD ME TO COME HERE AND...WHAT'S THE DIFFERENCE BETWEEN COLLATE AND COLLOCATE?
IT'S ALL RIGHT, JAN. CANDY WAS JUST ABOUT TO FIND ME THE POLICE COMMISSIONER.
NOW, PLEASE.

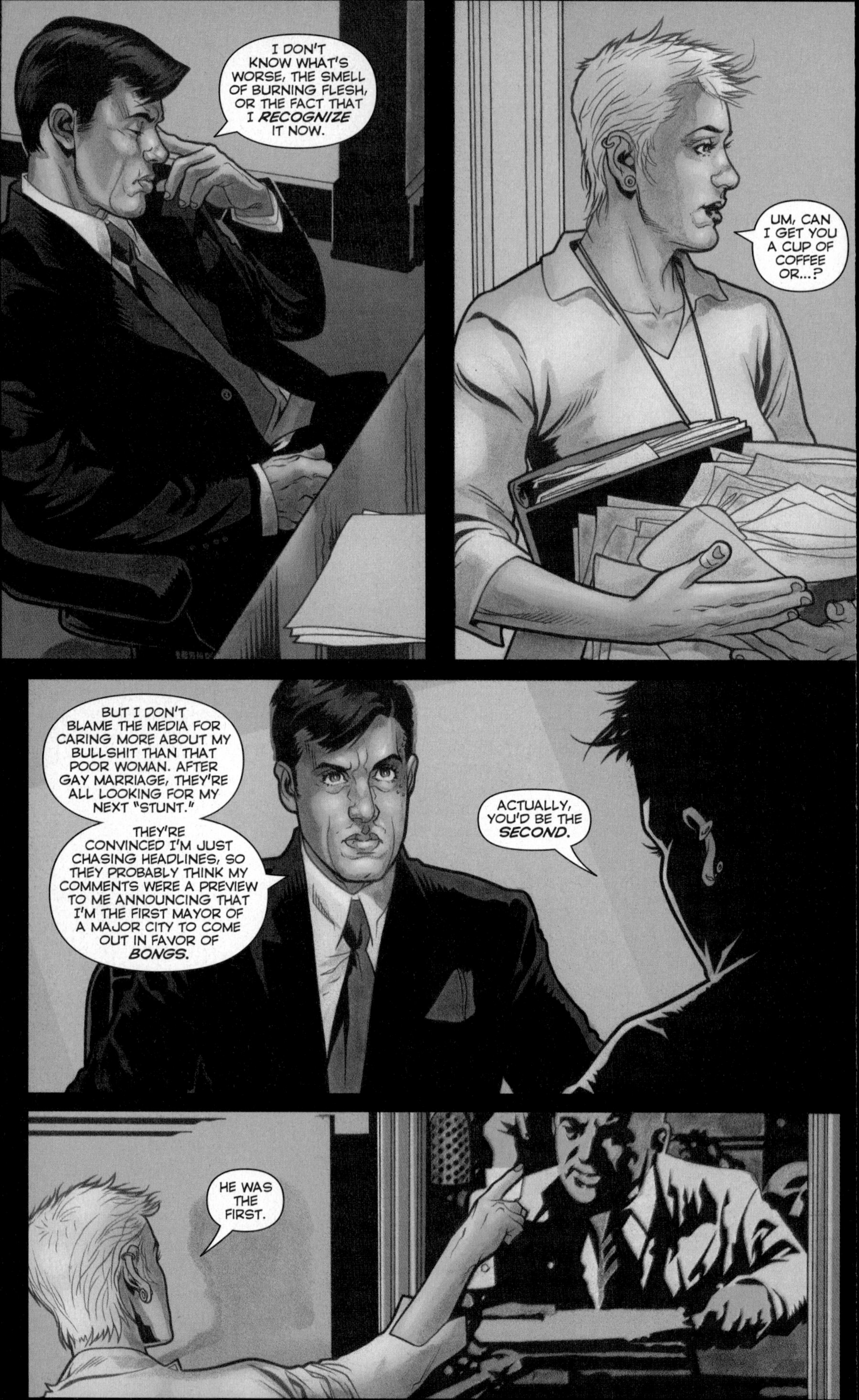
I DON'T KNOW WHAT'S WORSE, THE SMELL OF BURNING FLESH, OR THE FACT THAT I *RECOGNIZE* IT NOW.
UM, CAN I GET YOU A CUP OF COFFEE OR...?
BUT I DON'T BLAME THE MEDIA FOR CARING MORE ABOUT MY BULLSHIT THAN THAT POOR WOMAN. AFTER GAY MARRIAGE, THEY'RE ALL LOOKING FOR MY NEXT "STUNT."
THEY'RE CONVINCED I'M JUST CHASING HEADLINES, SO THEY PROBABLY THINK MY COMMENTS WERE A PREVIEW TO ME ANNOUNCING THAT I'M THE FIRST MAYOR OF A MAJOR CITY TO COME OUT IN FAVOR OF *BONGS*.
ACTUALLY, YOU'D BE THE *SECOND*.
HE WAS THE FIRST.

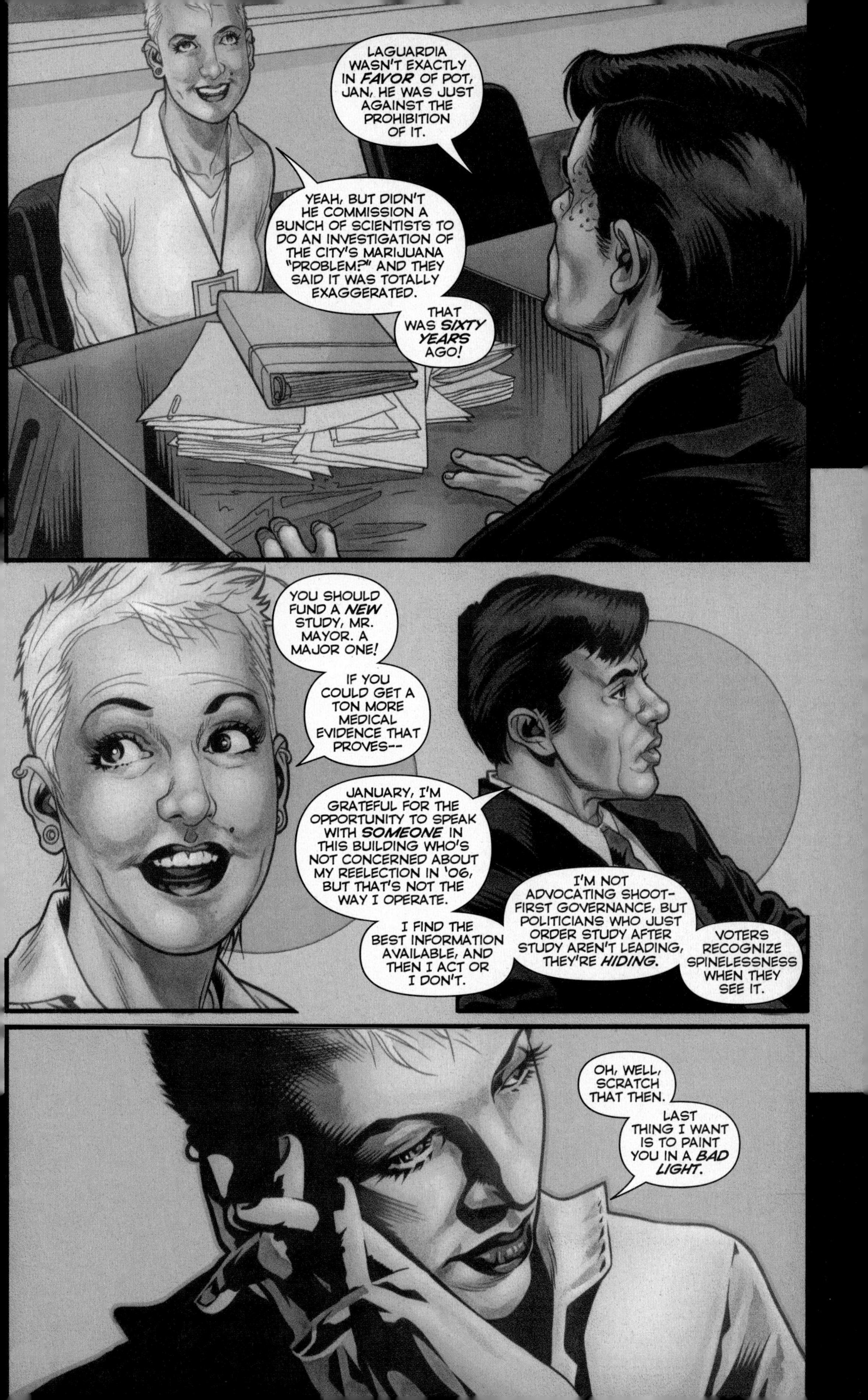
LAGUARDIA WASN'T EXACTLY IN FAVOR OF POT, JAN, HE WAS JUST AGAINST THE PROHIBITION OF IT.
YEAH, BUT DIDN'T HE COMMISSION A BUNCH OF SCIENTISTS TO DO AN INVESTIGATION OF THE CITY'S MARIJUANA "PROBLEM?" AND THEY SAID IT WAS TOTALLY EXAGGERATED.
THAT WAS SIXTY YEARS AGO!
YOU SHOULD FUND A NEW STUDY, MR. MAYOR. A MAJOR ONE!
IF YOU COULD GET A TON MORE MEDICAL EVIDENCE THAT PROVES--
JANUARY, I'M GRATEFUL FOR THE OPPORTUNITY TO SPEAK WITH SOMEONE IN THIS BUILDING WHO'S NOT CONCERNED ABOUT MY REELECTION IN '06, BUT THAT'S NOT THE WAY I OPERATE.
I FIND THE BEST INFORMATION AVAILABLE, AND THEN I ACT OR I DON'T.
I'M NOT ADVOCATING SHOOT-FIRST GOVERNANCE, BUT POLITICIANS WHO JUST ORDER STUDY AFTER STUDY AREN'T LEADING, THEY'RE HIDING.
VOTERS RECOGNIZE SPINELESSNESS WHEN THEY SEE IT.
OH, WELL, SCRATCH THAT THEN.
LAST THING I WANT IS TO PAINT YOU IN A BAD LIGHT.

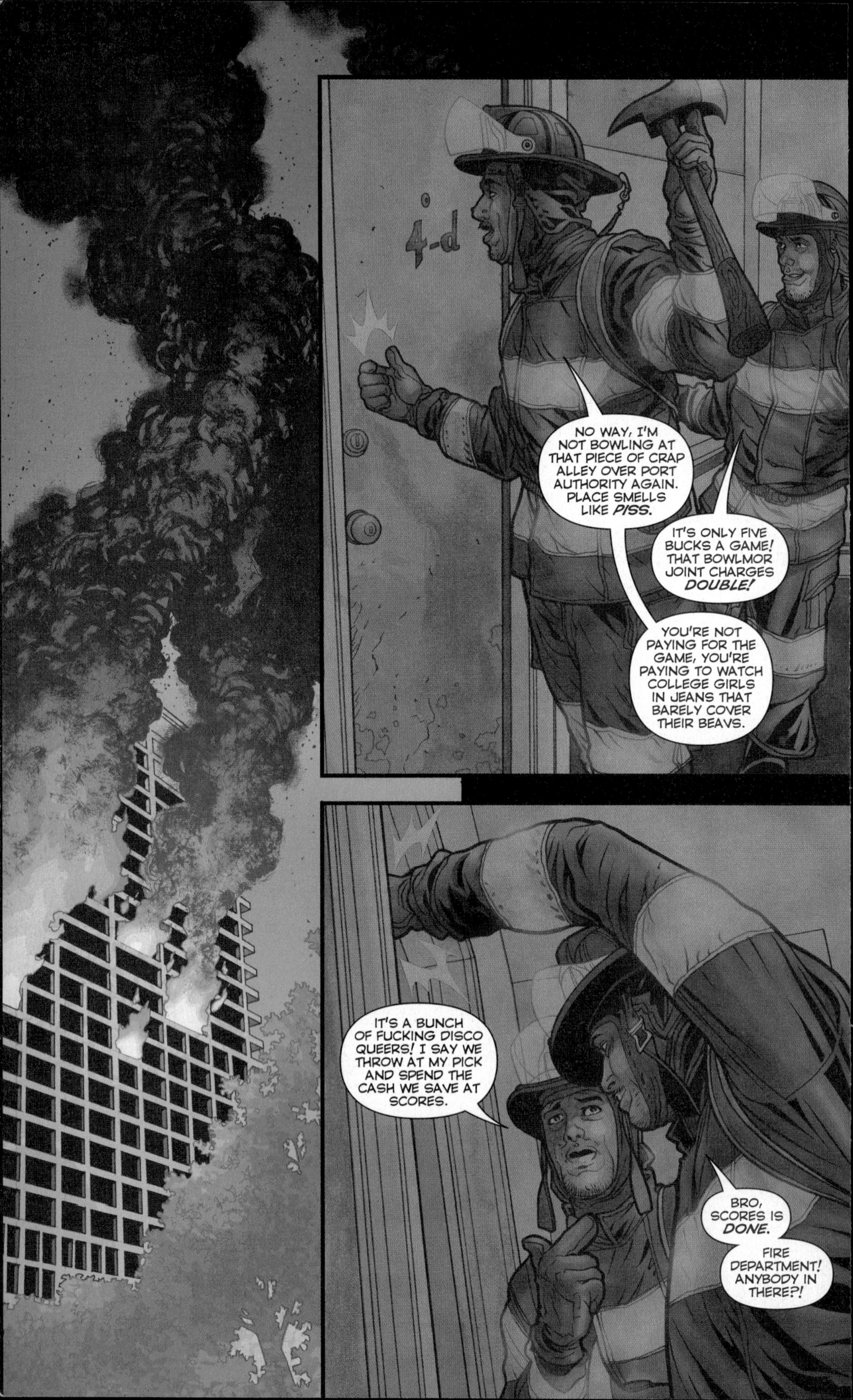
NO WAY, I'M NOT BOWLING AT THAT PIECE OF CRAP ALLEY OVER PORT AUTHORITY AGAIN. PLACE SMELLS LIKE *PISS*.
IT'S ONLY FIVE BUCKS A GAME! THAT BOWLMOR JOINT CHARGES *DOUBLE!*
YOU'RE NOT PAYING FOR THE GAME, YOU'RE PAYING TO WATCH COLLEGE GIRLS IN JEANS THAT BARELY COVER THEIR BEAVS.
IT'S A BUNCH OF FUCKING DISCO QUEERS! I SAY WE THROW AT MY PICK AND SPEND THE CASH WE SAVE AT SCORES.
BRO, SCORES IS *DONE*.
FIRE DEPARTMENT! ANYBODY IN THERE?!

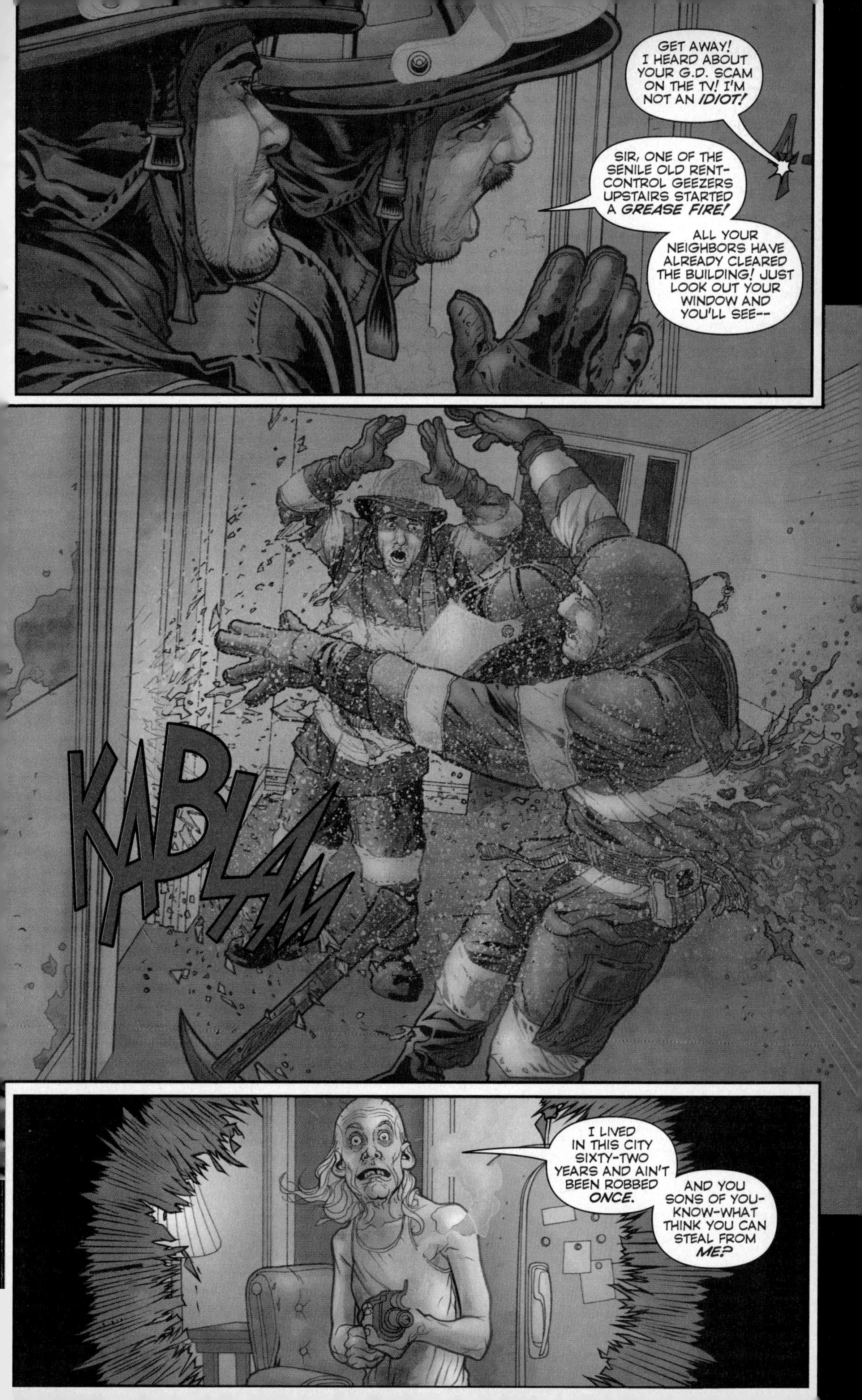
GET AWAY! I HEARD ABOUT YOUR G.D. SCAM ON THE TV! I'M NOT AN *IDIOT!*
SIR, ONE OF THE SENILE OLD RENT-CONTROL GEEZERS UPSTAIRS STARTED A *GREASE FIRE!*
ALL YOUR NEIGHBORS HAVE ALREADY CLEARED THE BUILDING! JUST LOOK OUT YOUR WINDOW AND YOU'LL SEE--
KABLAM
I LIVED IN THIS CITY SIXTY-TWO YEARS AND AIN'T BEEN ROBBED *ONCE*.
AND YOU SONS OF YOU-KNOW-WHAT THINK YOU CAN STEAL FROM *ME?*

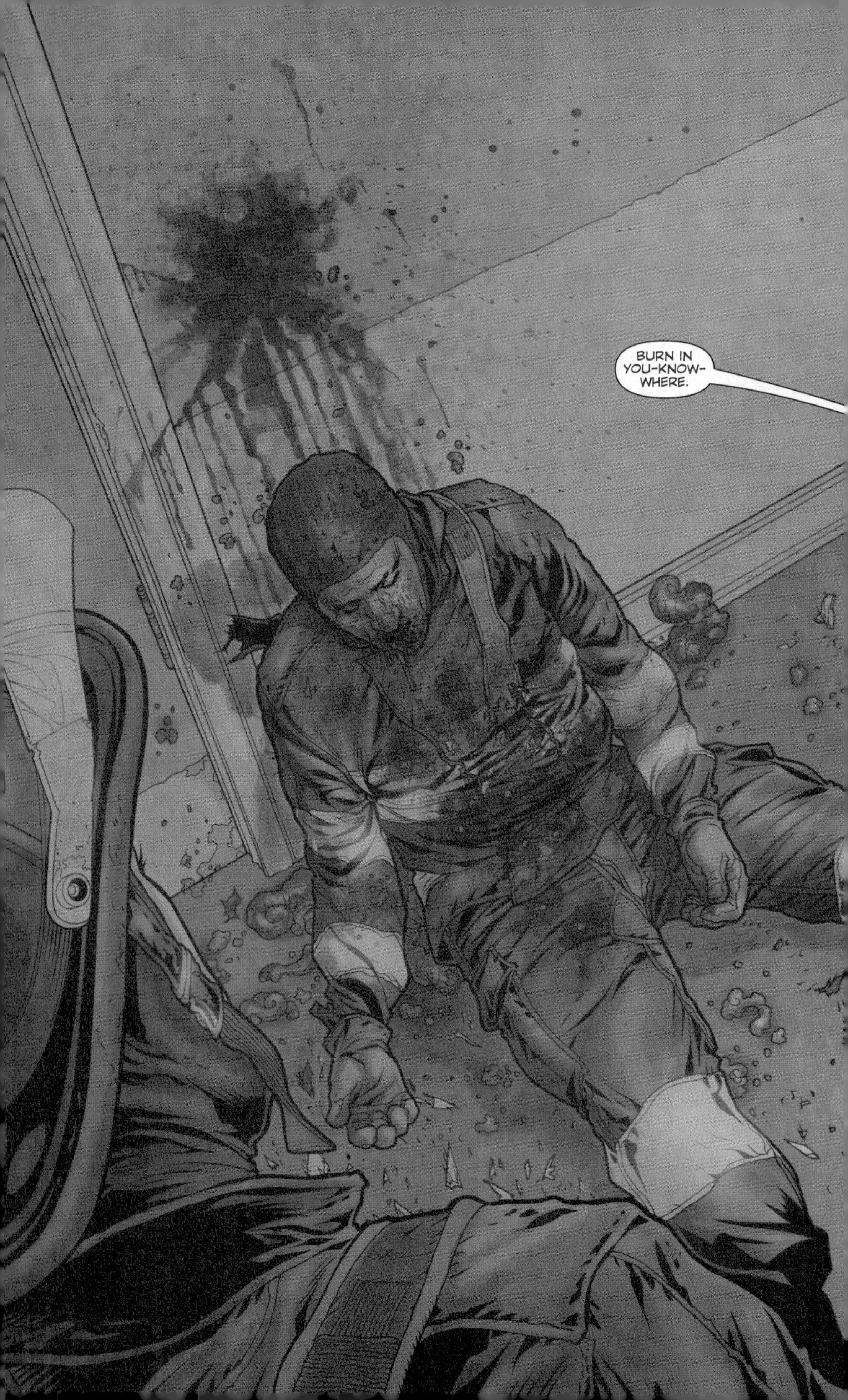
BURN IN YOU-KNOW-WHERE.

Smoke Smoke

Chapter 3

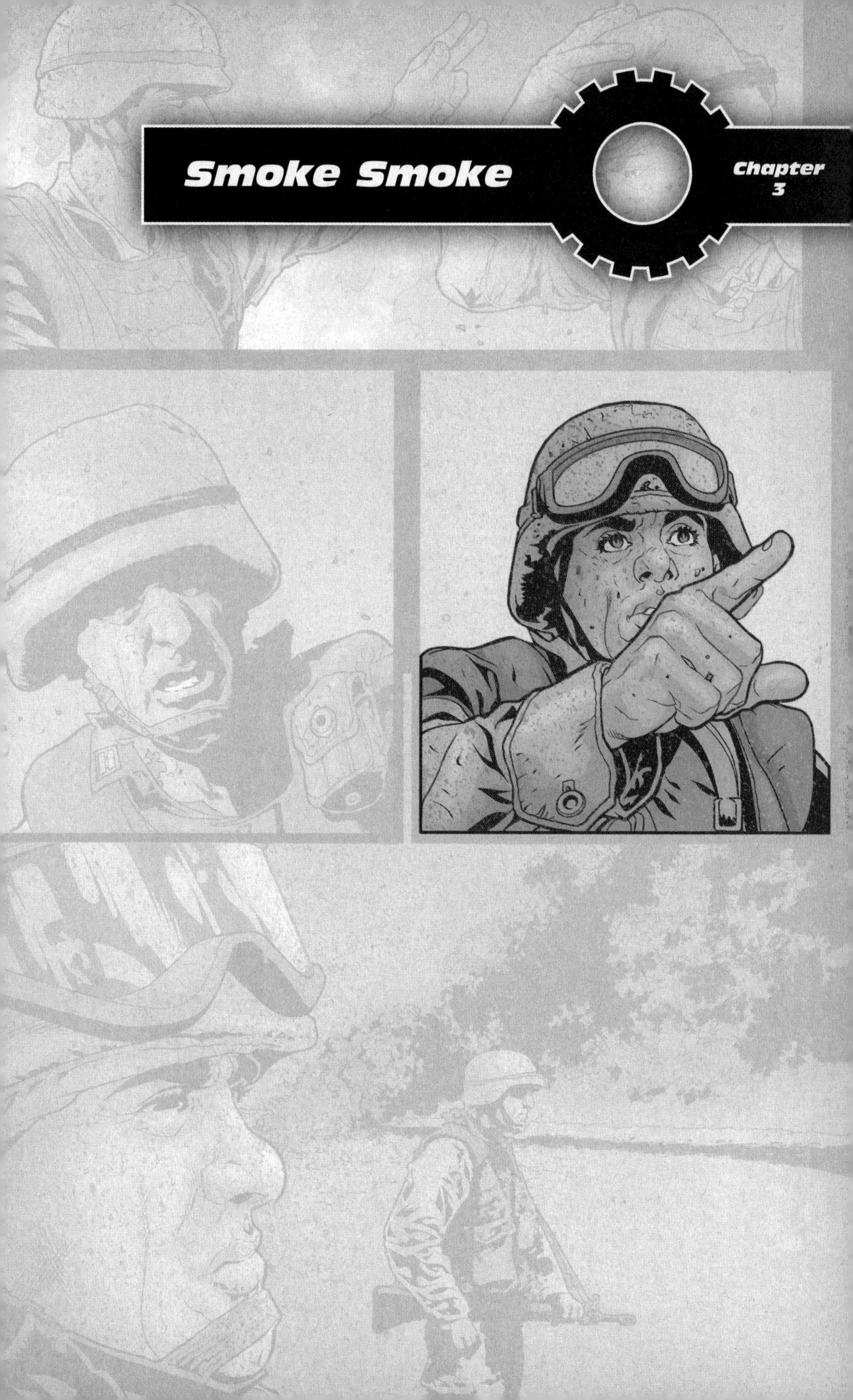

NEW ★ ★ ★ ★ YORK
DAILY ⚡ WIRE
New York's Most Respected Newspaper

★ **EXCLUSIVE** ★

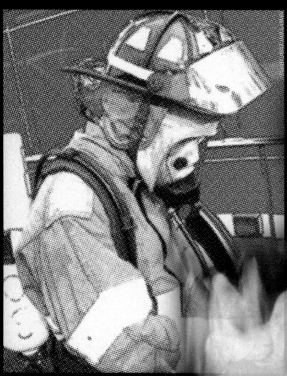

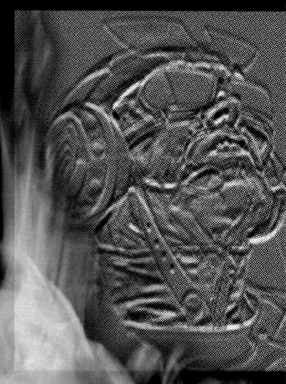

FIREFIGHTER THIEF STRIKES!

Sources at the N.Y.P.D. say that a man is posing as a New York City FireFighter and under that guise then enters peoples homes and robs them. He is allegedly targeting the upscale residents in the Soho area. Police are sorting through hundreds of leads, and phone calls from New Yorkers saying the (page 2)

NYC LOCAL 2507 HONOR MACHINE!

Sunday evening the Uniformed E.MT.'s and Paramedics of the Local 2507 will Honor The Great Machine and his efforts to save Tower 2 on 9/11. The ceremony will include a Banquet followed by the Unveiling of a relief plaque featuring a stunning likeness of The Great Machine. The Banquet is expected (page 6)

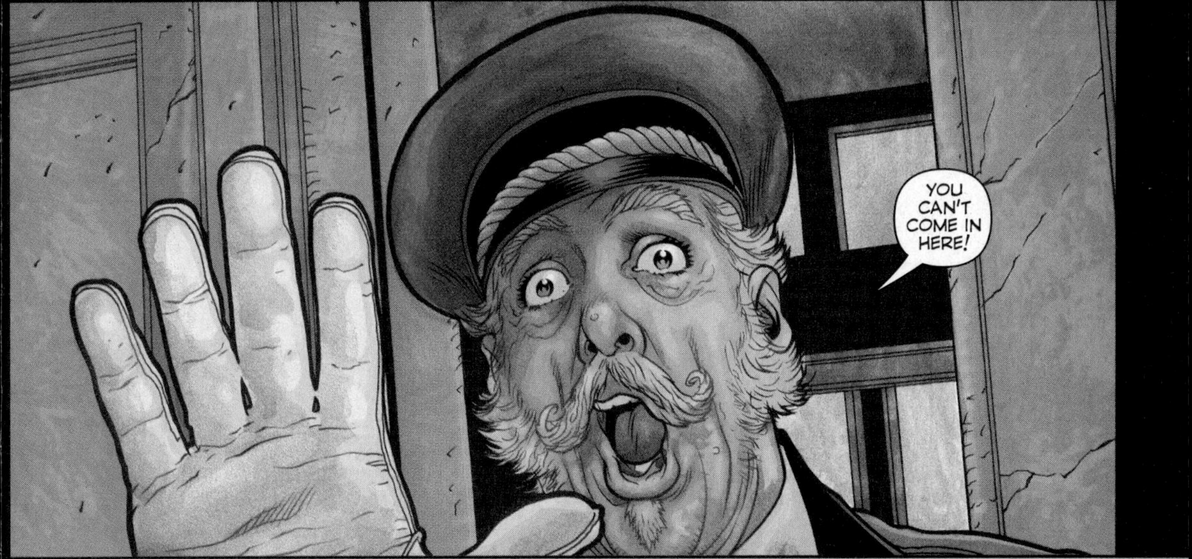
YOU CAN'T COME IN HERE!

MONDAY, APRIL 2, 2001

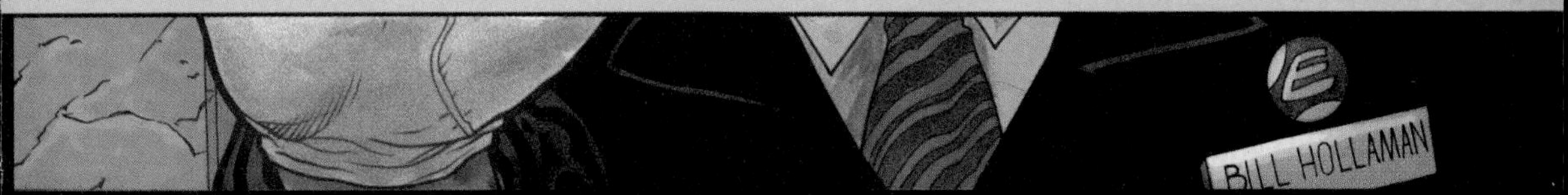
BILL HOLLAMAN

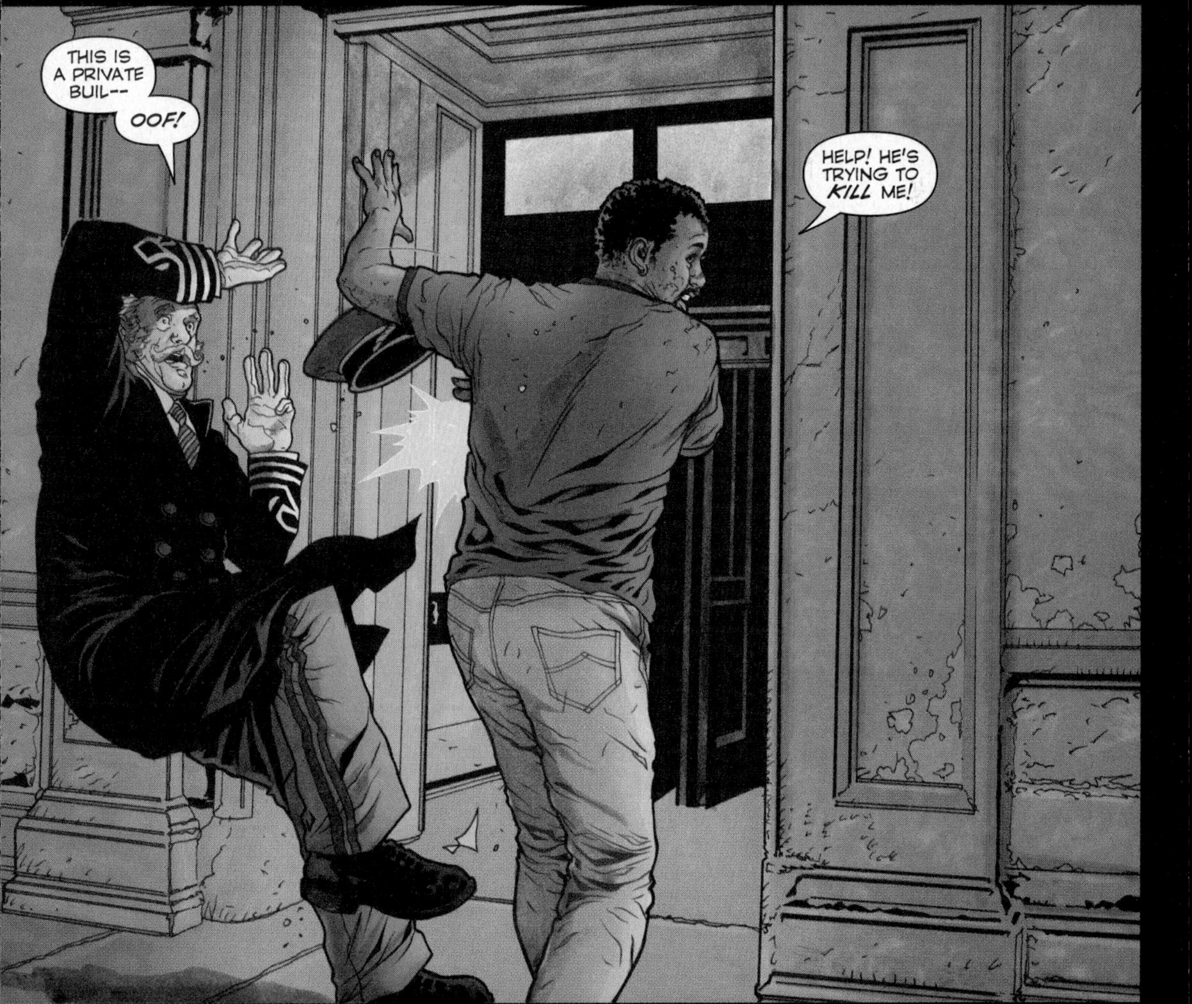
THIS IS A PRIVATE BUIL-- OOF!
HELP! HE'S TRYING TO KILL ME!

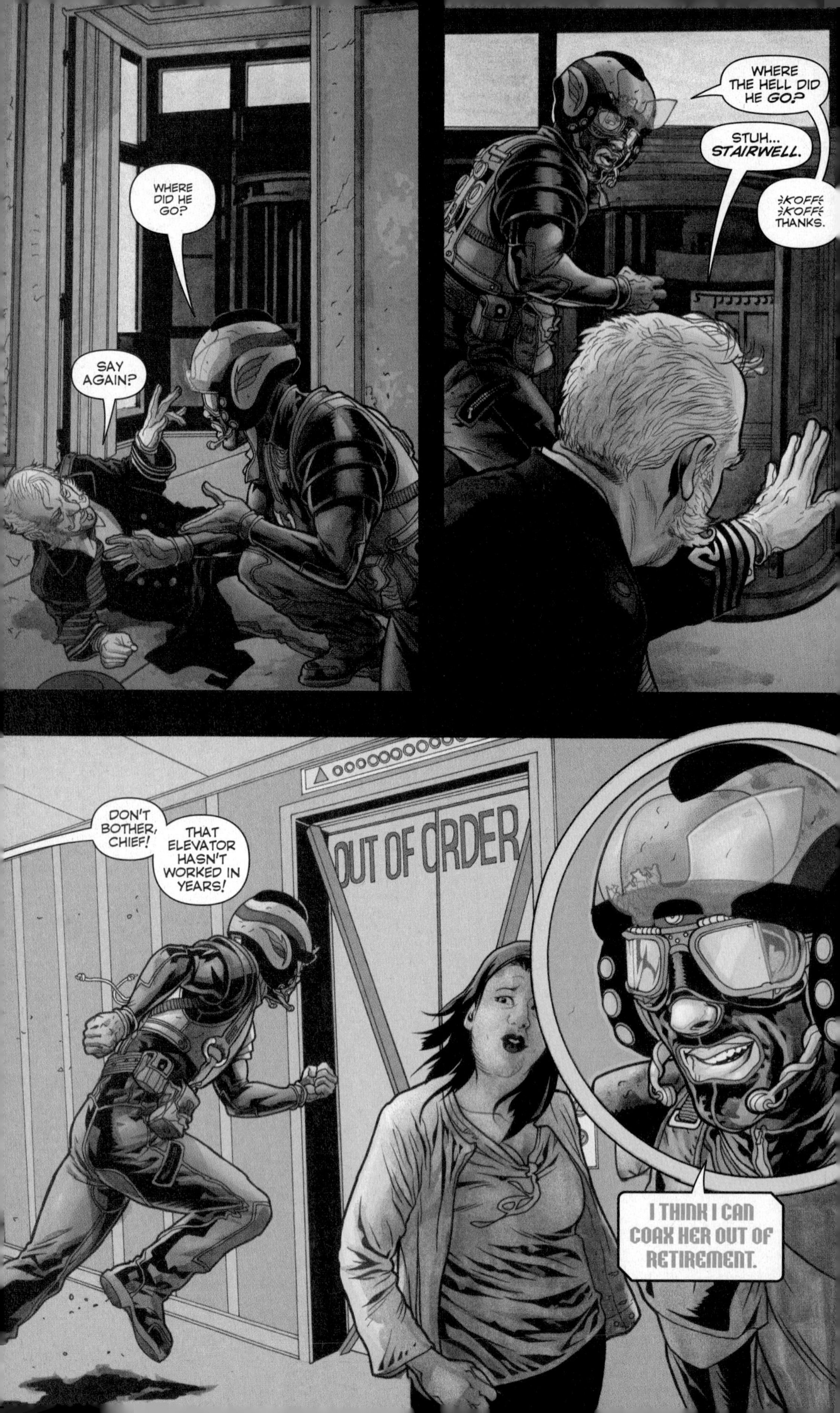
WHERE DID HE GO?
SAY AGAIN?
WHERE THE HELL DID HE GO?
STUH... STAIRWELL.
KOFF *KOFF* THANKS.
OUT OF ORDER
DON'T BOTHER, CHIEF!
THAT ELEVATOR HASN'T WORKED IN YEARS!
I THINK I CAN COAX HER OUT OF RETIREMENT.

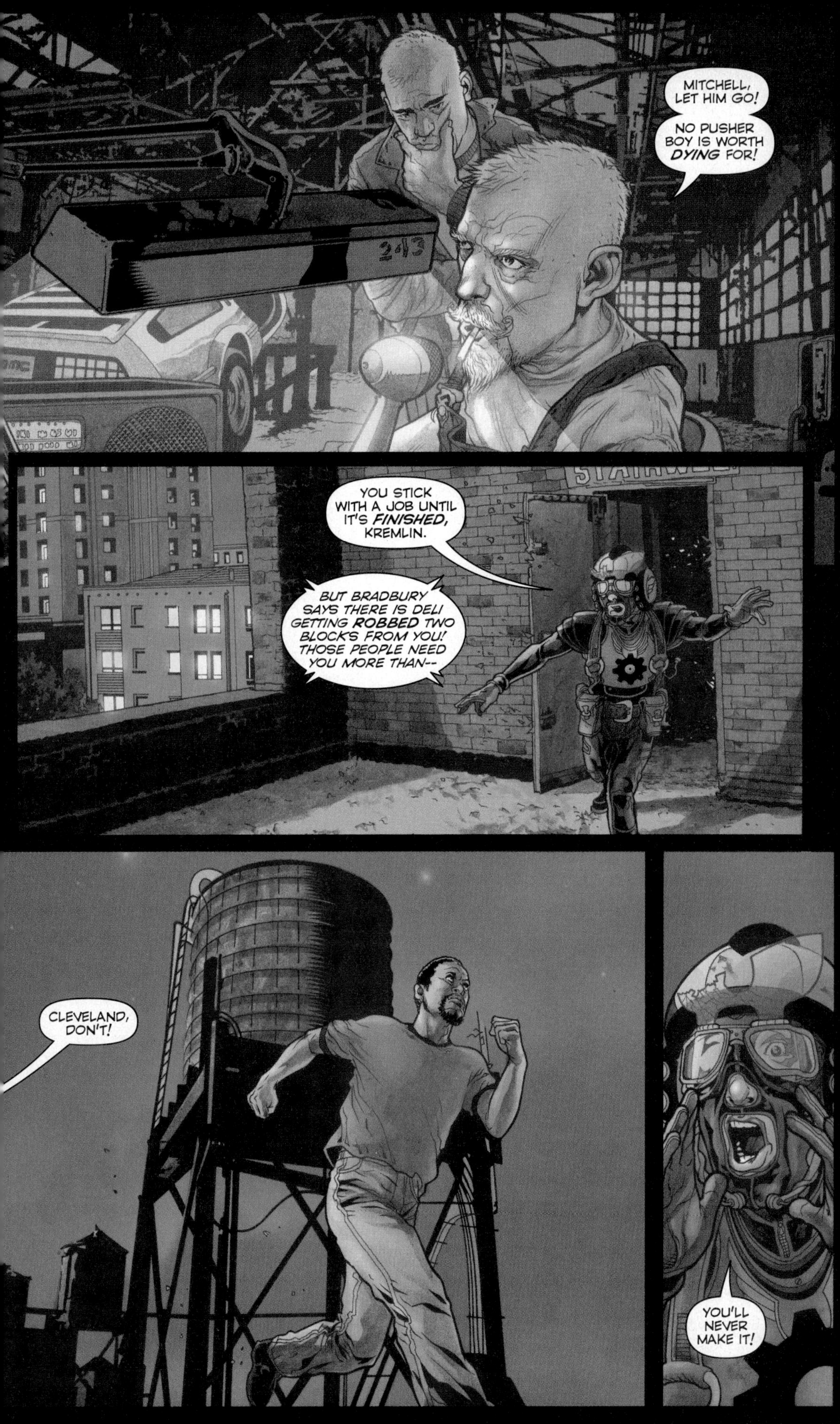
MITCHELL, LET HIM GO!
NO PUSHER BOY IS WORTH *DYING* FOR!
2-13
YOU STICK WITH A JOB UNTIL IT'S *FINISHED,* KREMLIN.
*BUT BRADBURY SAYS THERE IS DELI GETTING **ROBBED** TWO BLOCKS FROM YOU! THOSE PEOPLE NEED YOU MORE THAN--*
CLEVELAND, DON'T!
YOU'LL NEVER MAKE IT!

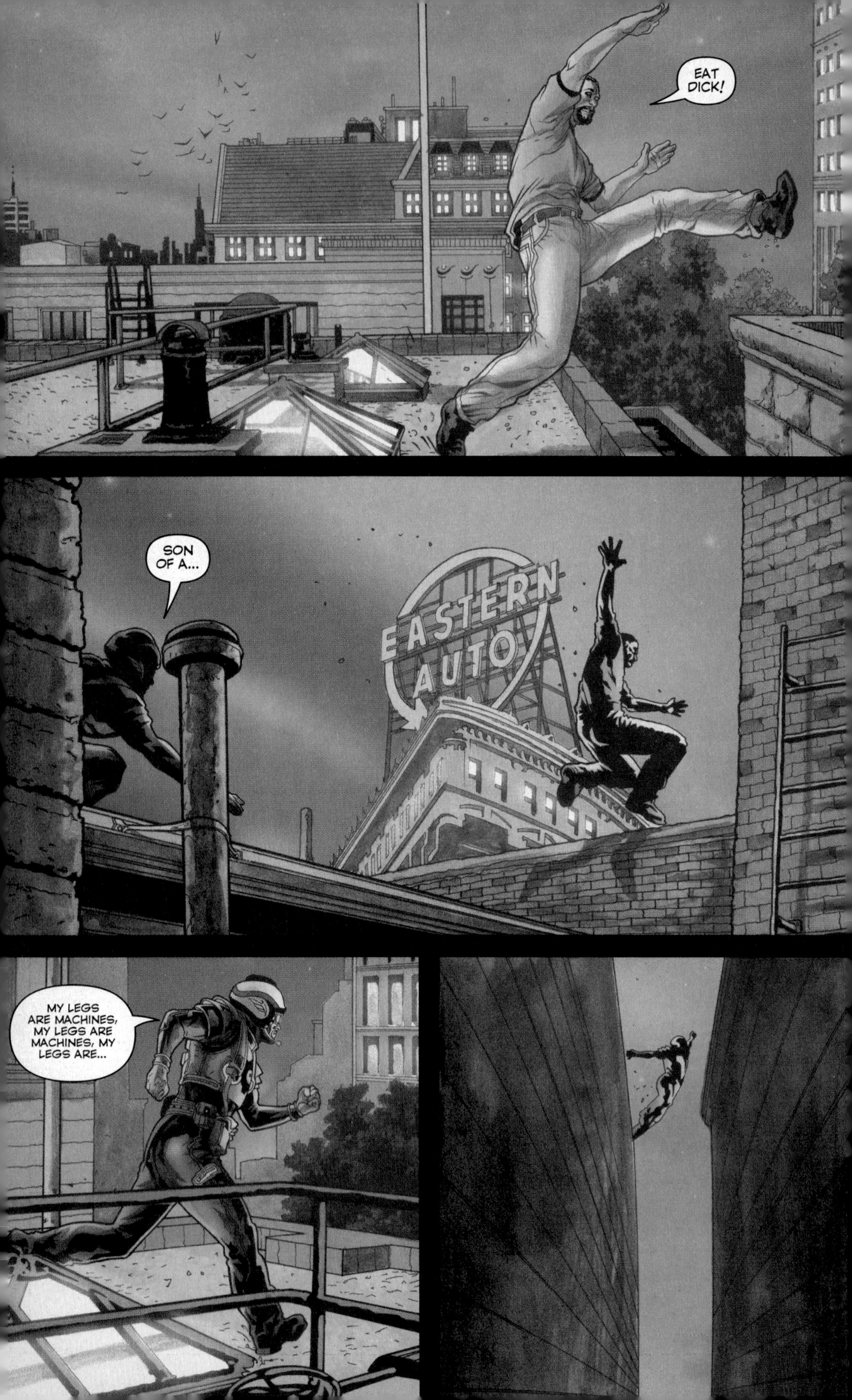
EAT DICK!
SON OF A...
EASTERN AUTO
MY LEGS ARE MACHINES, MY LEGS ARE MACHINES, MY LEGS ARE...

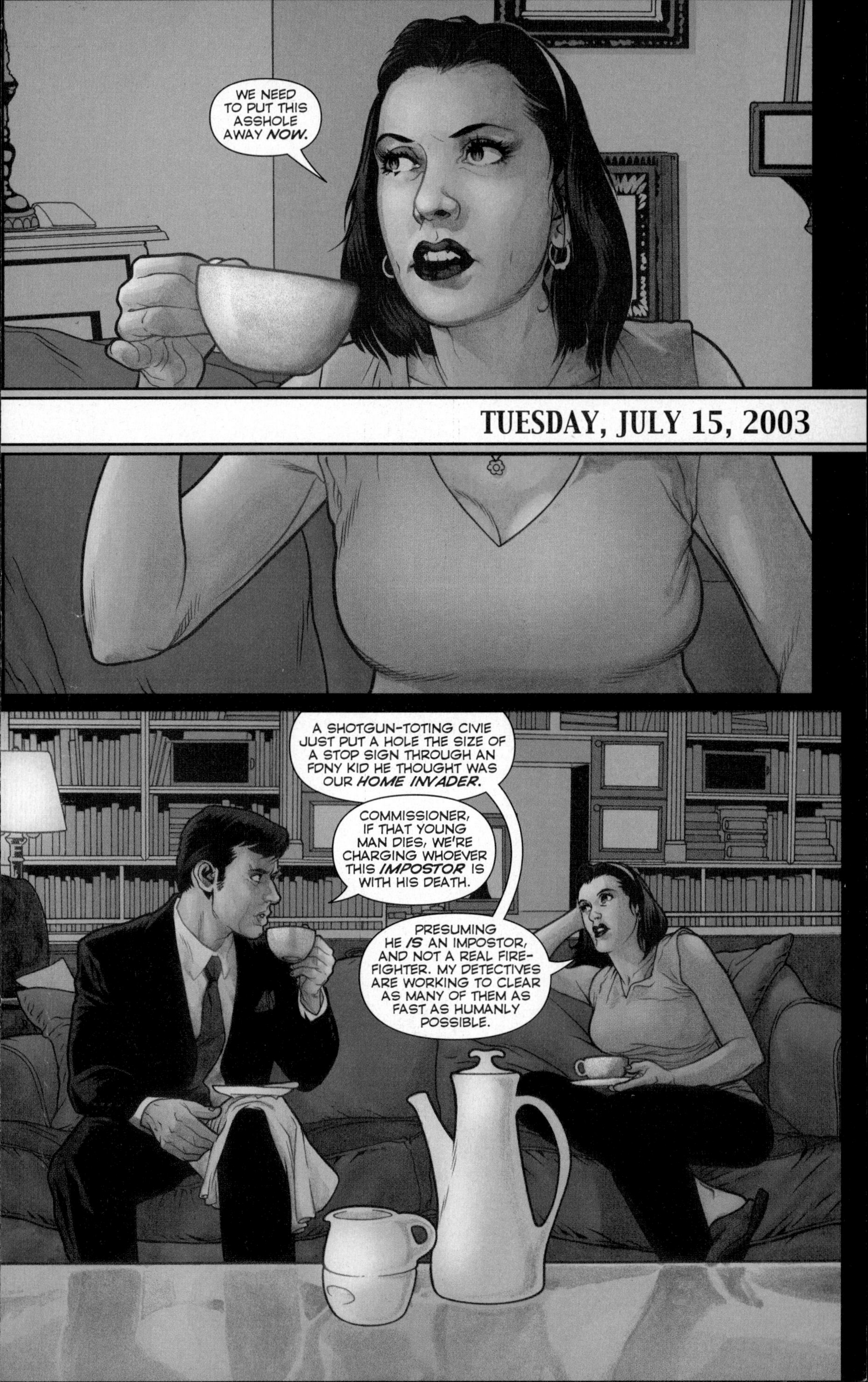
WE NEED TO PUT THIS ASSHOLE AWAY NOW.
TUESDAY, JULY 15, 2003
A SHOTGUN-TOTING CIVIE JUST PUT A HOLE THE SIZE OF A STOP SIGN THROUGH AN FDNY KID HE THOUGHT WAS OUR HOME INVADER.
COMMISSIONER, IF THAT YOUNG MAN DIES, WE'RE CHARGING WHOEVER THIS IMPOSTOR IS WITH HIS DEATH.
PRESUMING HE IS AN IMPOSTOR, AND NOT A REAL FIRE-FIGHTER. MY DETECTIVES ARE WORKING TO CLEAR AS MANY OF THEM AS FAST AS HUMANLY POSSIBLE.

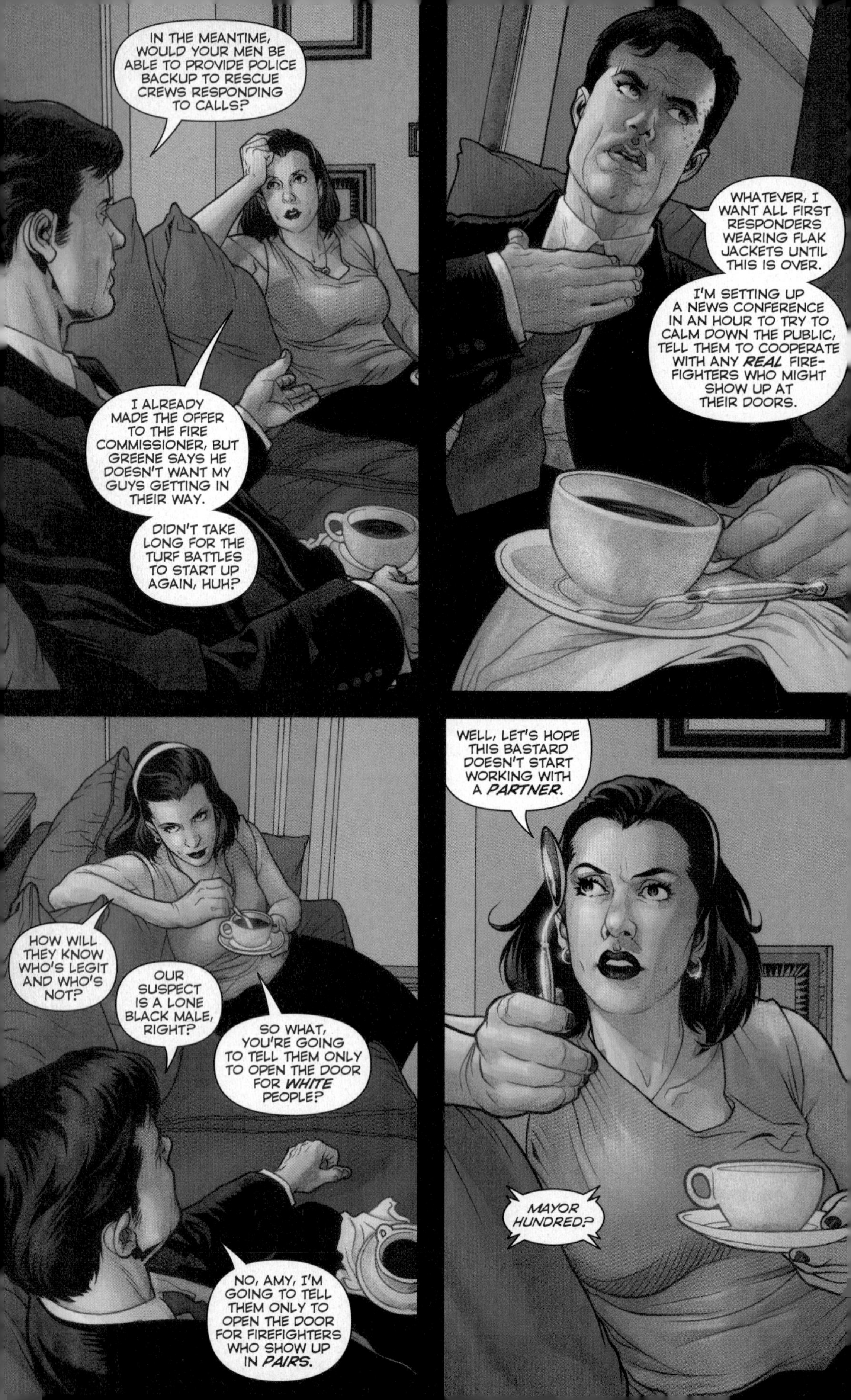
IN THE MEANTIME, WOULD YOUR MEN BE ABLE TO PROVIDE POLICE BACKUP TO RESCUE CREWS RESPONDING TO CALLS?
I ALREADY MADE THE OFFER TO THE FIRE COMMISSIONER, BUT GREENE SAYS HE DOESN'T WANT MY GUYS GETTING IN THEIR WAY.
DIDN'T TAKE LONG FOR THE TURF BATTLES TO START UP AGAIN, HUH?
WHATEVER, I WANT ALL FIRST RESPONDERS WEARING FLAK JACKETS UNTIL THIS IS OVER.
I'M SETTING UP A NEWS CONFERENCE IN AN HOUR TO TRY TO CALM DOWN THE PUBLIC, TELL THEM TO COOPERATE WITH ANY *REAL* FIRE-FIGHTERS WHO MIGHT SHOW UP AT THEIR DOORS.
HOW WILL THEY KNOW WHO'S LEGIT AND WHO'S NOT?
OUR SUSPECT IS A LONE BLACK MALE, RIGHT?
SO WHAT, YOU'RE GOING TO TELL THEM ONLY TO OPEN THE DOOR FOR *WHITE* PEOPLE?
NO, AMY, I'M GOING TO TELL THEM ONLY TO OPEN THE DOOR FOR FIREFIGHTERS WHO SHOW UP IN *PAIRS*.
WELL, LET'S HOPE THIS BASTARD DOESN'T START WORKING WITH A *PARTNER*.
MAYOR HUNDRED?

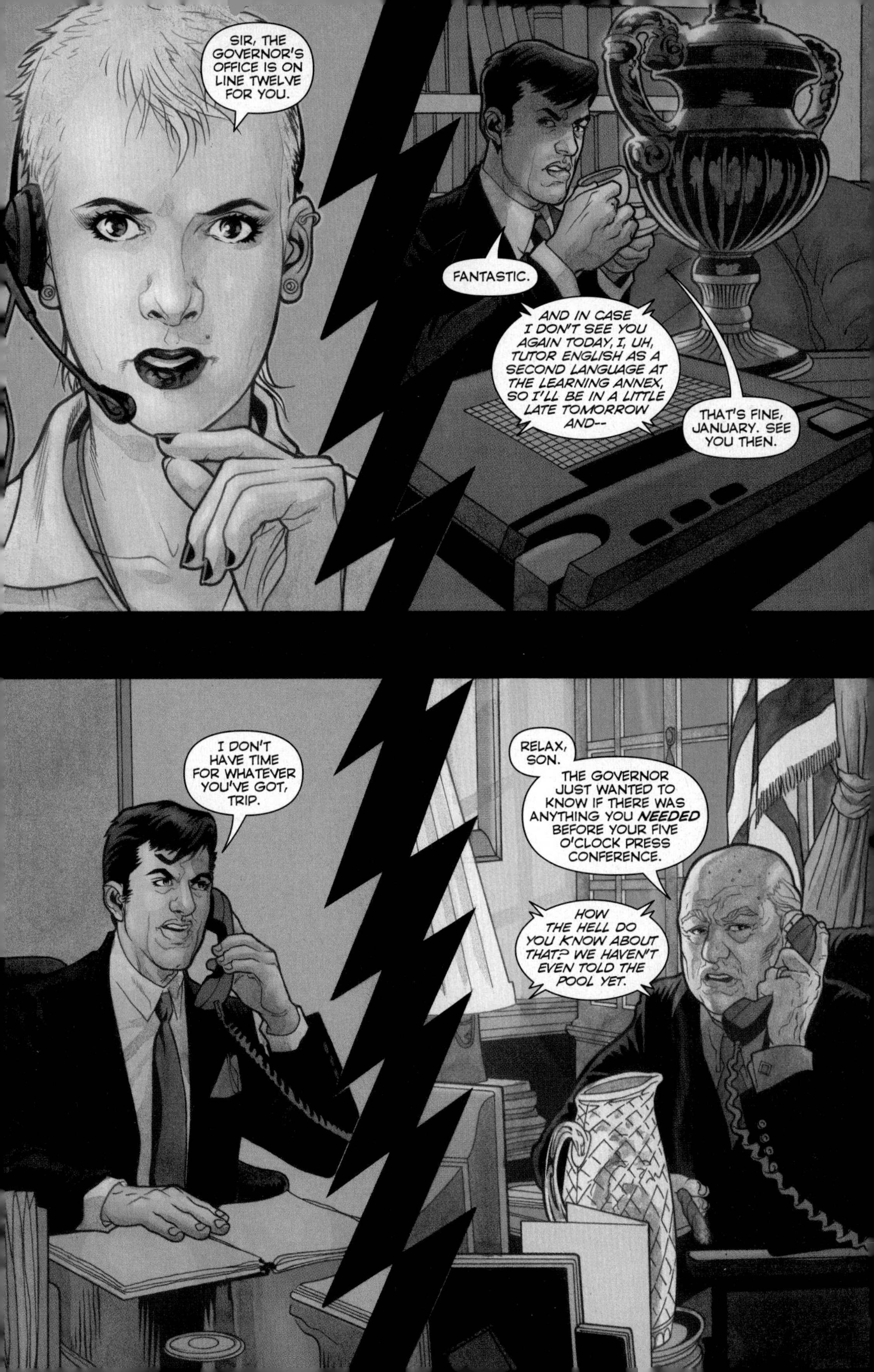
SIR, THE GOVERNOR'S OFFICE IS ON LINE TWELVE FOR YOU.
FANTASTIC.
AND IN CASE I DON'T SEE YOU AGAIN TODAY, I, UH, TUTOR ENGLISH AS A SECOND LANGUAGE AT THE LEARNING ANNEX, SO I'LL BE IN A LITTLE LATE TOMORROW AND--
THAT'S FINE, JANUARY. SEE YOU THEN.
I DON'T HAVE TIME FOR WHATEVER YOU'VE GOT, TRIP.
RELAX, SON.
THE GOVERNOR JUST WANTED TO KNOW IF THERE WAS ANYTHING YOU NEEDED BEFORE YOUR FIVE O'CLOCK PRESS CONFERENCE.
HOW THE HELL DO YOU KNOW ABOUT THAT? WE HAVEN'T EVEN TOLD THE POOL YET.

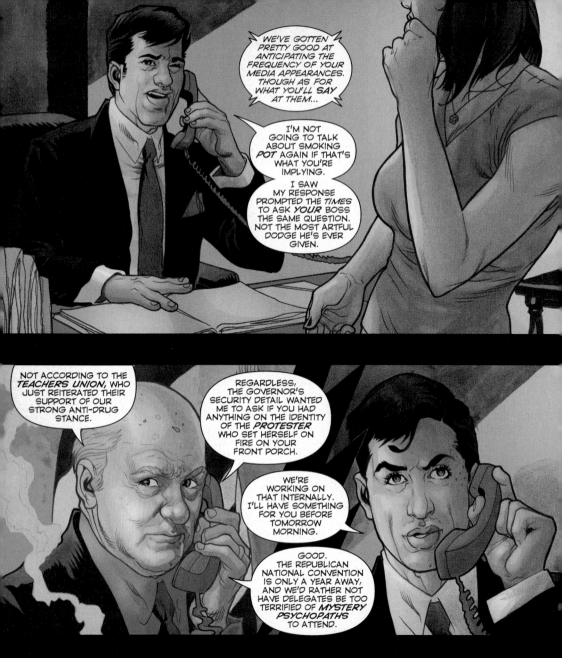

WE'VE GOTTEN PRETTY GOOD AT ANTICIPATING THE FREQUENCY OF YOUR MEDIA APPEARANCES. THOUGH AS FOR WHAT YOU'LL *SAY* AT THEM...

I'M NOT GOING TO TALK ABOUT SMOKING *POT* AGAIN IF THAT'S WHAT YOU'RE IMPLYING.

I SAW MY RESPONSE PROMPTED THE *TIMES* TO ASK *YOUR* BOSS THE SAME QUESTION. NOT THE MOST ARTFUL DODGE HE'S EVER GIVEN.

NOT ACCORDING TO THE *TEACHERS UNION*, WHO JUST REITERATED THEIR SUPPORT OF OUR STRONG ANTI-DRUG STANCE.

REGARDLESS, THE GOVERNOR'S SECURITY DETAIL WANTED ME TO ASK IF YOU HAD ANYTHING ON THE IDENTITY OF THE *PROTESTER* WHO SET HERSELF ON FIRE ON YOUR FRONT PORCH.

WE'RE WORKING ON THAT INTERNALLY. I'LL HAVE SOMETHING FOR YOU BEFORE TOMORROW MORNING.

GOOD. THE REPUBLICAN NATIONAL CONVENTION IS ONLY A YEAR AWAY, AND WE'D RATHER NOT HAVE DELEGATES BE TOO TERRIFIED OF *MYSTERY PSYCHOPATHS* TO ATTEND.

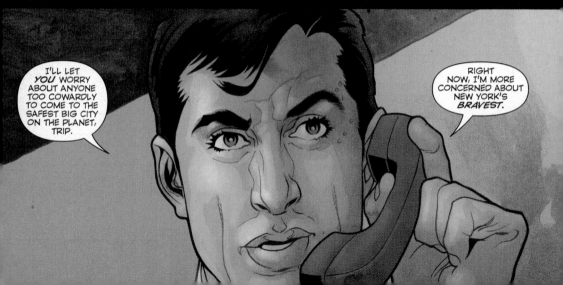

I'LL LET *YOU* WORRY ABOUT ANYONE TOO COWARDLY TO COME TO THE SAFEST BIG CITY ON THE PLANET, TRIP.

RIGHT NOW, I'M MORE CONCERNED ABOUT NEW YORK'S *BRAVEST*.

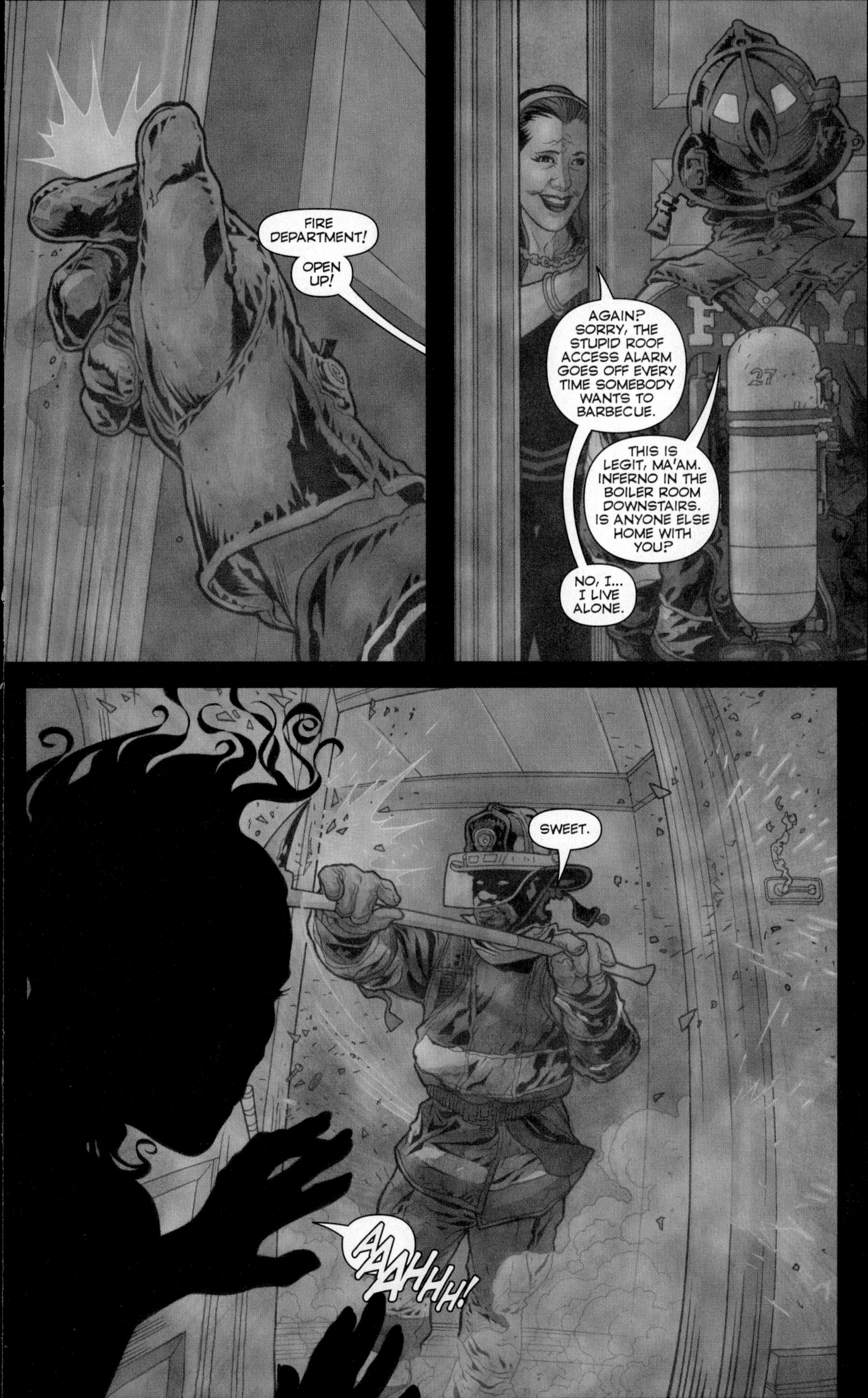
FIRE DEPARTMENT!
OPEN UP!
AGAIN? SORRY, THE STUPID ROOF ACCESS ALARM GOES OFF EVERY TIME SOMEBODY WANTS TO BARBECUE.
THIS IS LEGIT, MA'AM. INFERNO IN THE BOILER ROOM DOWNSTAIRS. IS ANYONE ELSE HOME WITH YOU?
NO, I... I LIVE ALONE.
SWEET.
AAAHHH!

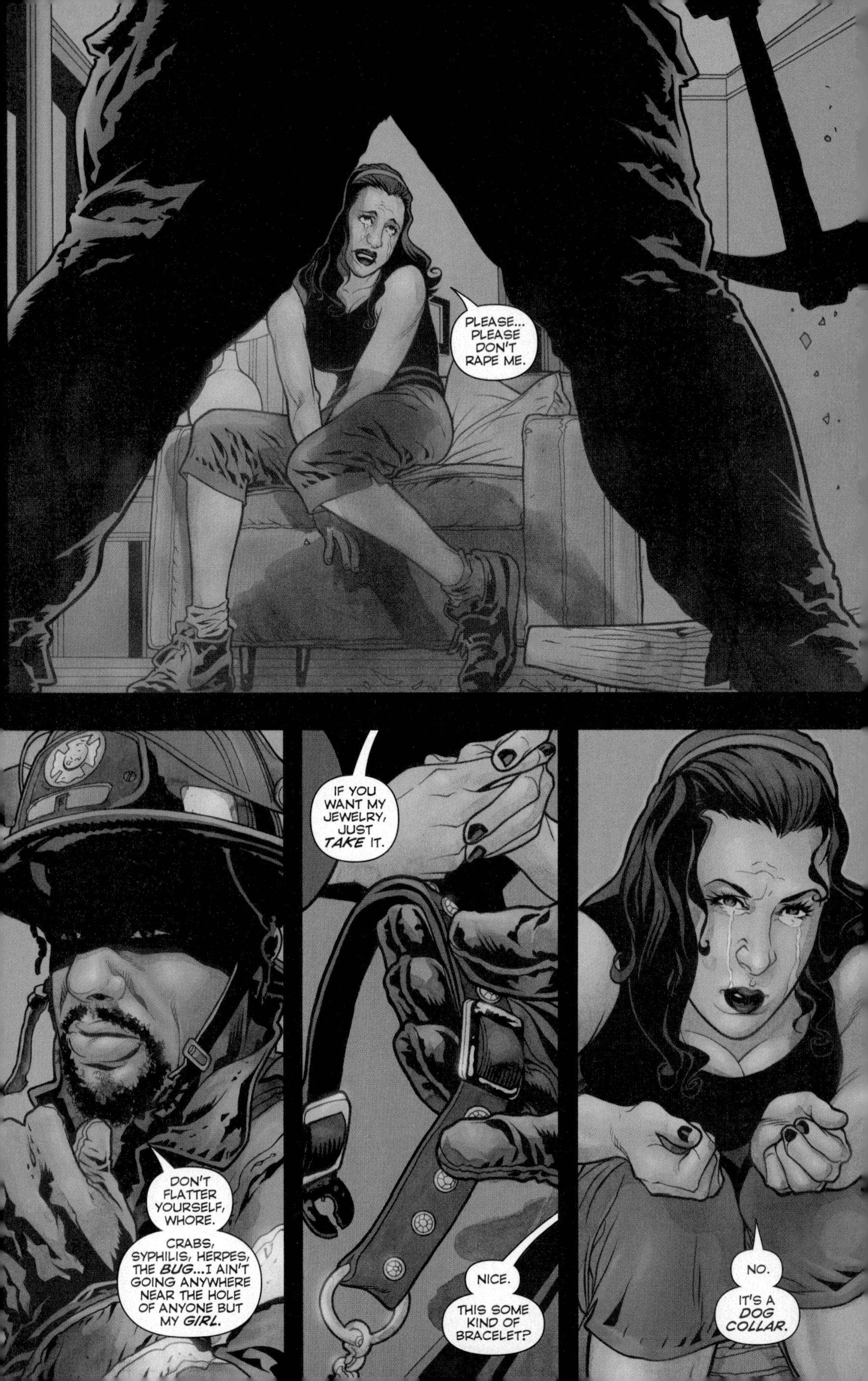
PLEASE... PLEASE DON'T RAPE ME.
DON'T FLATTER YOURSELF, WHORE.
CRABS, SYPHILIS, HERPES, THE BUG...I AIN'T GOING ANYWHERE NEAR THE HOLE OF ANYONE BUT MY GIRL.
IF YOU WANT MY JEWELRY, JUST TAKE IT.
NICE.
THIS SOME KIND OF BRACELET?
NO.
IT'S A DOG COLLAR.

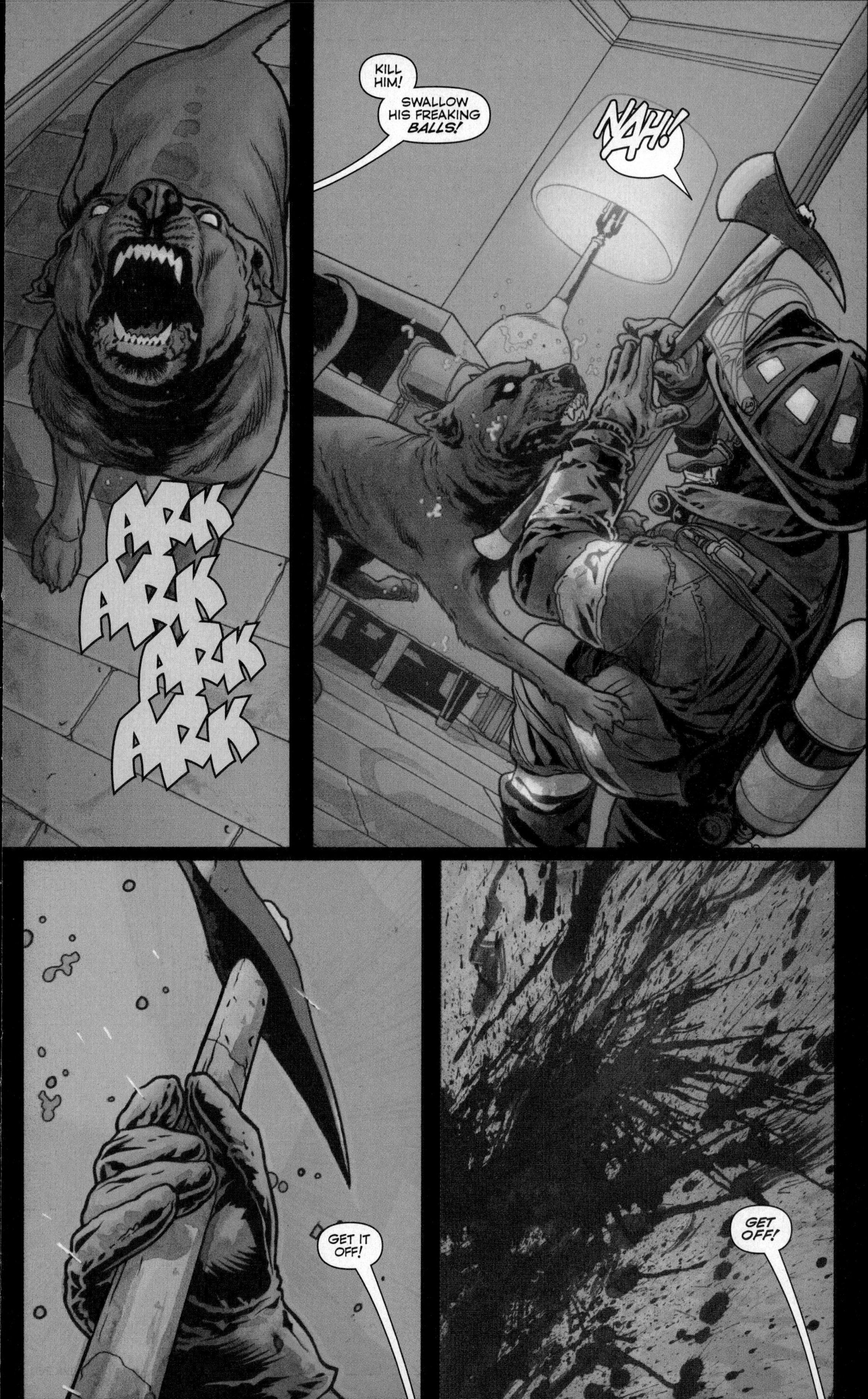
ARK
ARK
ARK
ARK
KILL HIM!
SWALLOW HIS FREAKING BALLS!
NAH!
GET IT OFF!
GET OFF!

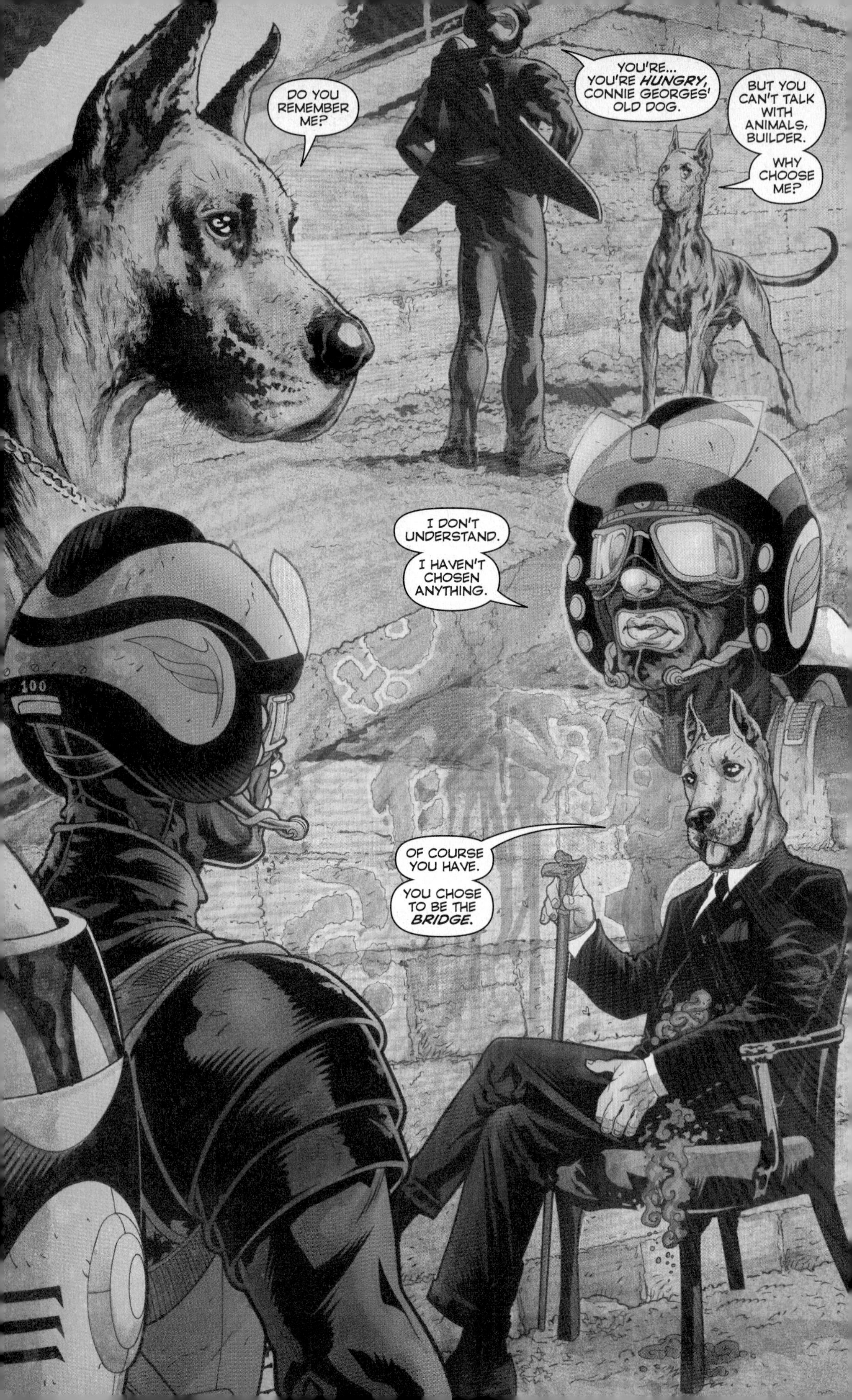
DO YOU REMEMBER ME?
YOU'RE... YOU'RE *HUNGRY*, CONNIE GEORGES' OLD DOG.
BUT YOU CAN'T TALK WITH ANIMALS, BUILDER.
WHY CHOOSE ME?
I DON'T UNDERSTAND.
I HAVEN'T CHOSEN ANYTHING.
OF COURSE YOU HAVE.
YOU CHOSE TO BE THE *BRIDGE*.
100

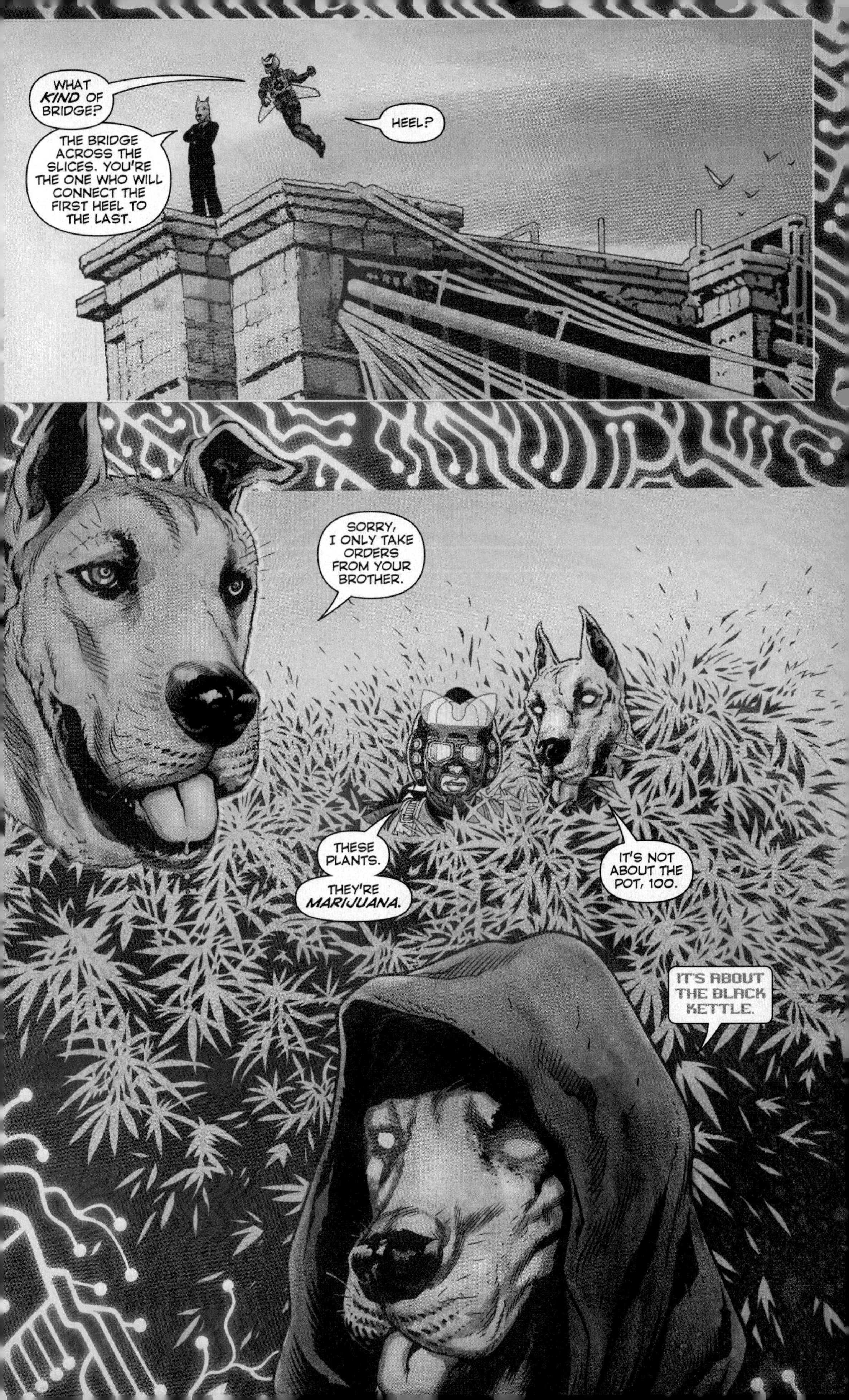
WHAT KIND OF BRIDGE?
THE BRIDGE ACROSS THE SLICES. YOU'RE THE ONE WHO WILL CONNECT THE FIRST HEEL TO THE LAST.
HEEL?
SORRY, I ONLY TAKE ORDERS FROM YOUR BROTHER.
THESE PLANTS.
THEY'RE *MARIJUANA.*
IT'S NOT ABOUT THE POT, 100.
IT'S ABOUT THE BLACK KETTLE.

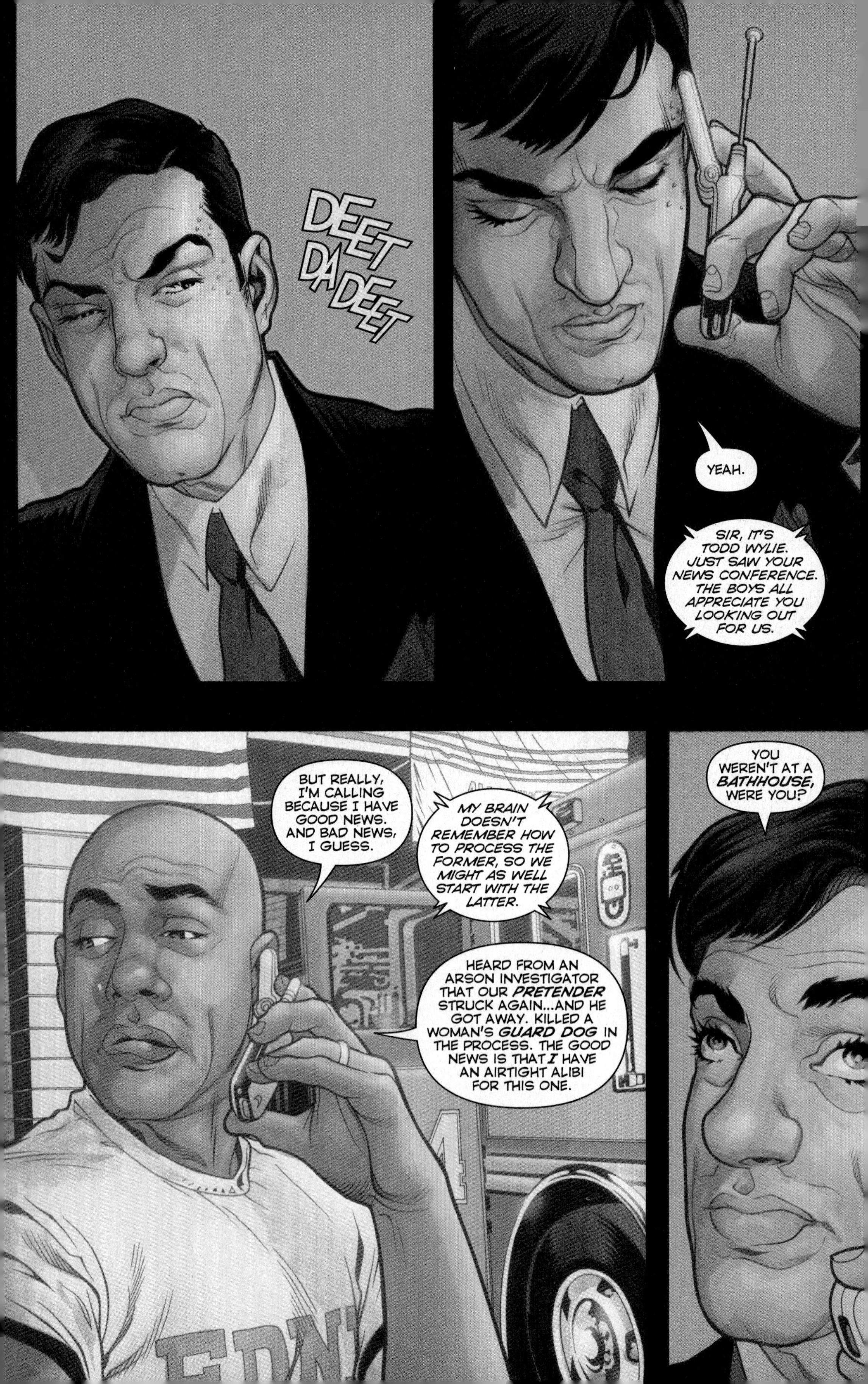
DEEET DA DEEET
YEAH.
SIR, IT'S TODD WYLIE. JUST SAW YOUR NEWS CONFERENCE. THE BOYS ALL APPRECIATE YOU LOOKING OUT FOR US.
BUT REALLY, I'M CALLING BECAUSE I HAVE GOOD NEWS. AND BAD NEWS, I GUESS.
MY BRAIN DOESN'T REMEMBER HOW TO PROCESS THE FORMER, SO WE MIGHT AS WELL START WITH THE LATTER.
HEARD FROM AN ARSON INVESTIGATOR THAT OUR PRETENDER STRUCK AGAIN...AND HE GOT AWAY. KILLED A WOMAN'S GUARD DOG IN THE PROCESS. THE GOOD NEWS IS THAT I HAVE AN AIRTIGHT ALIBI FOR THIS ONE.
YOU WEREN'T AT A BATHHOUSE, WERE YOU?

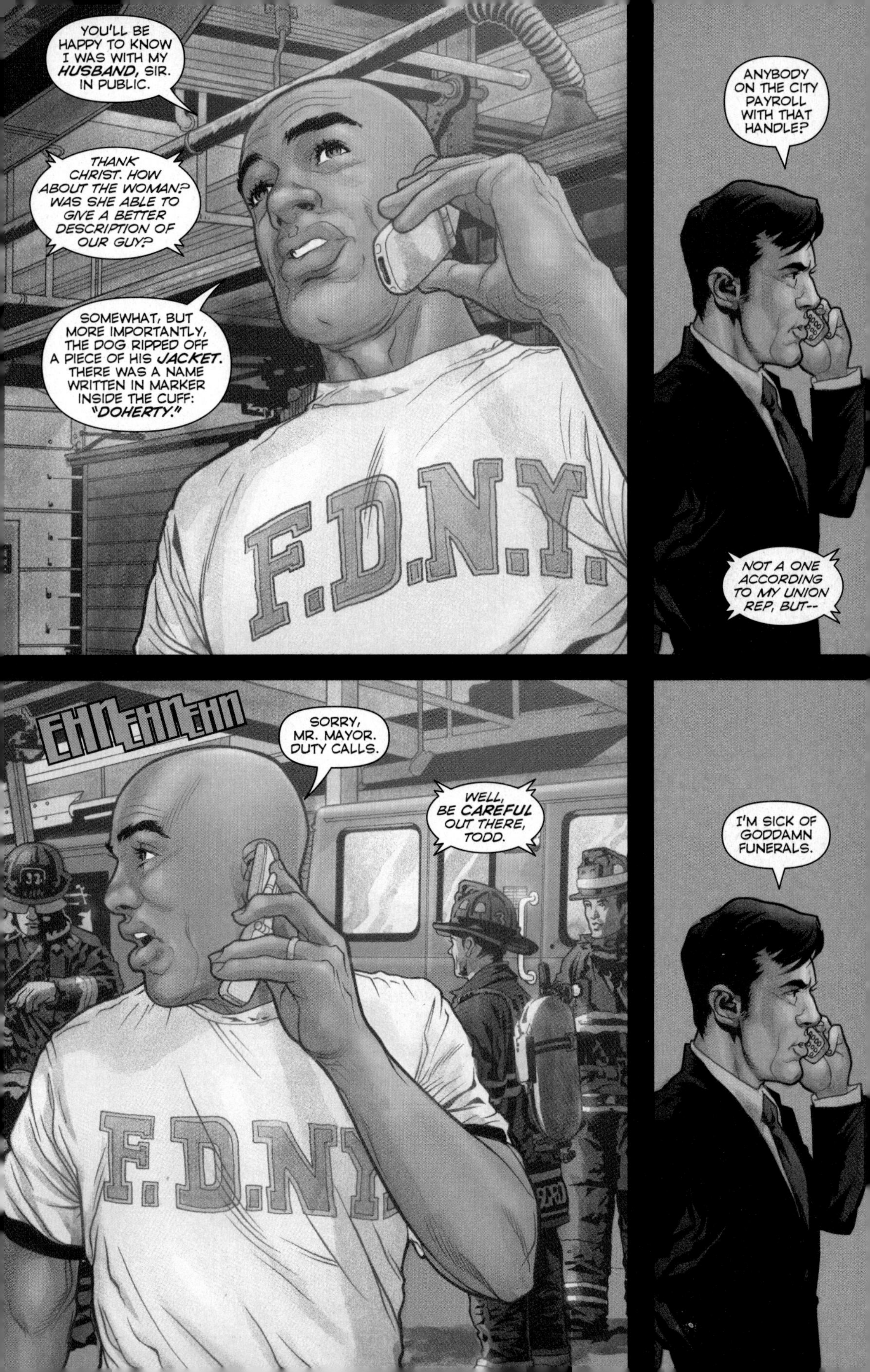
YOU'LL BE HAPPY TO KNOW I WAS WITH MY HUSBAND, SIR. IN PUBLIC.
ANYBODY ON THE CITY PAYROLL WITH THAT HANDLE?
THANK CHRIST. HOW ABOUT THE WOMAN? WAS SHE ABLE TO GIVE A BETTER DESCRIPTION OF OUR GUY?
SOMEWHAT, BUT MORE IMPORTANTLY, THE DOG RIPPED OFF A PIECE OF HIS JACKET. THERE WAS A NAME WRITTEN IN MARKER INSIDE THE CUFF: "DOHERTY."
F.D.N.Y.
NOT A ONE ACCORDING TO MY UNION REP, BUT--
EHN EHN EHN
SORRY, MR. MAYOR. DUTY CALLS.
WELL, BE CAREFUL OUT THERE, TODD.
I'M SICK OF GODDAMN FUNERALS.

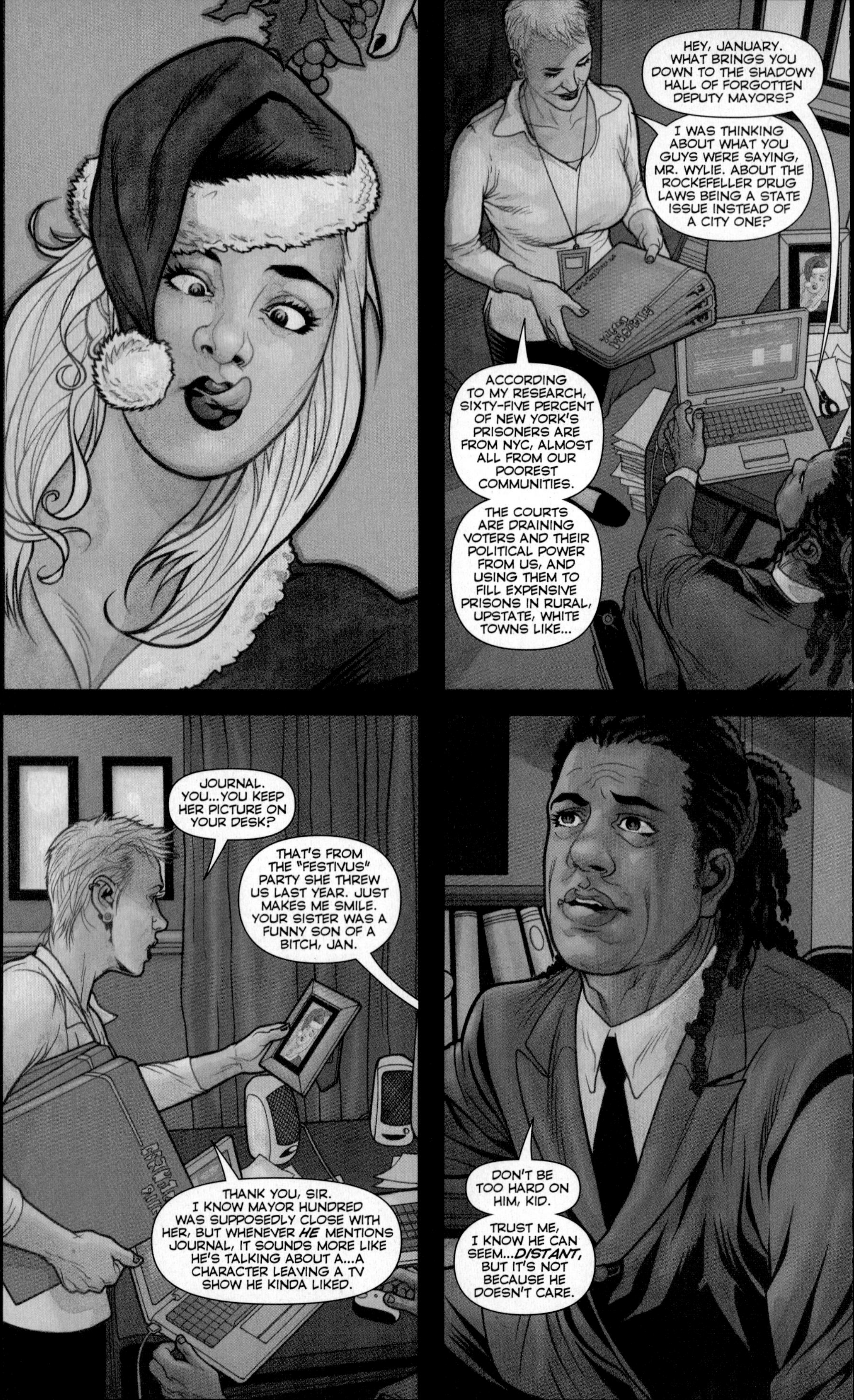
HEY, JANUARY. WHAT BRINGS YOU DOWN TO THE SHADOWY HALL OF FORGOTTEN DEPUTY MAYORS?
I WAS THINKING ABOUT WHAT YOU GUYS WERE SAYING, MR. WYLIE. ABOUT THE ROCKEFELLER DRUG LAWS BEING A STATE ISSUE INSTEAD OF A CITY ONE?
ACCORDING TO MY RESEARCH, SIXTY-FIVE PERCENT OF NEW YORK'S PRISONERS ARE FROM NYC, ALMOST ALL FROM OUR POOREST COMMUNITIES.
THE COURTS ARE DRAINING VOTERS AND THEIR POLITICAL POWER FROM US, AND USING THEM TO FILL EXPENSIVE PRISONS IN RURAL, UPSTATE, WHITE TOWNS LIKE...
JOURNAL. YOU...YOU KEEP HER PICTURE ON YOUR DESK?
THAT'S FROM THE "FESTIVUS" PARTY SHE THREW US LAST YEAR. JUST MAKES ME SMILE. YOUR SISTER WAS A FUNNY SON OF A BITCH, JAN.
THANK YOU, SIR. I KNOW MAYOR HUNDRED WAS SUPPOSEDLY CLOSE WITH HER, BUT WHENEVER *HE* MENTIONS JOURNAL, IT SOUNDS MORE LIKE HE'S TALKING ABOUT A...A CHARACTER LEAVING A TV SHOW HE KINDA LIKED.
DON'T BE TOO HARD ON HIM, KID.
TRUST ME, I KNOW HE CAN SEEM...*DISTANT,* BUT IT'S NOT BECAUSE HE DOESN'T CARE.

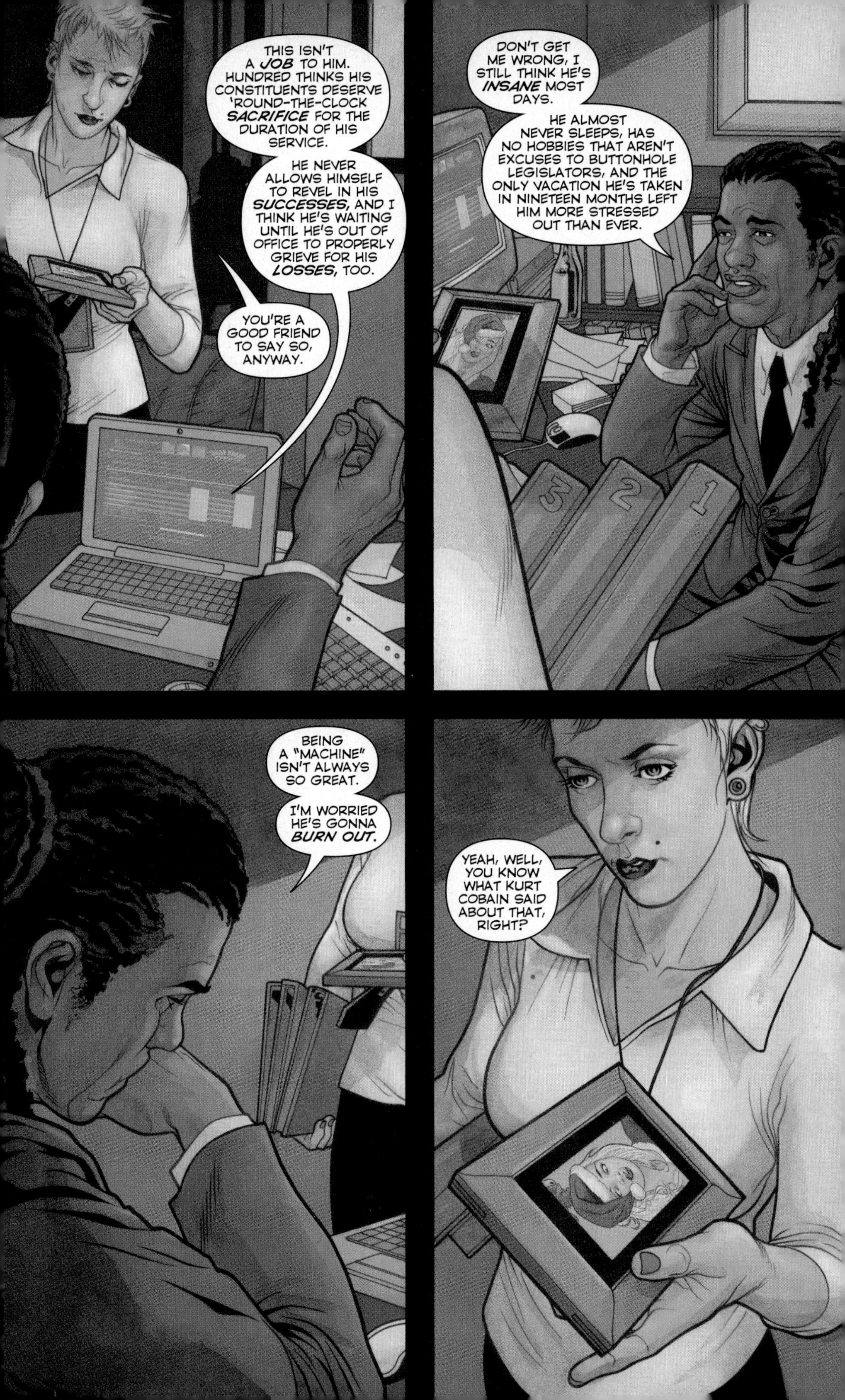

THIS ISN'T A JOB TO HIM. HUNDRED THINKS HIS CONSTITUENTS DESERVE 'ROUND-THE-CLOCK SACRIFICE FOR THE DURATION OF HIS SERVICE.
HE NEVER ALLOWS HIMSELF TO REVEL IN HIS SUCCESSES, AND I THINK HE'S WAITING UNTIL HE'S OUT OF OFFICE TO PROPERLY GRIEVE FOR HIS LOSSES, TOO.
YOU'RE A GOOD FRIEND TO SAY SO, ANYWAY.
DON'T GET ME WRONG, I STILL THINK HE'S INSANE MOST DAYS.
HE ALMOST NEVER SLEEPS, HAS NO HOBBIES THAT AREN'T EXCUSES TO BUTTONHOLE LEGISLATORS, AND THE ONLY VACATION HE'S TAKEN IN NINETEEN MONTHS LEFT HIM MORE STRESSED OUT THAN EVER.
3
2
1
BEING A "MACHINE" ISN'T ALWAYS SO GREAT.
I'M WORRIED HE'S GONNA BURN OUT.
YEAH, WELL, YOU KNOW WHAT KURT COBAIN SAID ABOUT THAT, RIGHT?

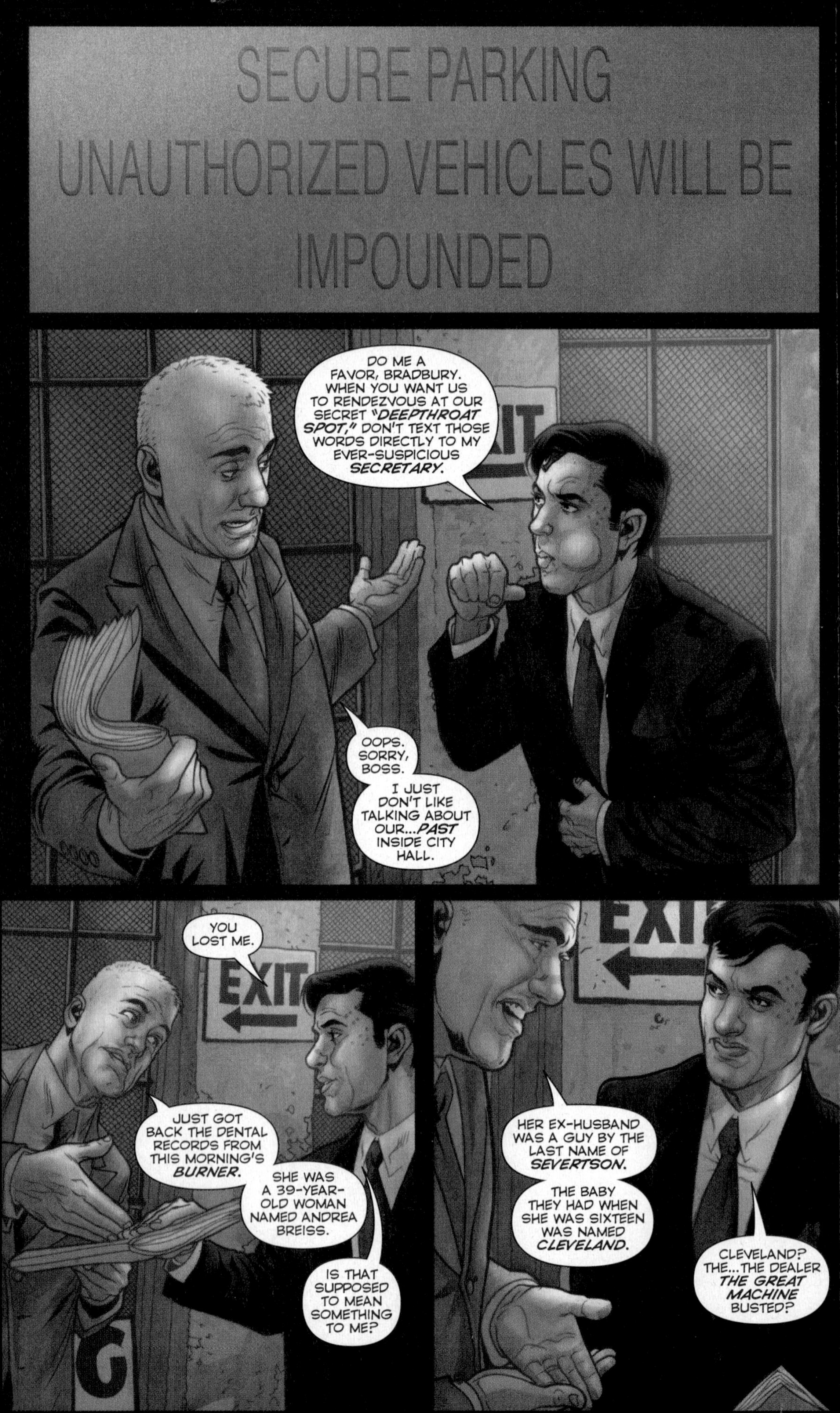
SECURE PARKING
UNAUTHORIZED VEHICLES WILL BE IMPOUNDED
DO ME A FAVOR, BRADBURY. WHEN YOU WANT US TO RENDEZVOUS AT OUR SECRET "DEEPTHROAT SPOT," DON'T TEXT THOSE WORDS DIRECTLY TO MY EVER-SUSPICIOUS SECRETARY.
EXIT
OOPS. SORRY, BOSS.
I JUST DON'T LIKE TALKING ABOUT OUR...PAST INSIDE CITY HALL.
YOU LOST ME.
EXIT
JUST GOT BACK THE DENTAL RECORDS FROM THIS MORNING'S BURNER.
SHE WAS A 39-YEAR-OLD WOMAN NAMED ANDREA BREISS.
IS THAT SUPPOSED TO MEAN SOMETHING TO ME?
EXIT
HER EX-HUSBAND WAS A GUY BY THE LAST NAME OF SEVERTSON.
THE BABY THEY HAD WHEN SHE WAS SIXTEEN WAS NAMED CLEVELAND.
CLEVELAND? THE...THE DEALER THE GREAT MACHINE BUSTED?

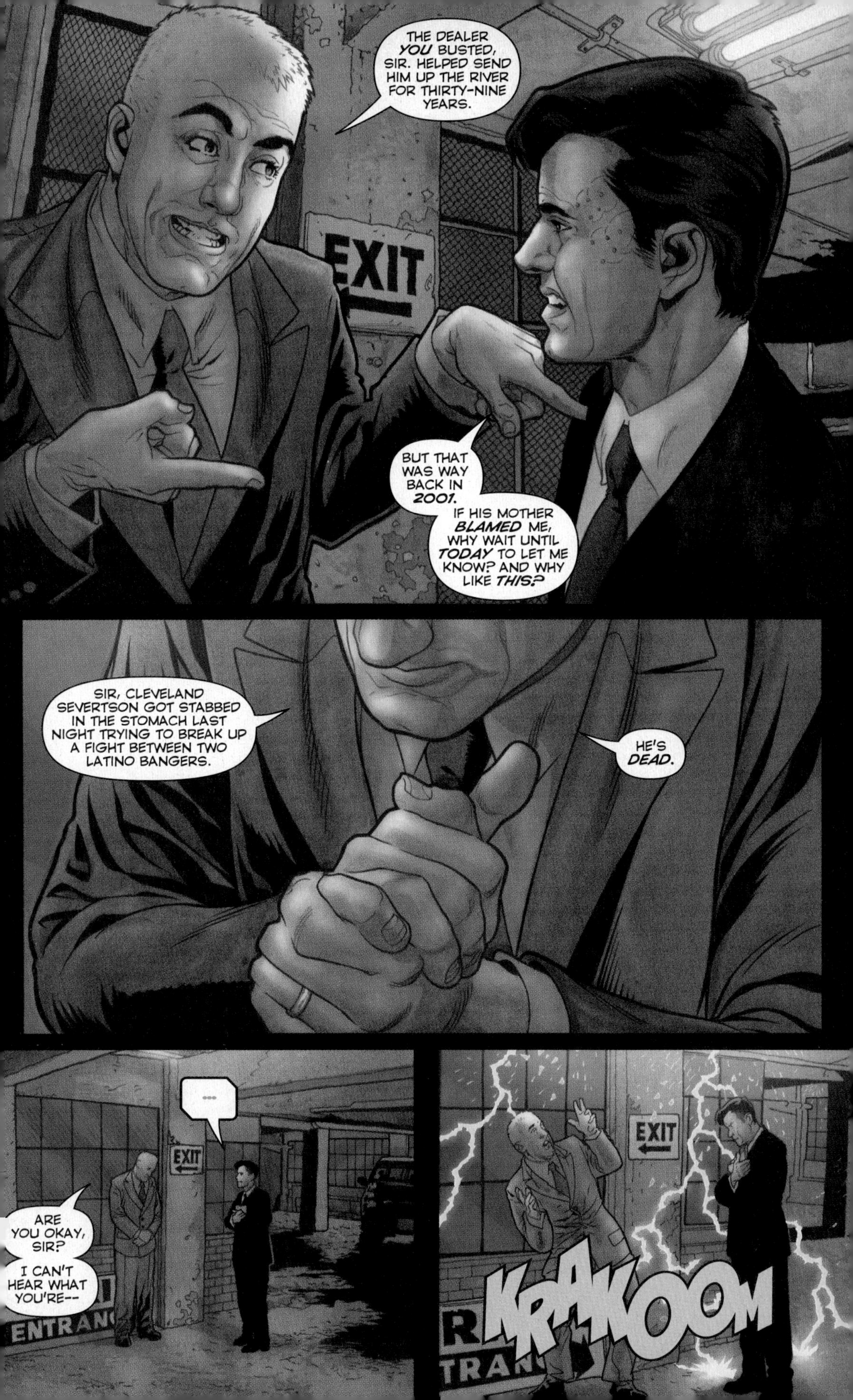
THE DEALER YOU BUSTED, SIR. HELPED SEND HIM UP THE RIVER FOR THIRTY-NINE YEARS.
EXIT
BUT THAT WAS WAY BACK IN 2001.
IF HIS MOTHER BLAMED ME, WHY WAIT UNTIL TODAY TO LET ME KNOW? AND WHY LIKE THIS?
SIR, CLEVELAND SEVERTSON GOT STABBED IN THE STOMACH LAST NIGHT TRYING TO BREAK UP A FIGHT BETWEEN TWO LATINO BANGERS.
HE'S DEAD.
...
EXIT
ARE YOU OKAY, SIR?
I CAN'T HEAR WHAT YOU'RE--
ENTRAN
EXIT
KRAKOOM
TRAN

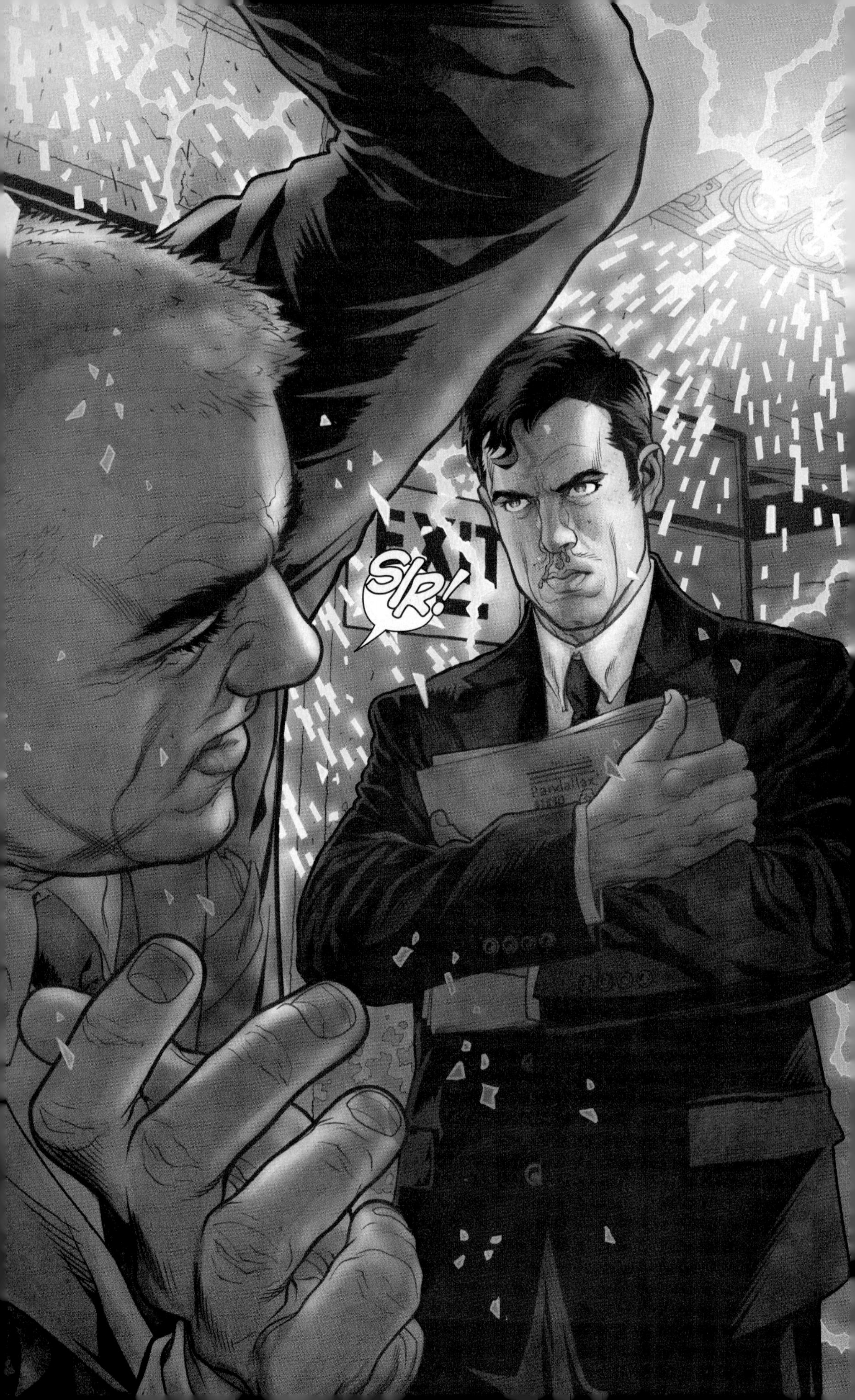
SIR!
Pandallax

Smoke Smoke

Chapter 4

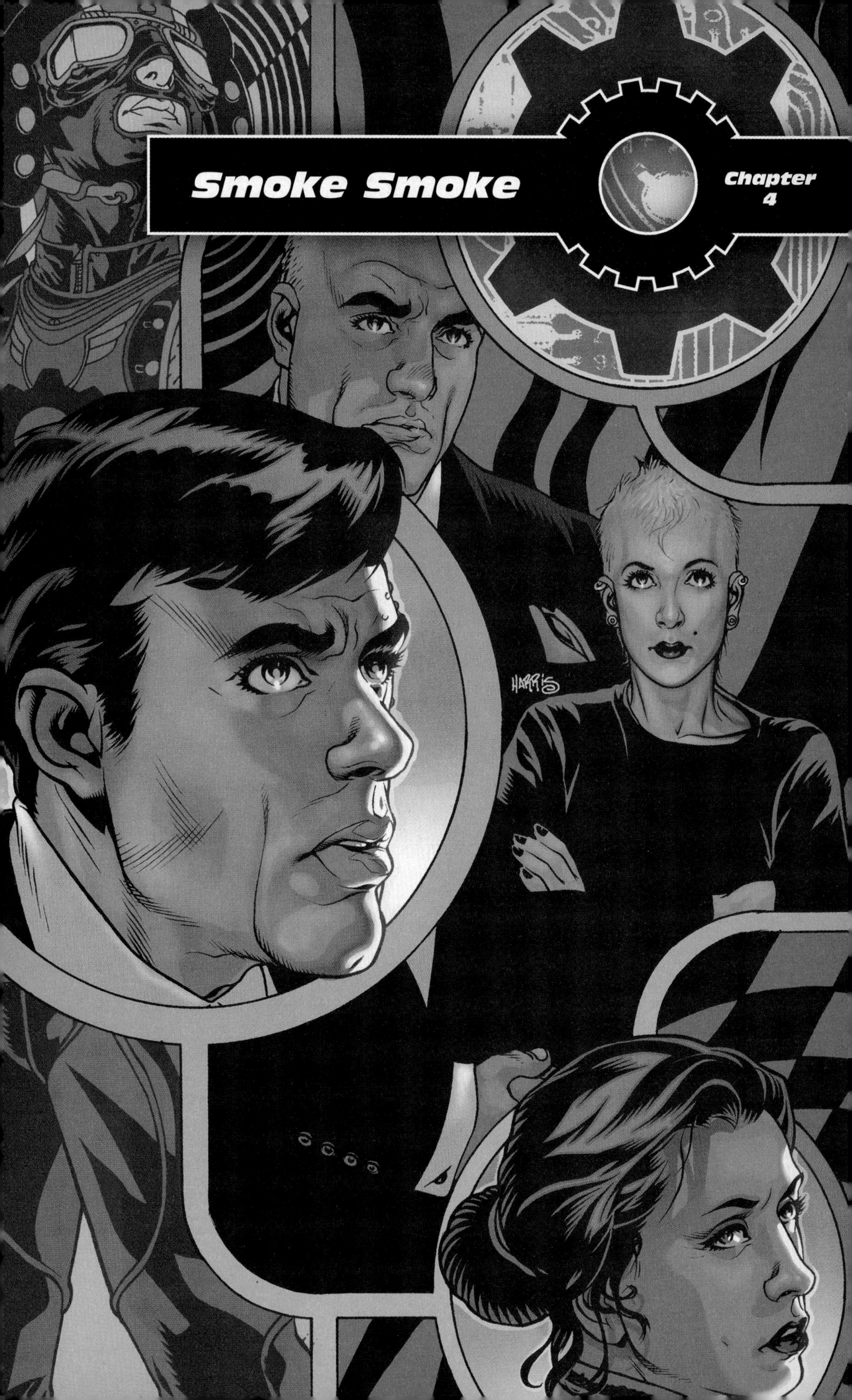

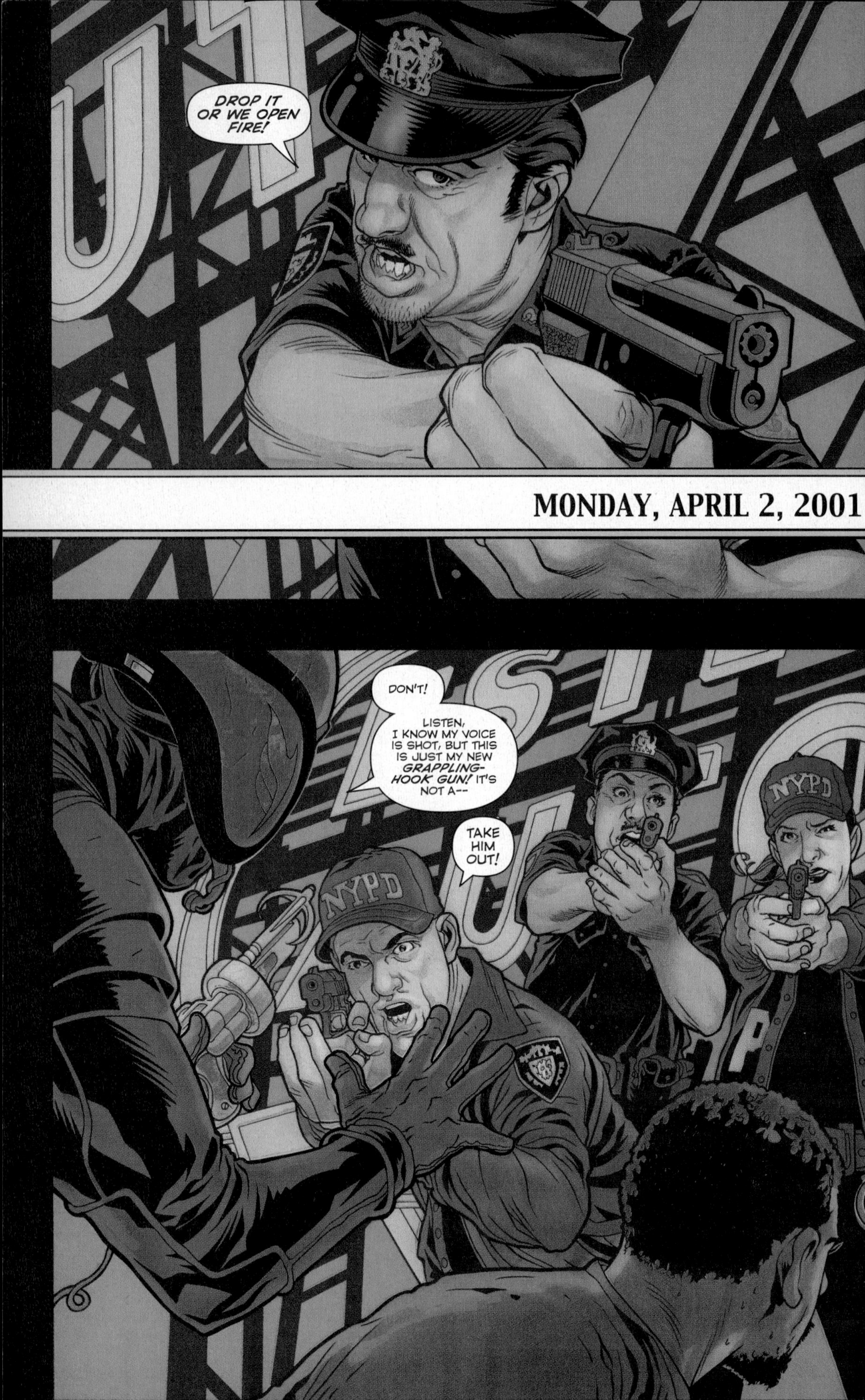

DROP IT OR WE OPEN FIRE!
MONDAY, APRIL 2, 2001
DON'T!
LISTEN, I KNOW MY VOICE IS SHOT, BUT THIS IS JUST MY NEW GRAPPLING-HOOK GUN! IT'S NOT A--
TAKE HIM OUT!
NYPD
NYPD

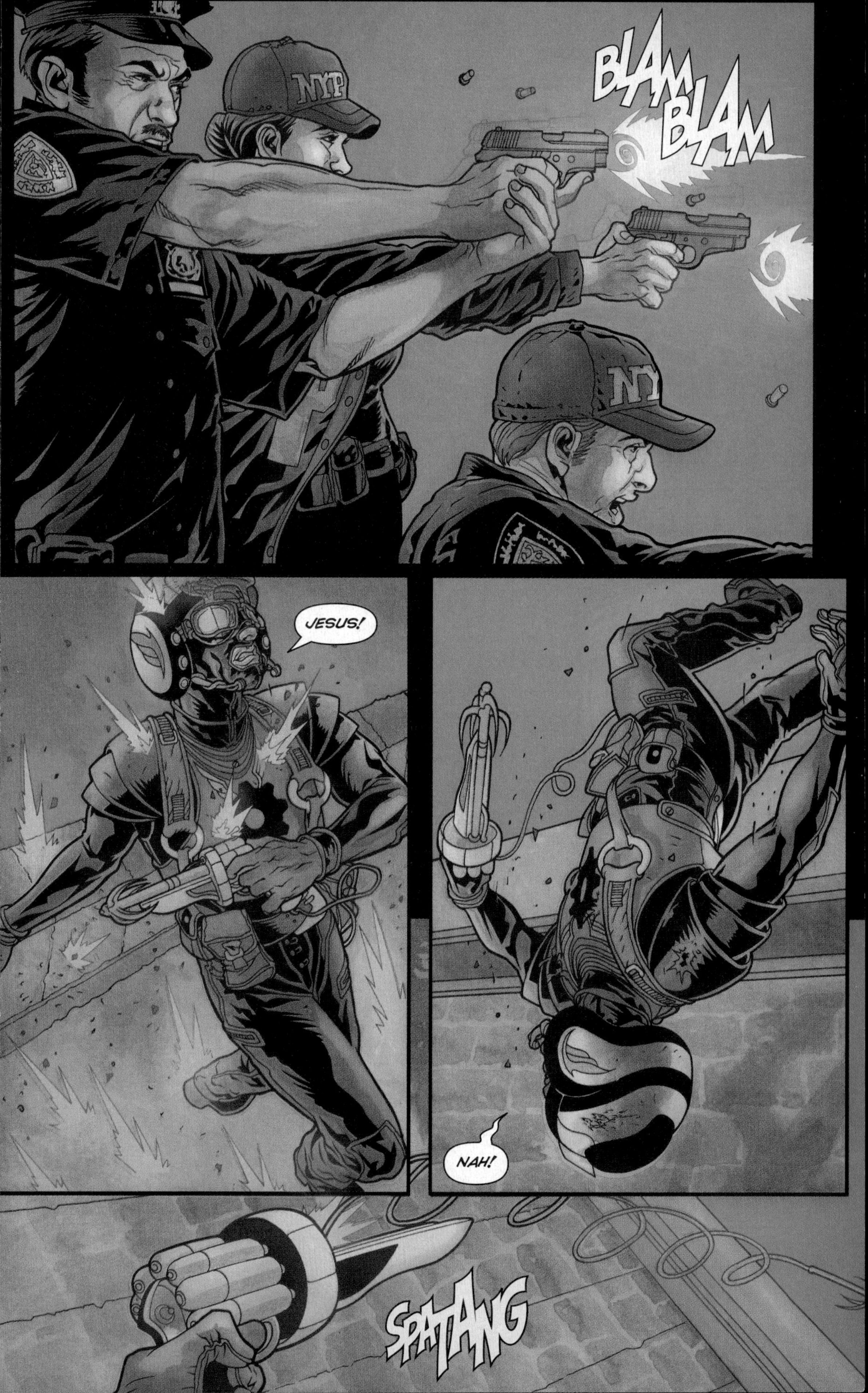
BLAM BLAM
JESUS!
NAH!
SPATANG

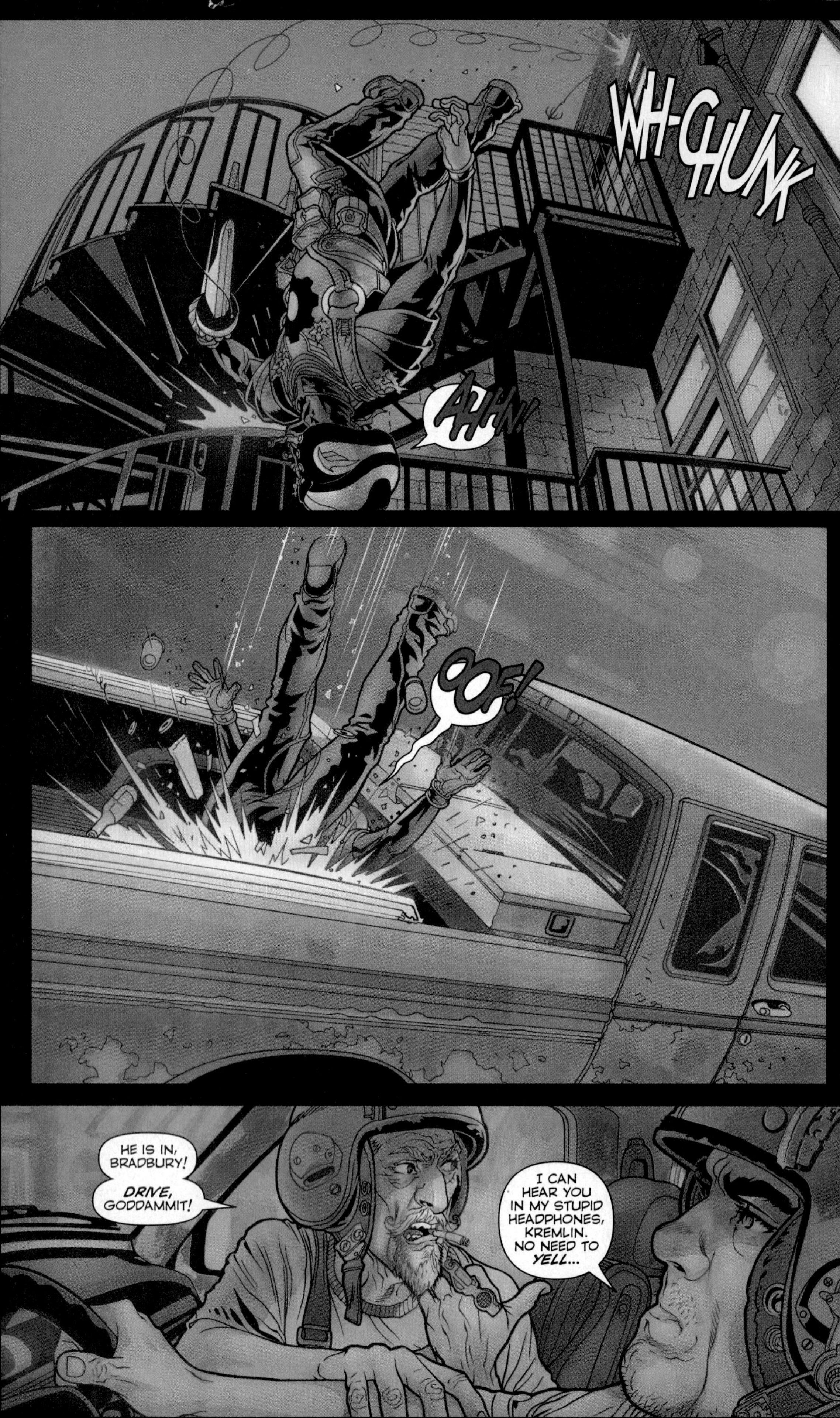

WH-CHUNK
AHHN!
OOF!
HE IS IN, BRADBURY!
DRIVE, GODDAMMIT!
I CAN HEAR YOU IN MY STUPID HEADPHONES, KREMLIN. NO NEED TO YELL...

NNN, KEVLAR STOPPED THE ROUNDS, BUT I'M LOOKING AT A FEW BUSTED RIBS HERE.

BODY ARMOR WORKED BETTER THAN MY *NEW* TOY, AT LEAST.

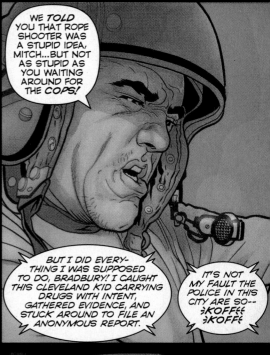

WE *TOLD* YOU THAT ROPE SHOOTER WAS A STUPID IDEA, MITCH...BUT NOT AS STUPID AS YOU WAITING AROUND FOR THE *COPS!*

BUT I DID EVERY-THING I WAS SUPPOSED TO DO, BRADBURY! I CAUGHT THIS CLEVELAND KID CARRYING DRUGS WITH INTENT, GATHERED EVIDENCE, AND STUCK AROUND TO FILE AN ANONYMOUS REPORT.

IT'S NOT MY FAULT THE POLICE IN THIS CITY ARE SO-- ≷KOFF≶ ≷KOFF≶

YOU'VE WASTED ENOUGH OF YOUR VOICE ON MEANINGLESS BULLSHIT LIKE THE MARIJUANA.

THIS CITY NEEDS YOU, BOY. SAVE YOUR WORDS FOR FIGHT THAT REALLY MATTERS.

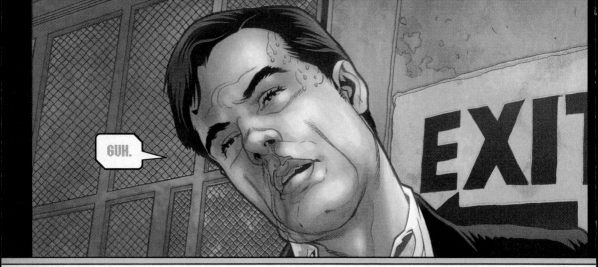

GUH.

TUESDAY, JULY 15, 2003

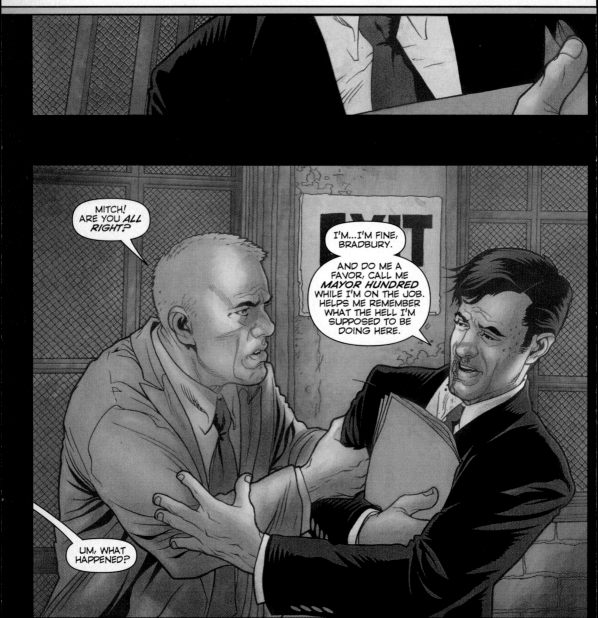

MITCH! ARE YOU *ALL RIGHT?*

I'M...I'M FINE, BRADBURY.

AND DO ME A FAVOR, CALL ME *MAYOR HUNDRED* WHILE I'M ON THE JOB. HELPS ME REMEMBER WHAT THE HELL I'M SUPPOSED TO BE DOING HERE.

UM, WHAT HAPPENED?

IS MY CAR OKAY?

GET THE FUCK OUT OF HERE, MAN!

A...A *TRANSFORMER* BLEW UP AND WE GOT LIVE WIRES ALL OVER!

WHO WAS THAT?

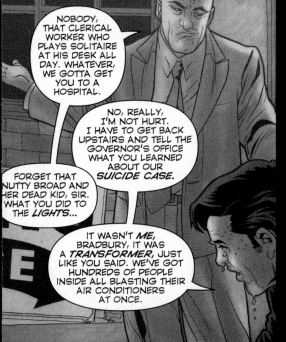

NOBODY, THAT CLERICAL WORKER WHO PLAYS SOLITAIRE AT HIS DESK ALL DAY. WHATEVER, WE GOTTA GET YOU TO A HOSPITAL.

NO, REALLY, I'M NOT HURT. I HAVE TO GET BACK UPSTAIRS AND TELL THE GOVERNOR'S OFFICE WHAT YOU LEARNED ABOUT OUR *SUICIDE CASE*.

FORGET THAT NUTTY BROAD AND HER DEAD KID, SIR. WHAT YOU DID TO THE *LIGHTS*...

IT WASN'T *ME*, BRADBURY, IT WAS A *TRANSFORMER*, JUST LIKE YOU SAID. WE'VE GOT HUNDREDS OF PEOPLE INSIDE ALL BLASTING THEIR AIR CONDITIONERS AT ONCE.

IT'S JUST STRESS ON THE SYSTEM.

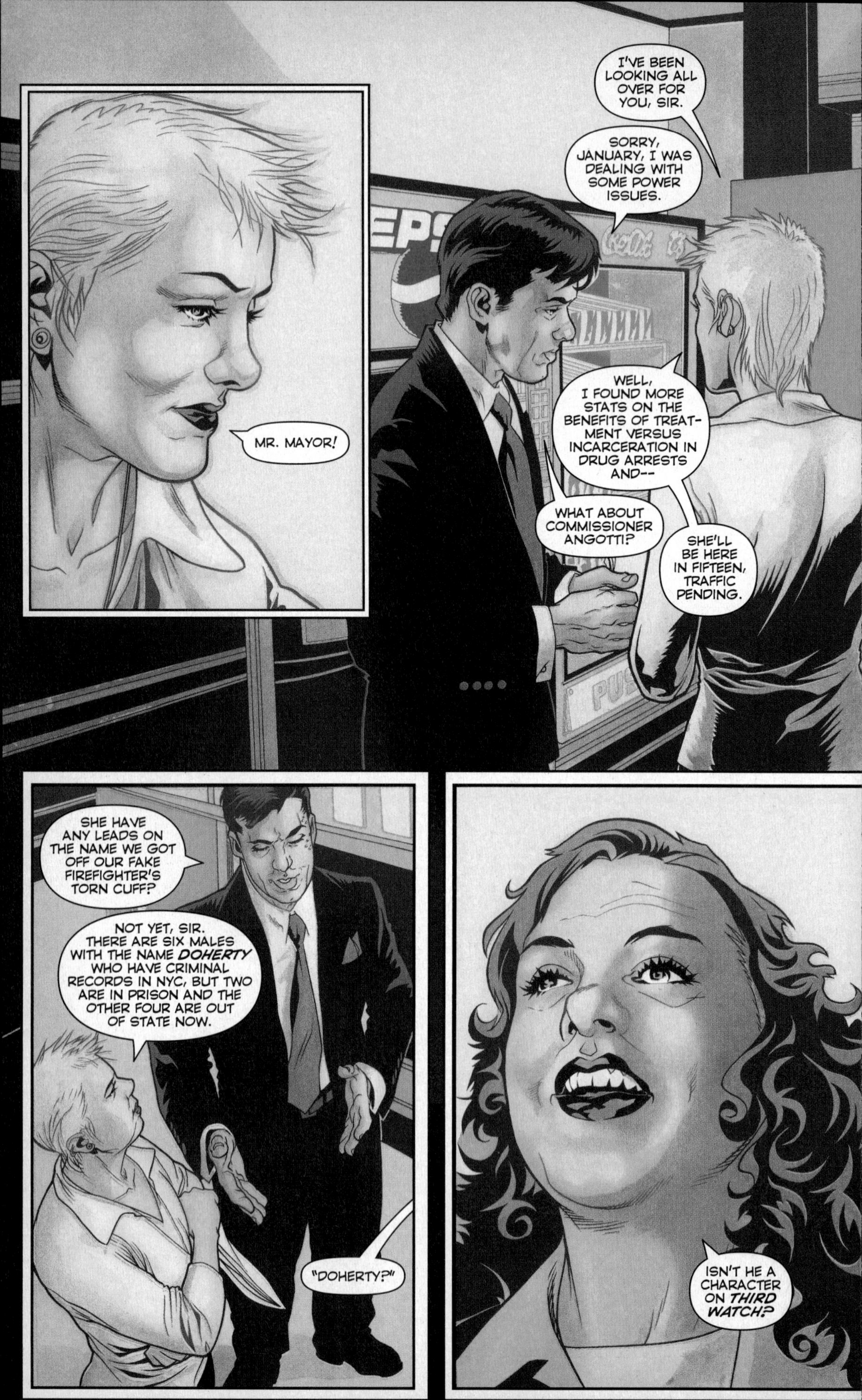
MR. MAYOR!
I'VE BEEN LOOKING ALL OVER FOR YOU, SIR.
SORRY, JANUARY, I WAS DEALING WITH SOME POWER ISSUES.
WELL, I FOUND MORE STATS ON THE BENEFITS OF TREAT-MENT VERSUS INCARCERATION IN DRUG ARRESTS AND--
WHAT ABOUT COMMISSIONER ANGOTTI?
SHE'LL BE HERE IN FIFTEEN, TRAFFIC PENDING.
SHE HAVE ANY LEADS ON THE NAME WE GOT OFF OUR FAKE FIREFIGHTER'S TORN CUFF?
NOT YET, SIR. THERE ARE SIX MALES WITH THE NAME *DOHERTY* WHO HAVE CRIMINAL RECORDS IN NYC, BUT TWO ARE IN PRISON AND THE OTHER FOUR ARE OUT OF STATE NOW.
"DOHERTY?"
ISN'T HE A CHARACTER ON *THIRD WATCH?*

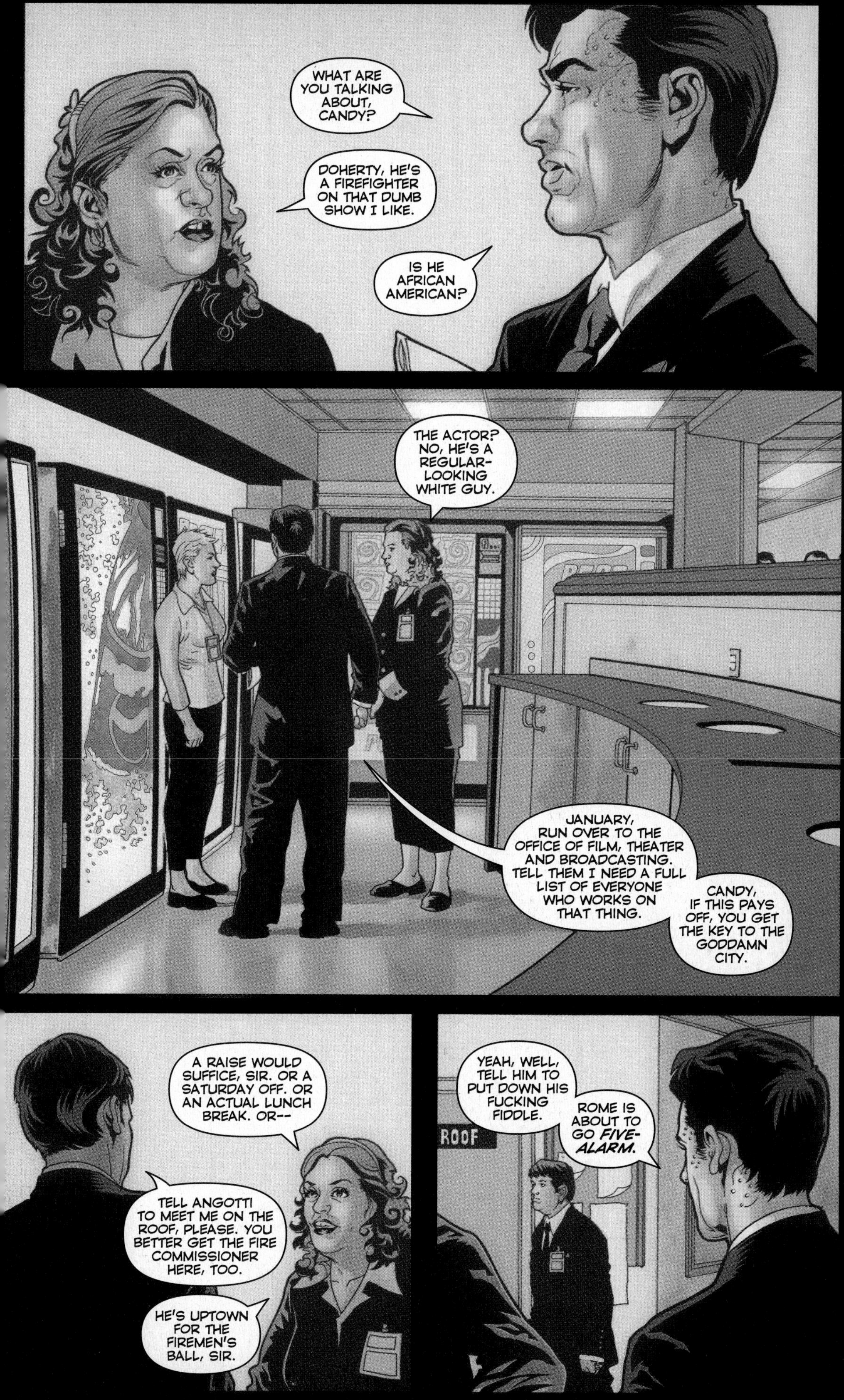
WHAT ARE YOU TALKING ABOUT, CANDY?
DOHERTY, HE'S A FIREFIGHTER ON THAT DUMB SHOW I LIKE.
IS HE AFRICAN AMERICAN?
THE ACTOR? NO, HE'S A REGULAR-LOOKING WHITE GUY.
JANUARY, RUN OVER TO THE OFFICE OF FILM, THEATER AND BROADCASTING. TELL THEM I NEED A FULL LIST OF EVERYONE WHO WORKS ON THAT THING.
CANDY, IF THIS PAYS OFF, YOU GET THE KEY TO THE GODDAMN CITY.
A RAISE WOULD SUFFICE, SIR. OR A SATURDAY OFF. OR AN ACTUAL LUNCH BREAK. OR--
TELL ANGOTTI TO MEET ME ON THE ROOF, PLEASE. YOU BETTER GET THE FIRE COMMISSIONER HERE, TOO.
HE'S UPTOWN FOR THE FIREMEN'S BALL, SIR.
ROOF
YEAH, WELL, TELL HIM TO PUT DOWN HIS FUCKING FIDDLE.
ROME IS ABOUT TO GO *FIVE-ALARM.*

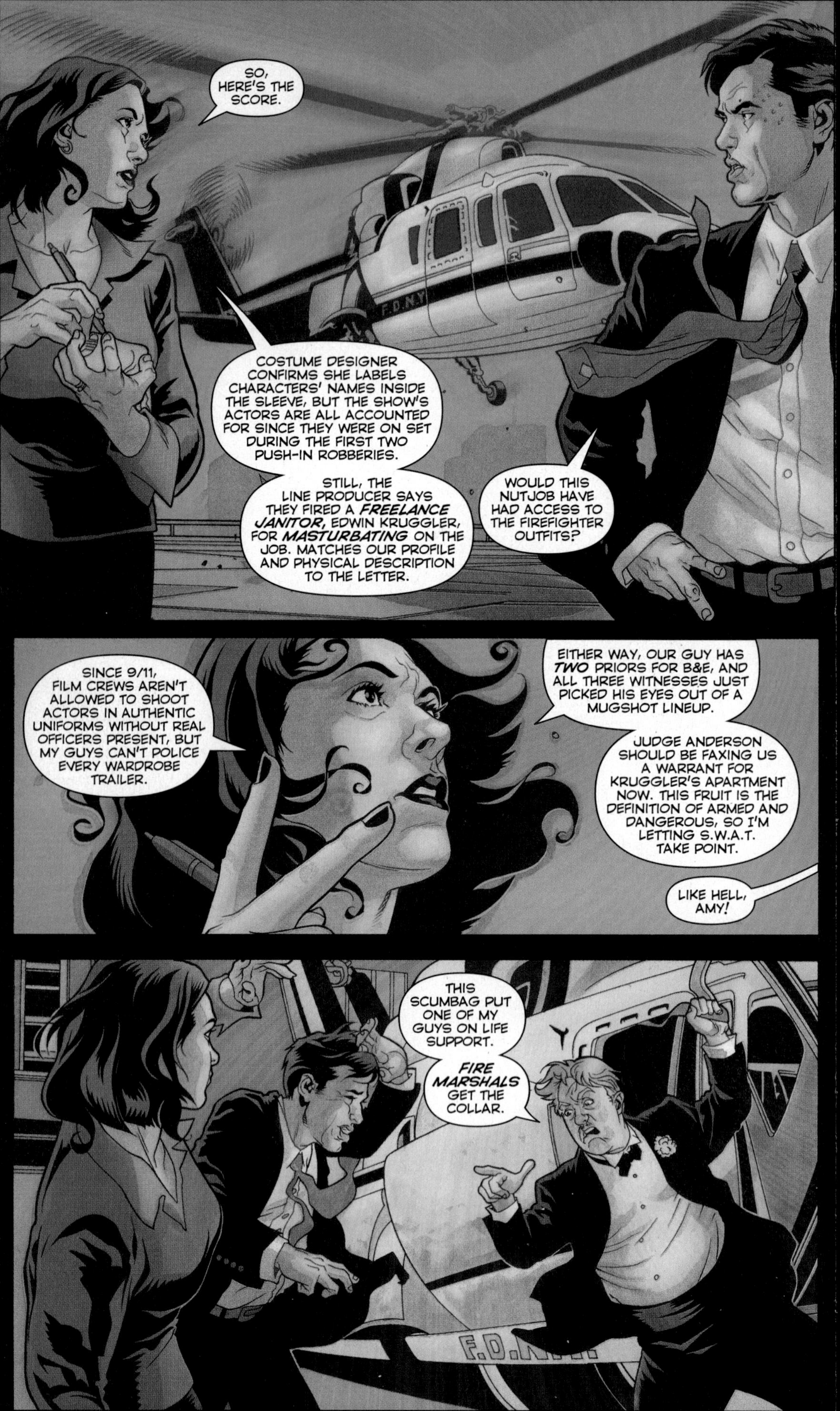
SO, HERE'S THE SCORE.
COSTUME DESIGNER CONFIRMS SHE LABELS CHARACTERS' NAMES INSIDE THE SLEEVE, BUT THE SHOW'S ACTORS ARE ALL ACCOUNTED FOR SINCE THEY WERE ON SET DURING THE FIRST TWO PUSH-IN ROBBERIES.
STILL, THE LINE PRODUCER SAYS THEY FIRED A *FREELANCE JANITOR,* EDWIN KRUGGLER, FOR *MASTURBATING* ON THE JOB. MATCHES OUR PROFILE AND PHYSICAL DESCRIPTION TO THE LETTER.
WOULD THIS NUTJOB HAVE HAD ACCESS TO THE FIREFIGHTER OUTFITS?
SINCE 9/11, FILM CREWS AREN'T ALLOWED TO SHOOT ACTORS IN AUTHENTIC UNIFORMS WITHOUT REAL OFFICERS PRESENT, BUT MY GUYS CAN'T POLICE EVERY WARDROBE TRAILER.
EITHER WAY, OUR GUY HAS *TWO* PRIORS FOR B&E, AND ALL THREE WITNESSES JUST PICKED HIS EYES OUT OF A MUGSHOT LINEUP.
JUDGE ANDERSON SHOULD BE FAXING US A WARRANT FOR KRUGGLER'S APARTMENT NOW. THIS FRUIT IS THE DEFINITION OF ARMED AND DANGEROUS, SO I'M LETTING S.W.A.T. TAKE POINT.
LIKE HELL, AMY!
THIS SCUMBAG PUT ONE OF MY GUYS ON LIFE SUPPORT.
FIRE MARSHALS GET THE COLLAR.
F.D.N.Y

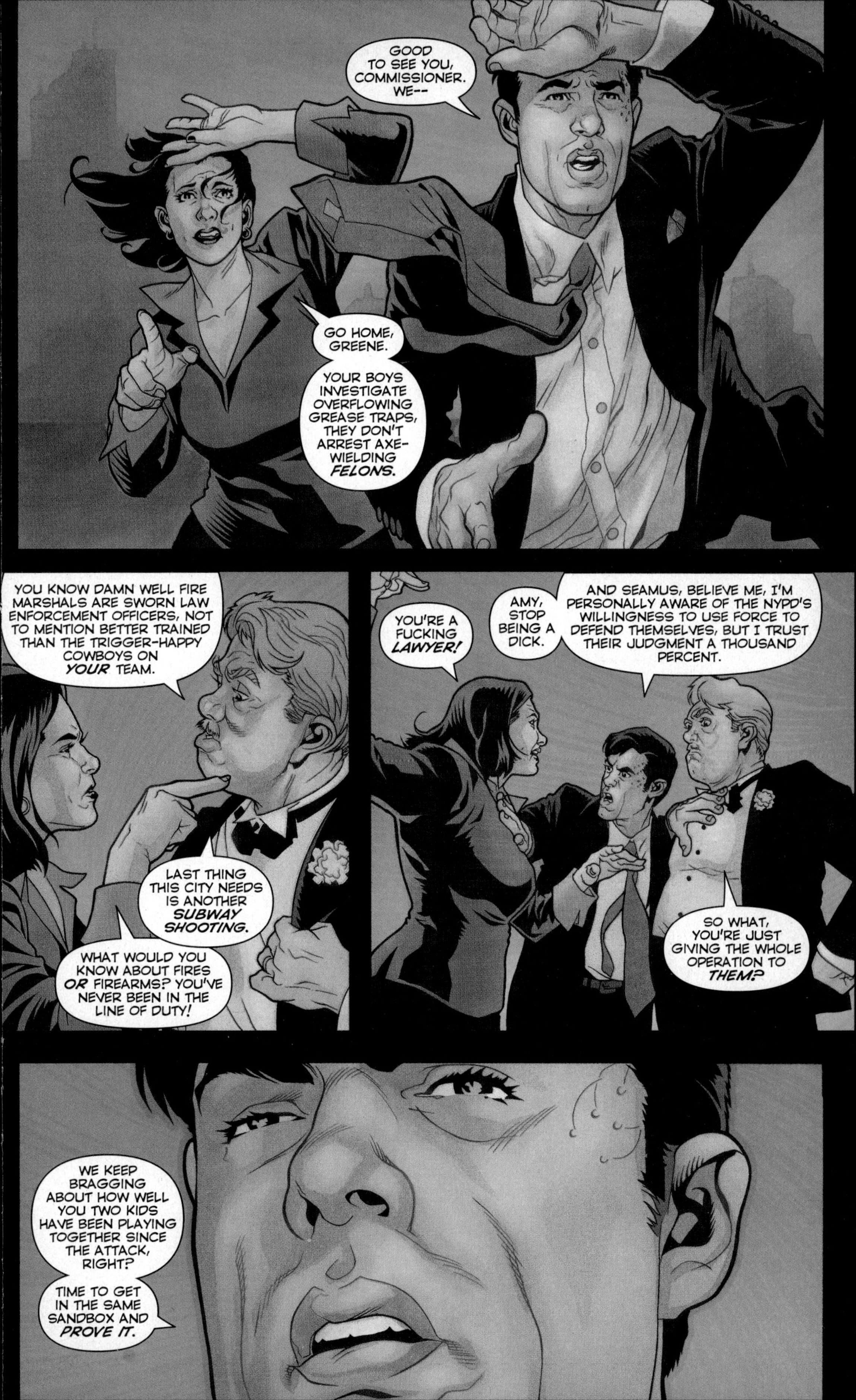
GOOD TO SEE YOU, COMMISSIONER. WE--
GO HOME, GREENE.
YOUR BOYS INVESTIGATE OVERFLOWING GREASE TRAPS, THEY DON'T ARREST AXE-WIELDING *FELONS*.
YOU KNOW DAMN WELL FIRE MARSHALS ARE SWORN LAW ENFORCEMENT OFFICERS, NOT TO MENTION BETTER TRAINED THAN THE TRIGGER-HAPPY COWBOYS ON *YOUR* TEAM.
LAST THING THIS CITY NEEDS IS ANOTHER *SUBWAY SHOOTING*.
WHAT WOULD YOU KNOW ABOUT FIRES *OR* FIREARMS? YOU'VE NEVER BEEN IN THE LINE OF DUTY!
YOU'RE A FUCKING *LAWYER!*
AMY, STOP BEING A DICK.
AND SEAMUS, BELIEVE ME, I'M PERSONALLY AWARE OF THE NYPD'S WILLINGNESS TO USE FORCE TO DEFEND THEMSELVES, BUT I TRUST THEIR JUDGMENT A THOUSAND PERCENT.
SO WHAT, YOU'RE JUST GIVING THE WHOLE OPERATION TO *THEM?*
WE KEEP BRAGGING ABOUT HOW WELL YOU TWO KIDS HAVE BEEN PLAYING TOGETHER SINCE THE ATTACK, RIGHT?
TIME TO GET IN THE SAME SANDBOX AND *PROVE IT*.

VRRM
VRRM
VRRM

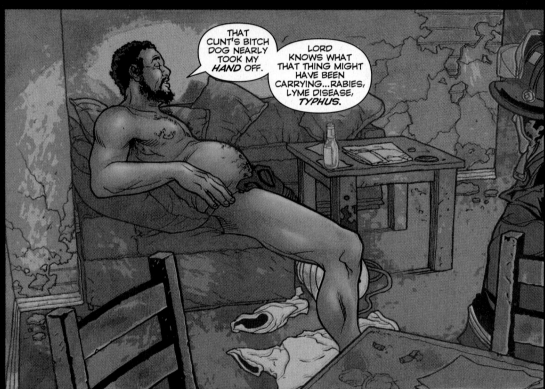

THAT CUNT'S BITCH DOG NEARLY TOOK MY *HAND* OFF.

LORD KNOWS WHAT THAT THING MIGHT HAVE BEEN CARRYING...RABIES, LYME DISEASE, *TYPHUS.*

I'LL NEVER FIGURE HOW PEOPLE LOVE OTHER ANIMALS.

HOW YOU *TRUST* SOMETHING WHEN IT'S JUST A BAG OF GERMS AND VIRUSES? NAH, LOVE IS *CLEAN*, RIGHT, BABY? LOVE IS--

SEARCH WARRANT, OPEN UP!

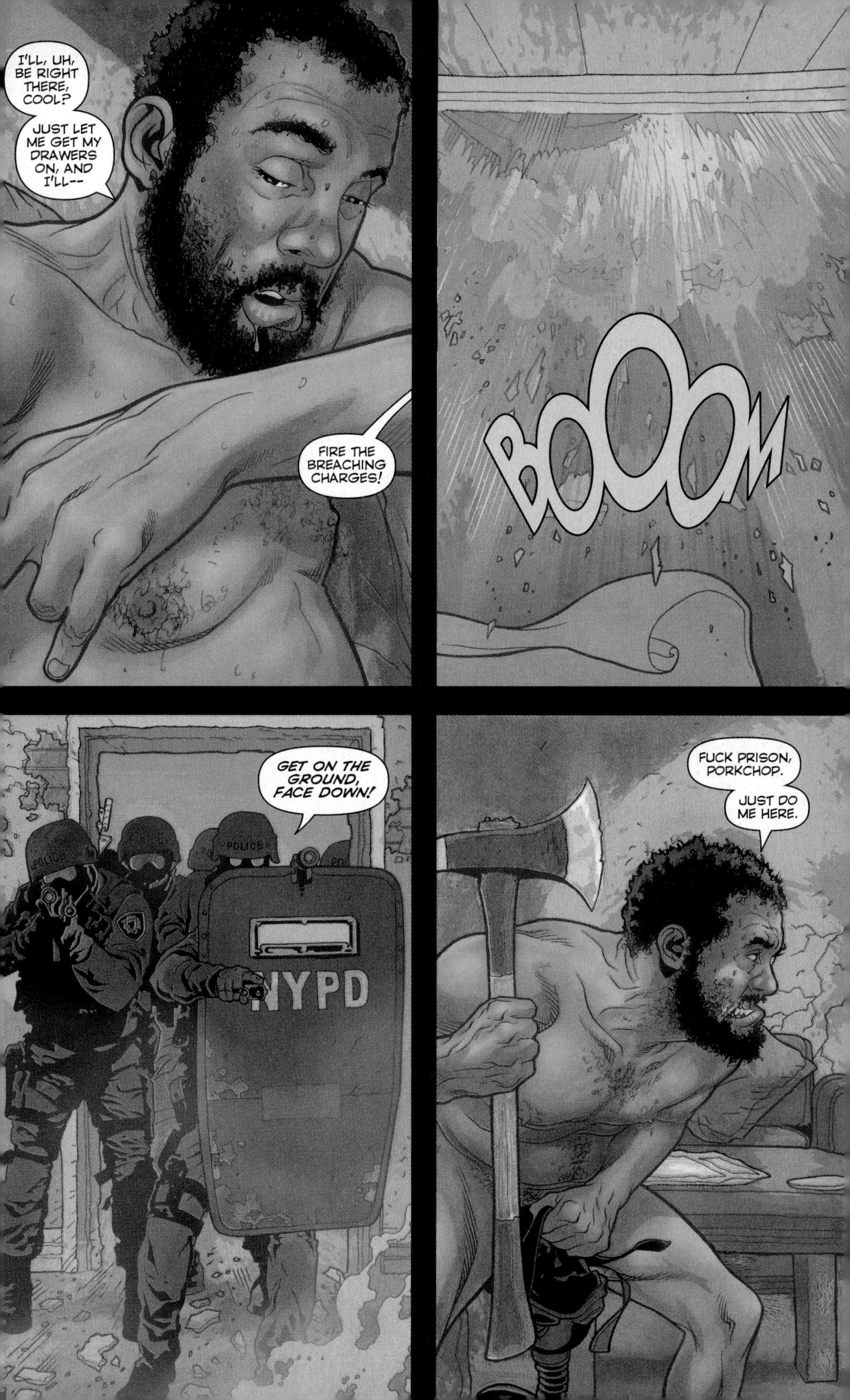
I'LL, UH, BE RIGHT THERE, COOL?
JUST LET ME GET MY DRAWERS ON, AND I'LL--
FIRE THE BREACHING CHARGES!
BOOOOM
GET ON THE GROUND, FACE DOWN!
POLICE
POLICE
NYPD
FUCK PRISON, PORKCHOP.
JUST DO ME HERE.

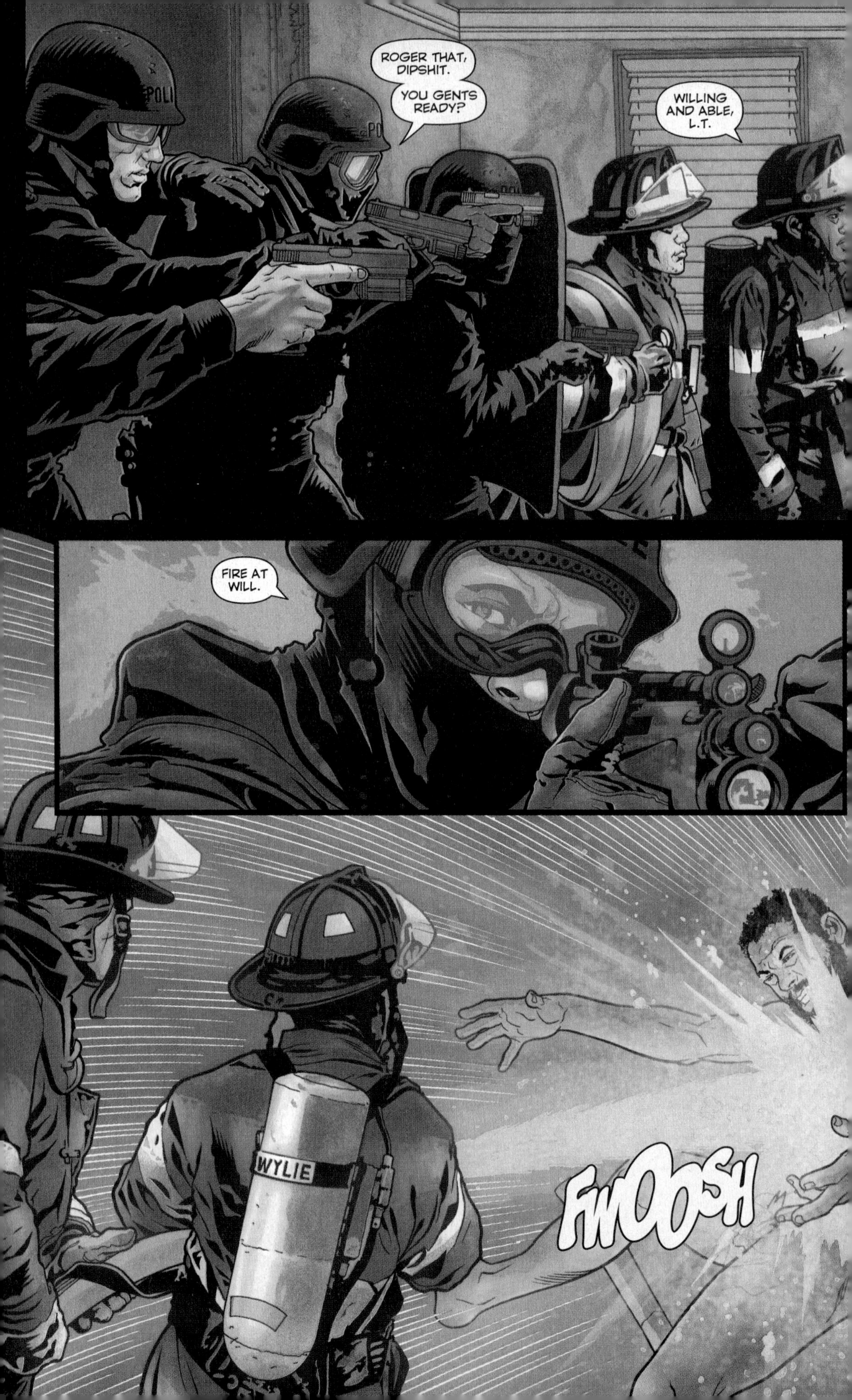
ROGER THAT, DIPSHIT.
YOU GENTS READY?
WILLING AND ABLE, L.T.
FIRE AT WILL.
WYLIE
FWOOSH

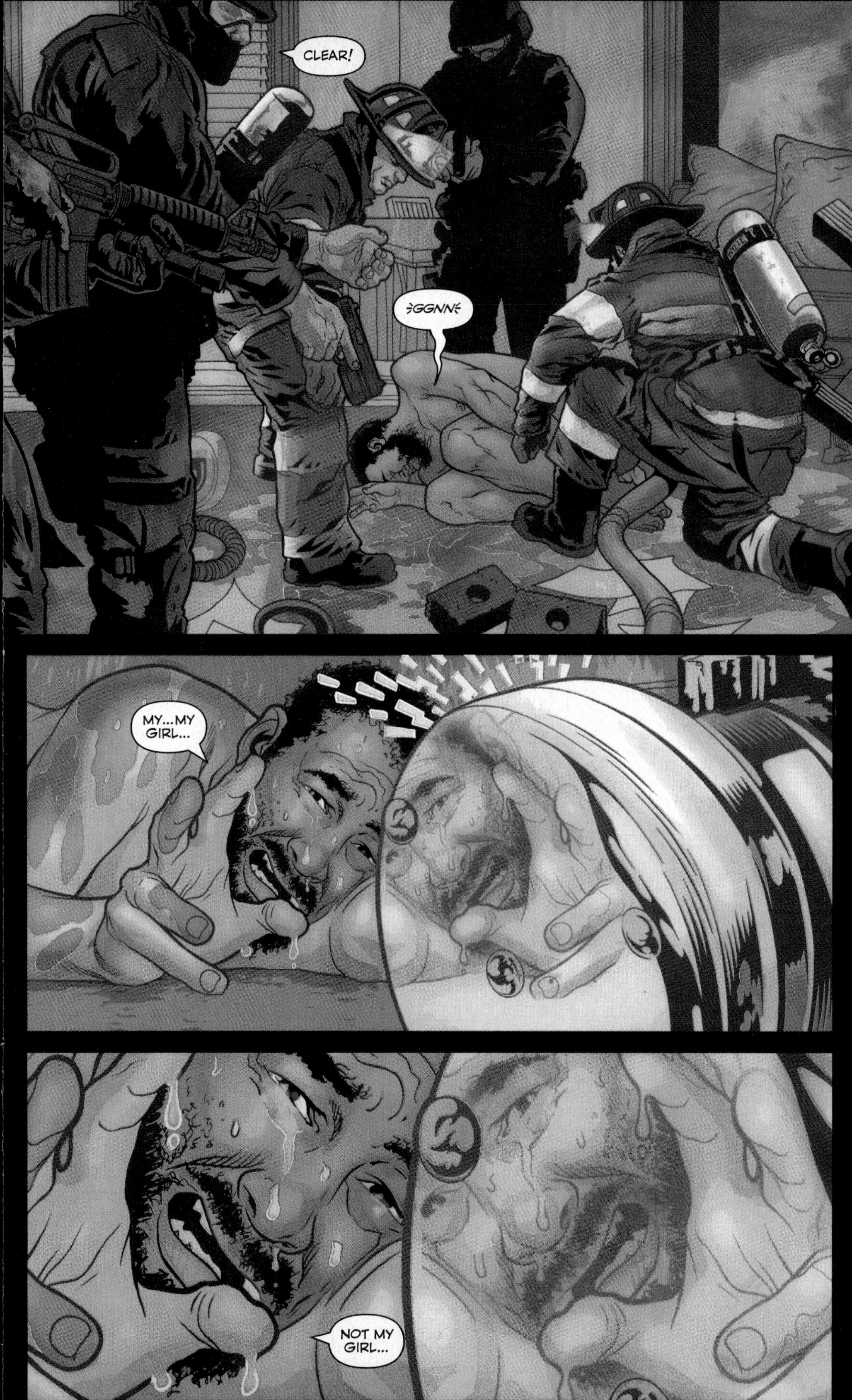
CLEAR!
GGNN
MY...MY GIRL...
NOT MY GIRL...

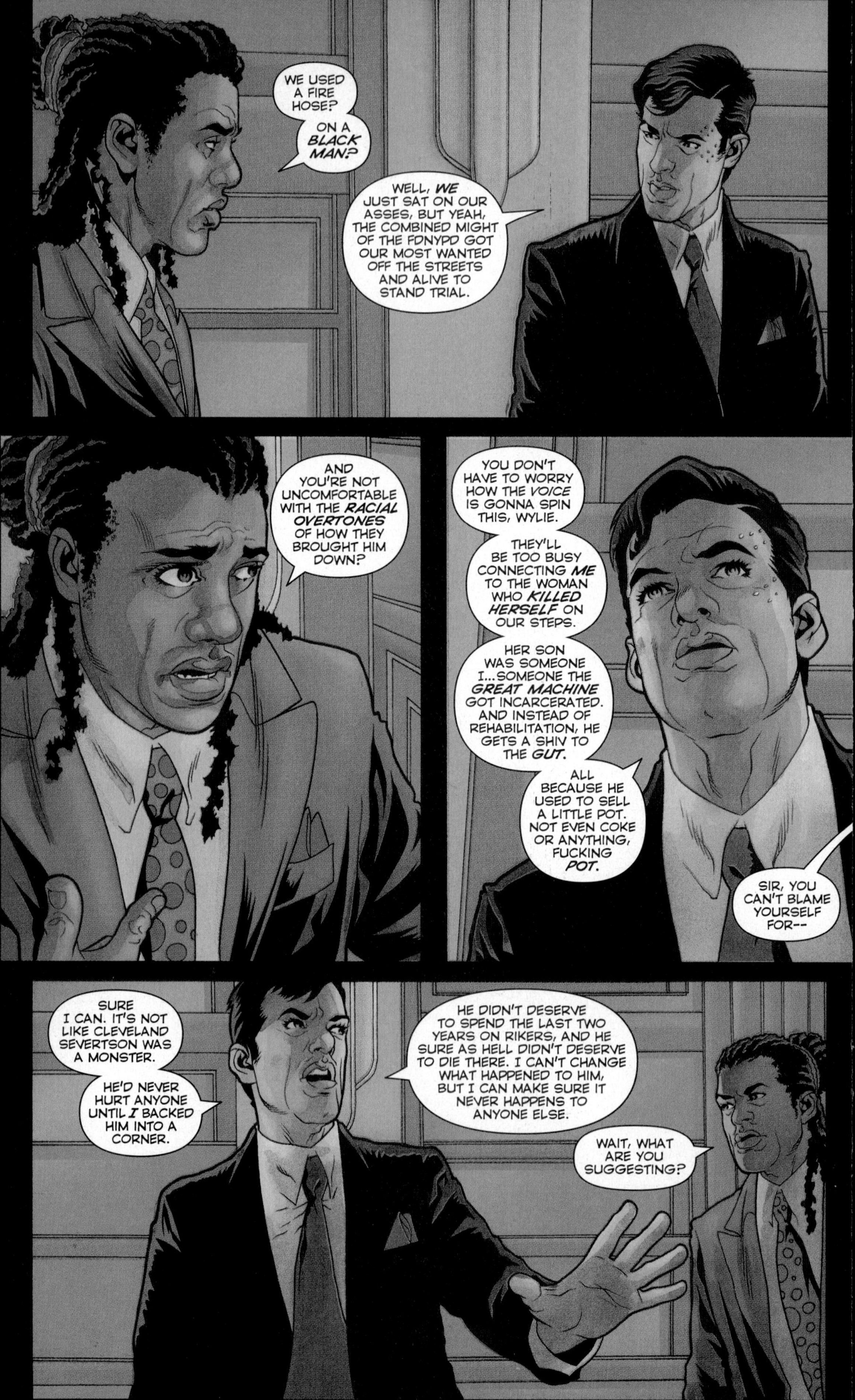
WE USED A FIRE HOSE?
ON A *BLACK MAN?*
WELL, *WE* JUST SAT ON OUR ASSES, BUT YEAH, THE COMBINED MIGHT OF THE FDNYPD GOT OUR MOST WANTED OFF THE STREETS AND ALIVE TO STAND TRIAL.
AND YOU'RE NOT UNCOMFORTABLE WITH THE *RACIAL OVERTONES* OF HOW THEY BROUGHT HIM DOWN?
YOU DON'T HAVE TO WORRY HOW THE *VOICE* IS GONNA SPIN THIS, WYLIE.
THEY'LL BE TOO BUSY CONNECTING *ME* TO THE WOMAN WHO *KILLED HERSELF* ON OUR STEPS.
HER SON WAS SOMEONE I...SOMEONE THE *GREAT MACHINE* GOT INCARCERATED. AND INSTEAD OF REHABILITATION, HE GETS A SHIV TO THE *GUT*.
ALL BECAUSE HE USED TO SELL A LITTLE POT. NOT EVEN COKE OR ANYTHING, FUCKING *POT*.
SIR, YOU CAN'T BLAME YOURSELF FOR--
SURE I CAN. IT'S NOT LIKE CLEVELAND SEVERTSON WAS A MONSTER.
HE'D NEVER HURT ANYONE UNTIL *I* BACKED HIM INTO A CORNER.
HE DIDN'T DESERVE TO SPEND THE LAST TWO YEARS ON RIKERS, AND HE SURE AS HELL DIDN'T DESERVE TO DIE THERE. I CAN'T CHANGE WHAT HAPPENED TO HIM, BUT I CAN MAKE SURE IT NEVER HAPPENS TO ANYONE ELSE.
WAIT, WHAT ARE YOU SUGGESTING?

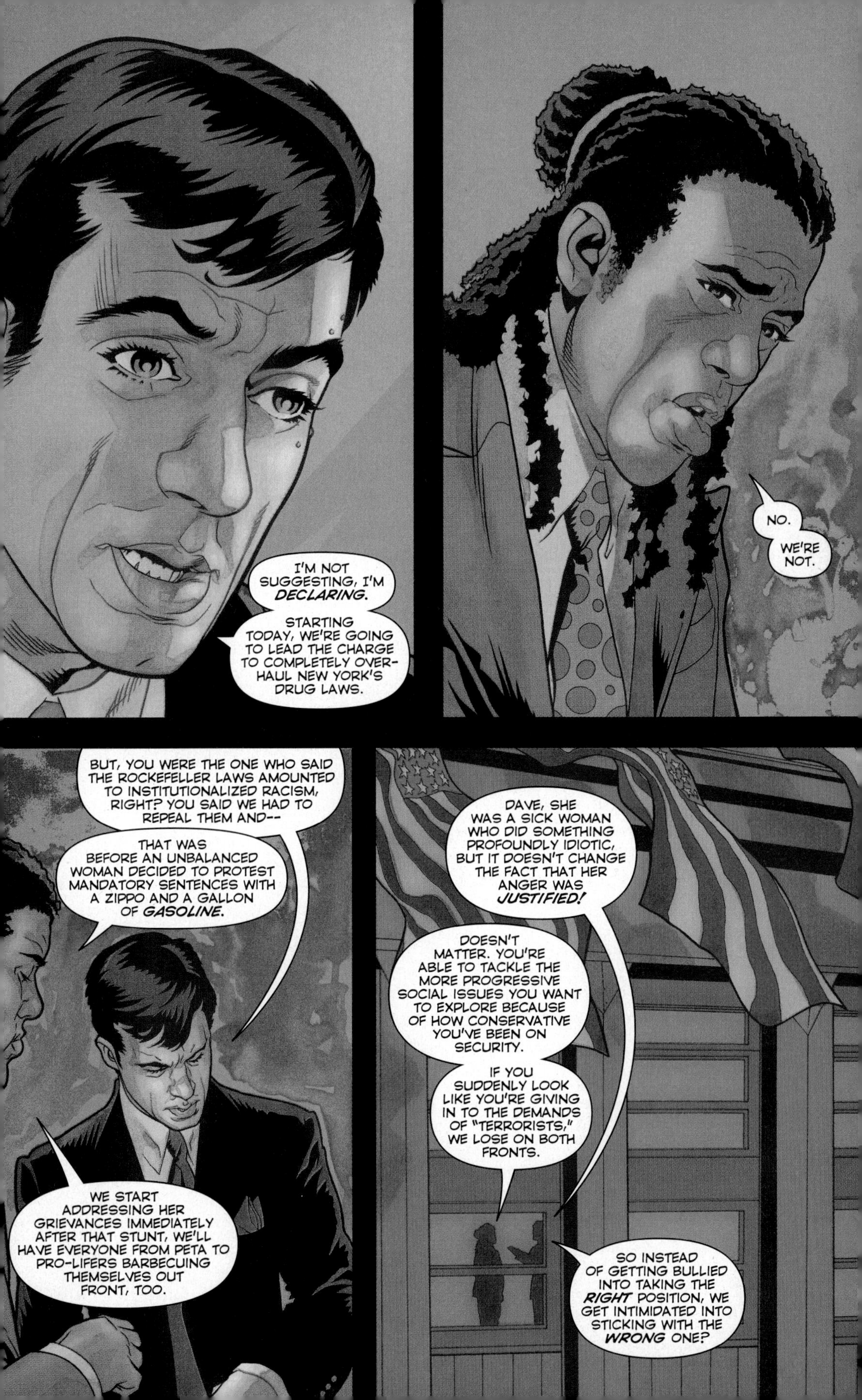
I'M NOT SUGGESTING, I'M *DECLARING*.
STARTING TODAY, WE'RE GOING TO LEAD THE CHARGE TO COMPLETELY OVER-HAUL NEW YORK'S DRUG LAWS.
NO.
WE'RE NOT.
BUT, YOU WERE THE ONE WHO SAID THE ROCKEFELLER LAWS AMOUNTED TO INSTITUTIONALIZED RACISM, RIGHT? YOU SAID WE HAD TO REPEAL THEM AND--
THAT WAS BEFORE AN UNBALANCED WOMAN DECIDED TO PROTEST MANDATORY SENTENCES WITH A ZIPPO AND A GALLON OF *GASOLINE*.
WE START ADDRESSING HER GRIEVANCES IMMEDIATELY AFTER THAT STUNT, WE'LL HAVE EVERYONE FROM PETA TO PRO-LIFERS BARBECUING THEMSELVES OUT FRONT, TOO.
DAVE, SHE WAS A SICK WOMAN WHO DID SOMETHING PROFOUNDLY IDIOTIC, BUT IT DOESN'T CHANGE THE FACT THAT HER ANGER WAS *JUSTIFIED!*
DOESN'T MATTER. YOU'RE ABLE TO TACKLE THE MORE PROGRESSIVE SOCIAL ISSUES YOU WANT TO EXPLORE BECAUSE OF HOW CONSERVATIVE YOU'VE BEEN ON SECURITY.
IF YOU SUDDENLY LOOK LIKE YOU'RE GIVING IN TO THE DEMANDS OF "TERRORISTS," WE LOSE ON BOTH FRONTS.
SO INSTEAD OF GETTING BULLIED INTO TAKING THE *RIGHT* POSITION, WE GET INTIMIDATED INTO STICKING WITH THE *WRONG* ONE?

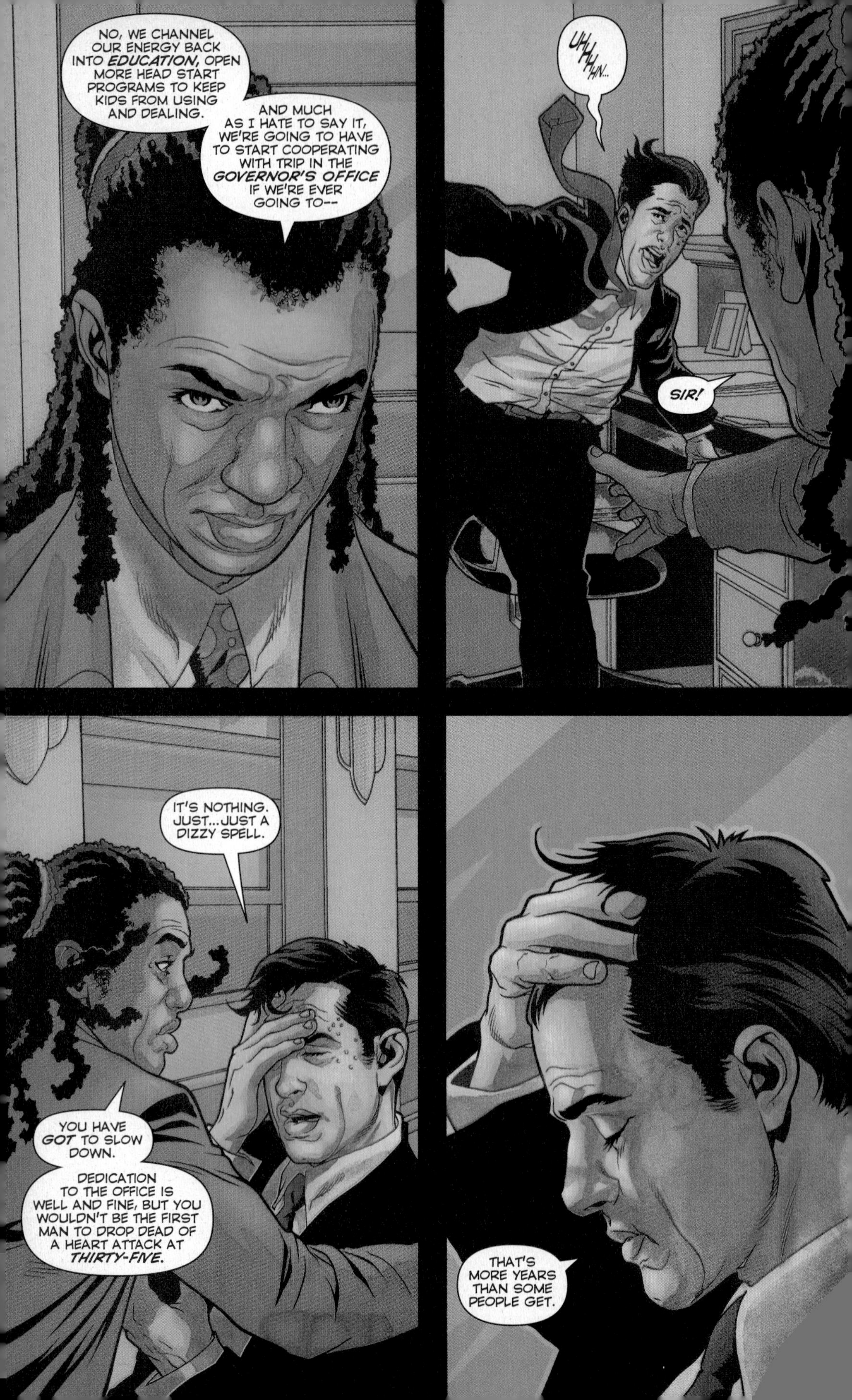
NO, WE CHANNEL OUR ENERGY BACK INTO EDUCATION, OPEN MORE HEAD START PROGRAMS TO KEEP KIDS FROM USING AND DEALING.
AND MUCH AS I HATE TO SAY IT, WE'RE GOING TO HAVE TO START COOPERATING WITH TRIP IN THE GOVERNOR'S OFFICE IF WE'RE EVER GOING TO--
UHHHHN...
SIR!
IT'S NOTHING. JUST...JUST A DIZZY SPELL.
YOU HAVE GOT TO SLOW DOWN.
DEDICATION TO THE OFFICE IS WELL AND FINE, BUT YOU WOULDN'T BE THE FIRST MAN TO DROP DEAD OF A HEART ATTACK AT THIRTY-FIVE.
THAT'S MORE YEARS THAN SOME PEOPLE GET.

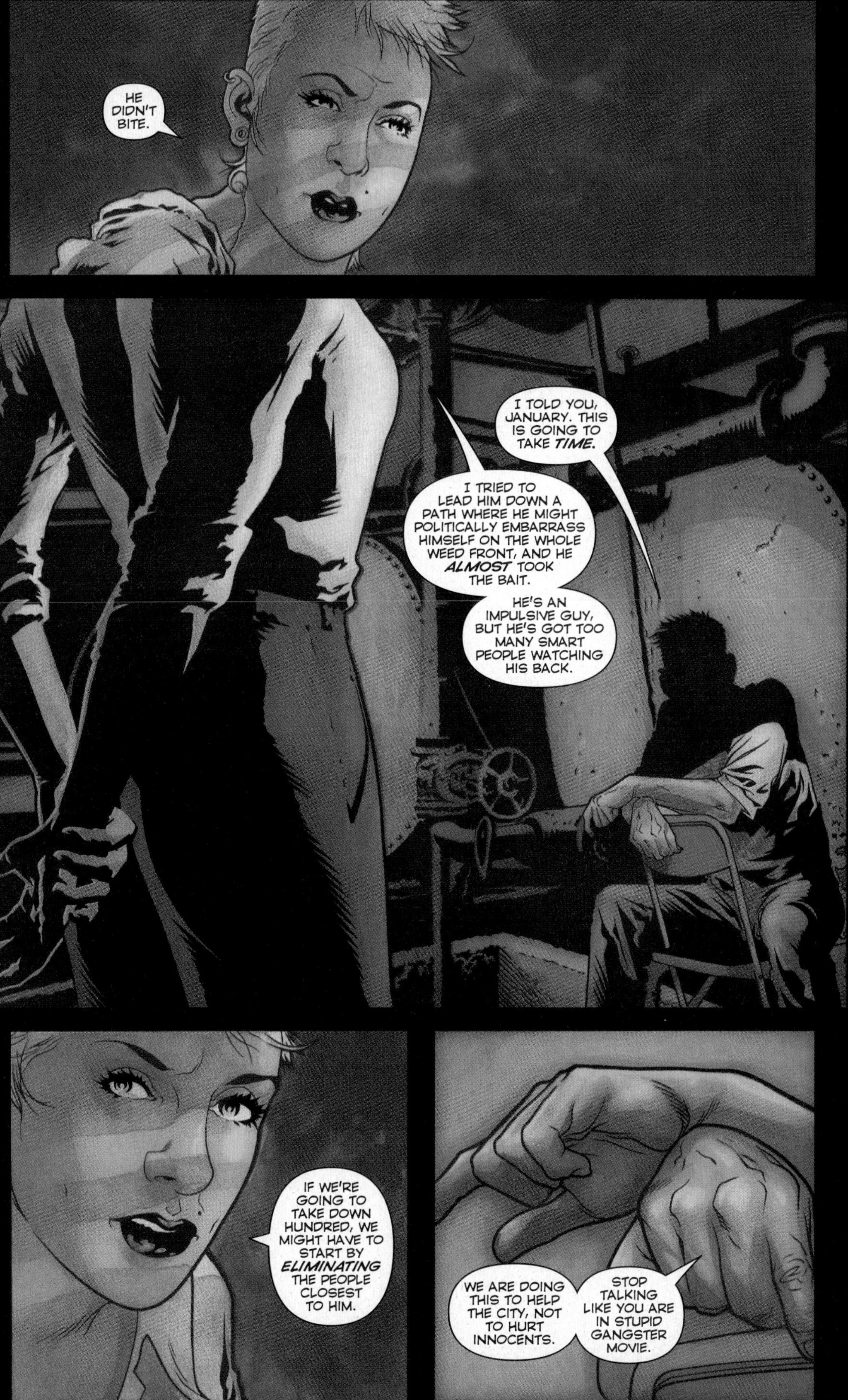
HE DIDN'T BITE.
I TOLD YOU, JANUARY. THIS IS GOING TO TAKE *TIME*.
I TRIED TO LEAD HIM DOWN A PATH WHERE HE MIGHT POLITICALLY EMBARRASS HIMSELF ON THE WHOLE WEED FRONT, AND HE *ALMOST* TOOK THE BAIT.
HE'S AN IMPULSIVE GUY, BUT HE'S GOT TOO MANY SMART PEOPLE WATCHING HIS BACK.
IF WE'RE GOING TO TAKE DOWN HUNDRED, WE MIGHT HAVE TO START BY *ELIMINATING* THE PEOPLE CLOSEST TO HIM.
STOP TALKING LIKE YOU ARE IN STUPID GANGSTER MOVIE.
WE ARE DOING THIS TO HELP THE CITY, NOT TO HURT INNOCENTS.

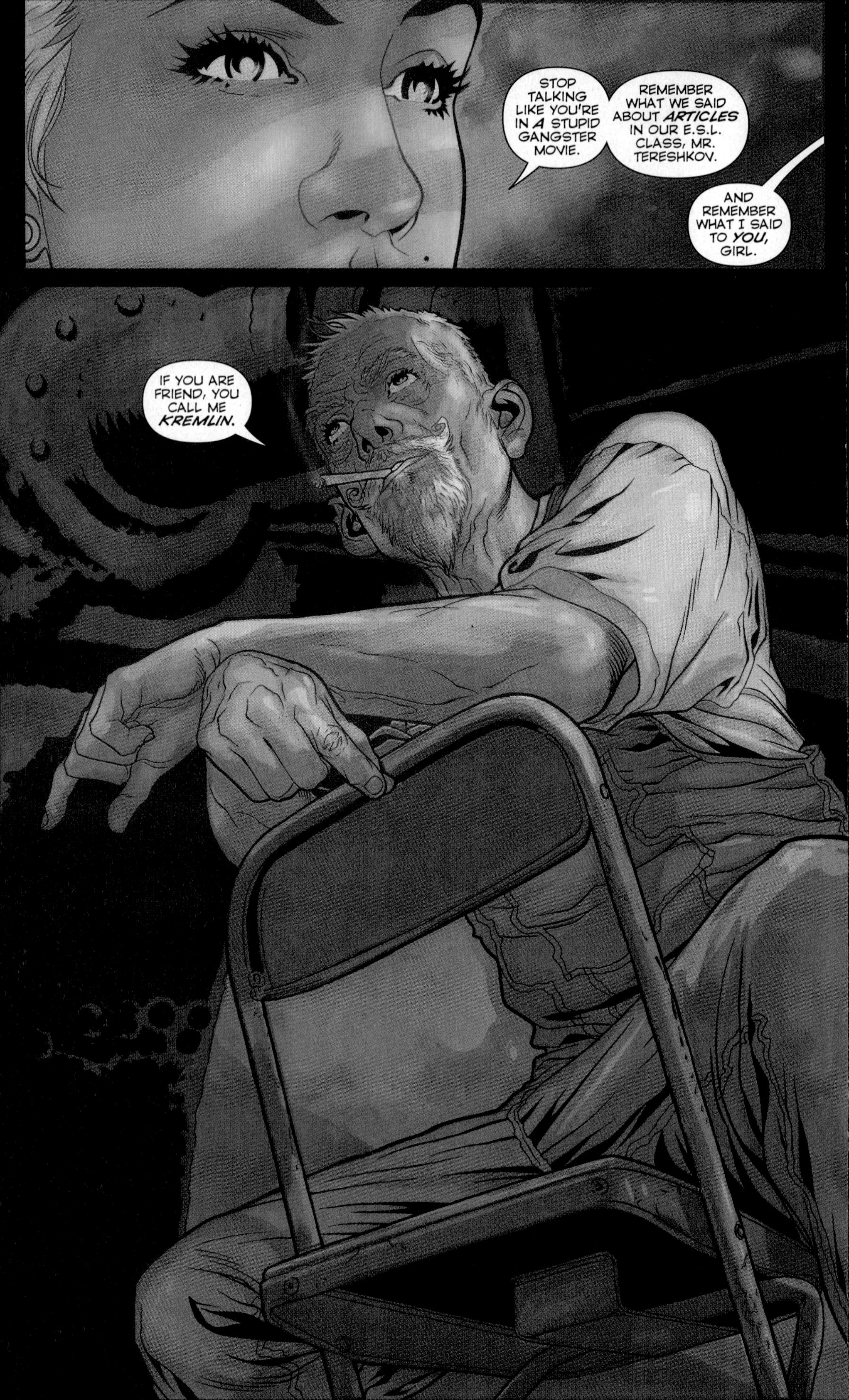
STOP TALKING LIKE YOU'RE IN *A* STUPID GANGSTER MOVIE.
REMEMBER WHAT WE SAID ABOUT *ARTICLES* IN OUR E.S.L. CLASS, MR. TERESHKOV.
AND REMEMBER WHAT I SAID TO *YOU,* GIRL.
IF YOU ARE FRIEND, YOU CALL ME *KREMLIN.*

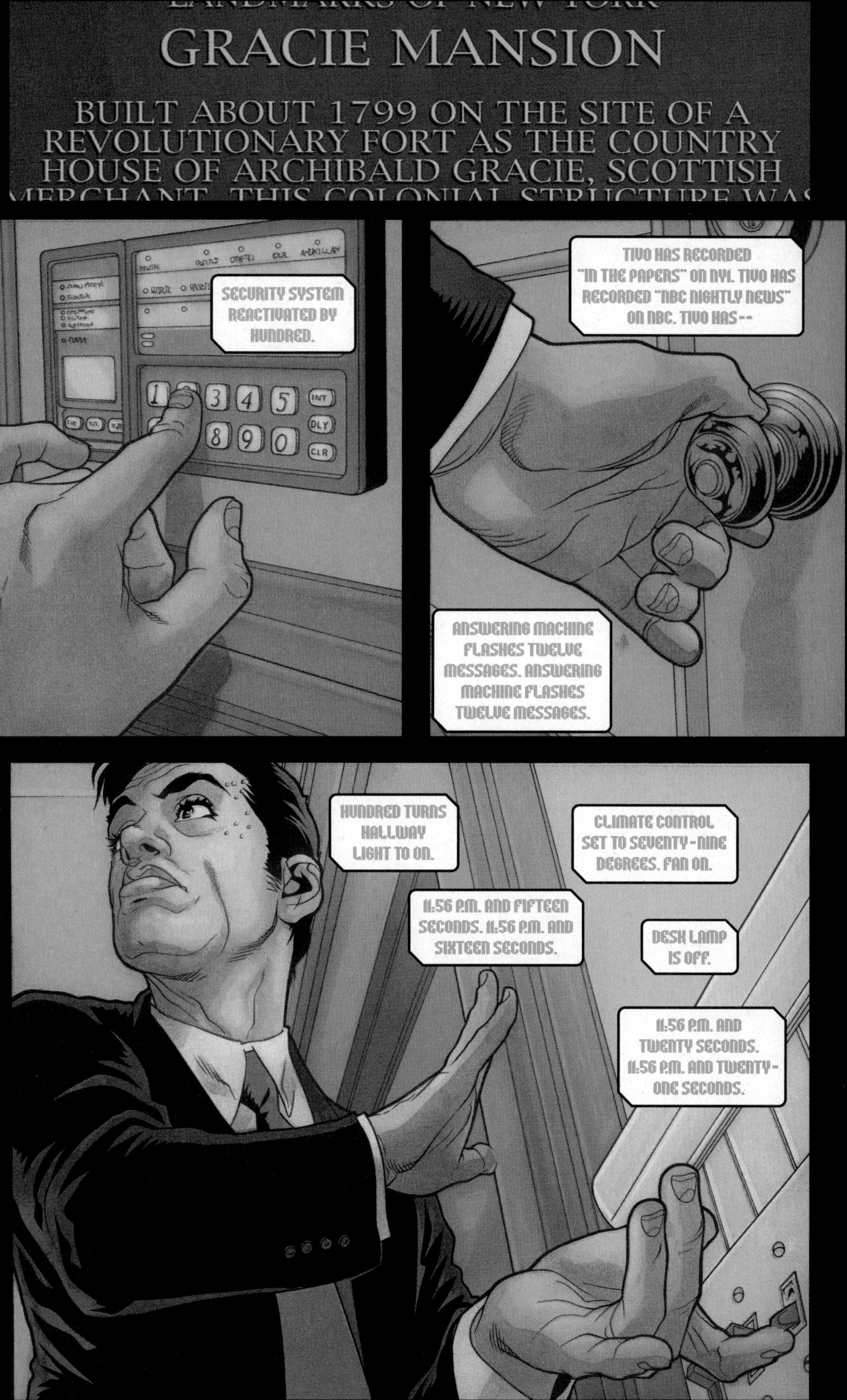
GRACIE MANSION
BUILT ABOUT 1799 ON THE SITE OF A
REVOLUTIONARY FORT AS THE COUNTRY
HOUSE OF ARCHIBALD GRACIE, SCOTTISH
SECURITY SYSTEM REACTIVATED BY HUNDRED.
TIVO HAS RECORDED "IN THE PAPERS" ON NY1. TIVO HAS RECORDED "NBC NIGHTLY NEWS" ON NBC. TIVO HAS--
ANSWERING MACHINE FLASHES TWELVE MESSAGES. ANSWERING MACHINE FLASHES TWELVE MESSAGES.
HUNDRED TURNS HALLWAY LIGHT TO ON.
CLIMATE CONTROL SET TO SEVENTY-NINE DEGREES. FAN ON.
11:56 P.M. AND FIFTEEN SECONDS. 11:56 P.M. AND SIXTEEN SECONDS.
DESK LAMP IS OFF.
11:56 P.M. AND TWENTY SECONDS. 11:56 P.M. AND TWENTY-ONE SECONDS.

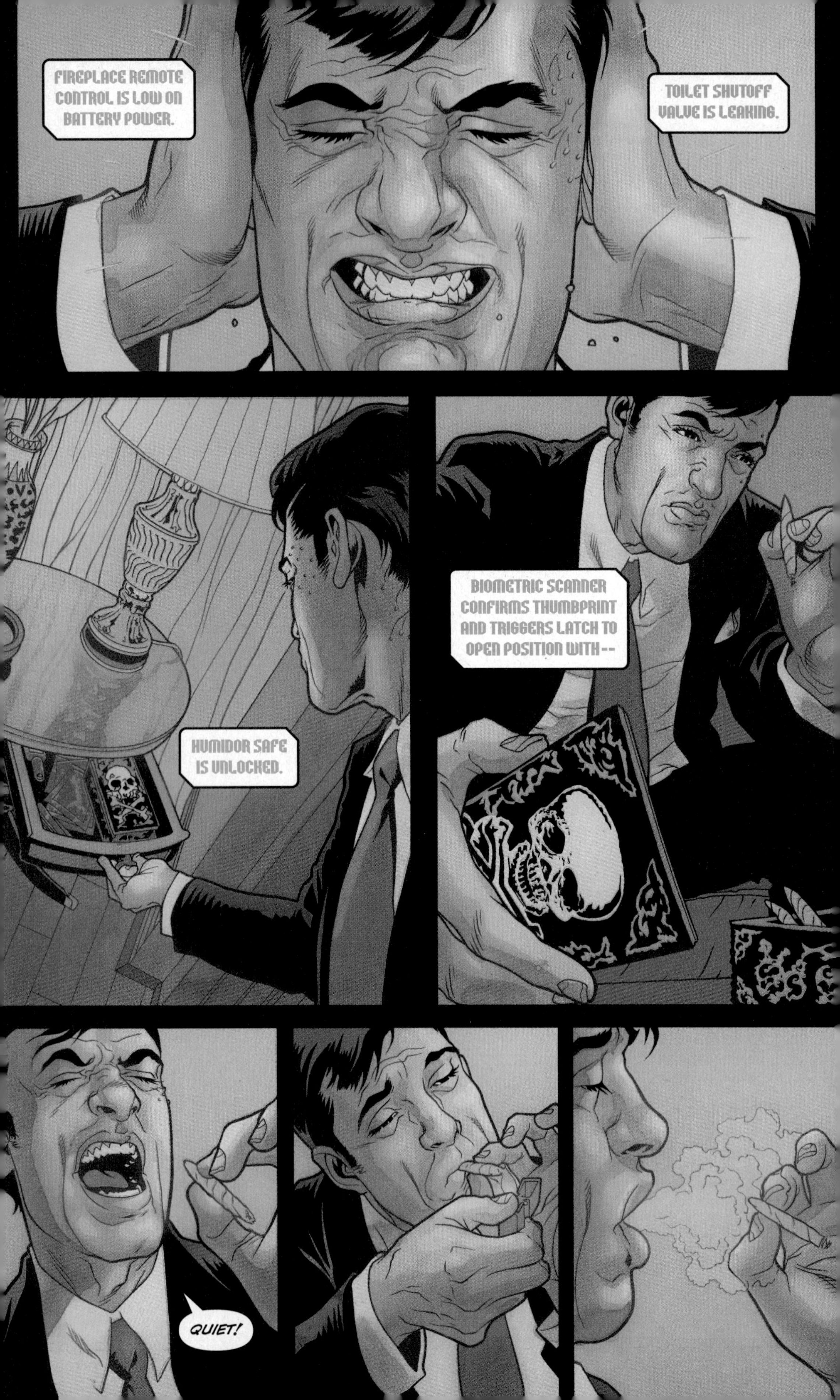
FIREPLACE REMOTE CONTROL IS LOW ON BATTERY POWER.
TOILET SHUTOFF VALVE IS LEAKING.
HUMIDOR SAFE IS UNLOCKED.
BIOMETRIC SCANNER CONFIRMS THUMBPRINT AND TRIGGERS LATCH TO OPEN POSITION WITH--
QUIET!

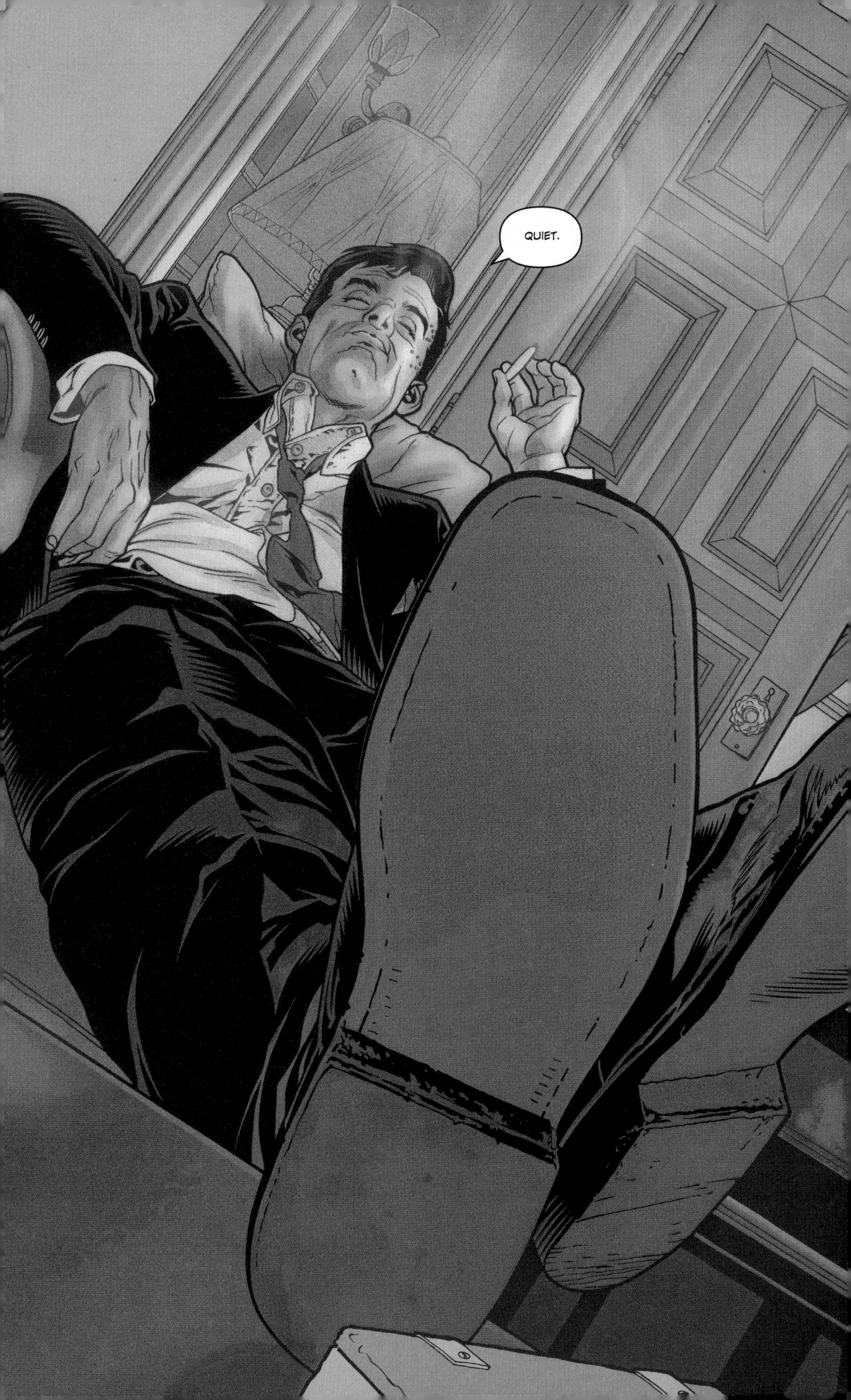
QUIET.

Chapter 5
Standalone

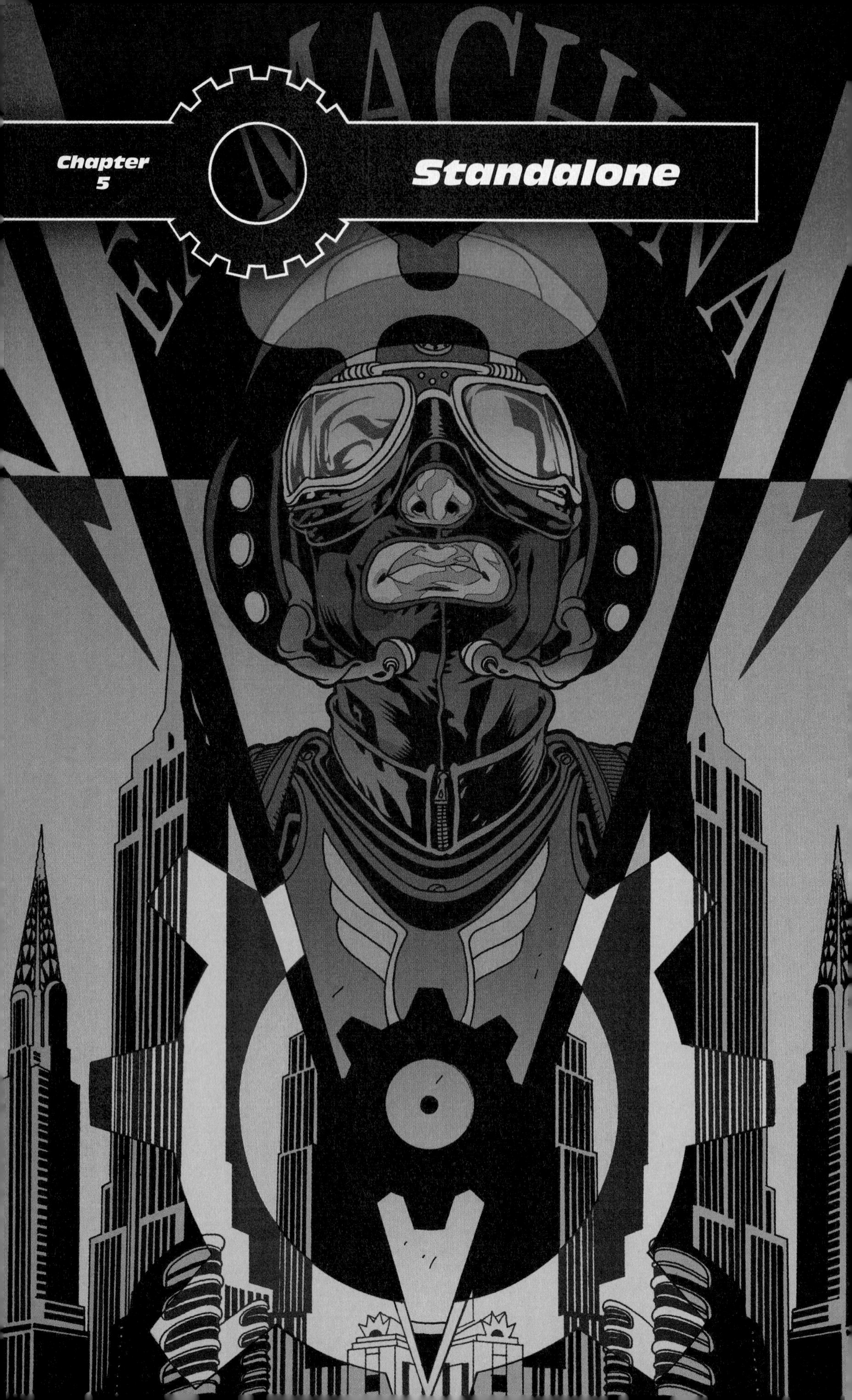

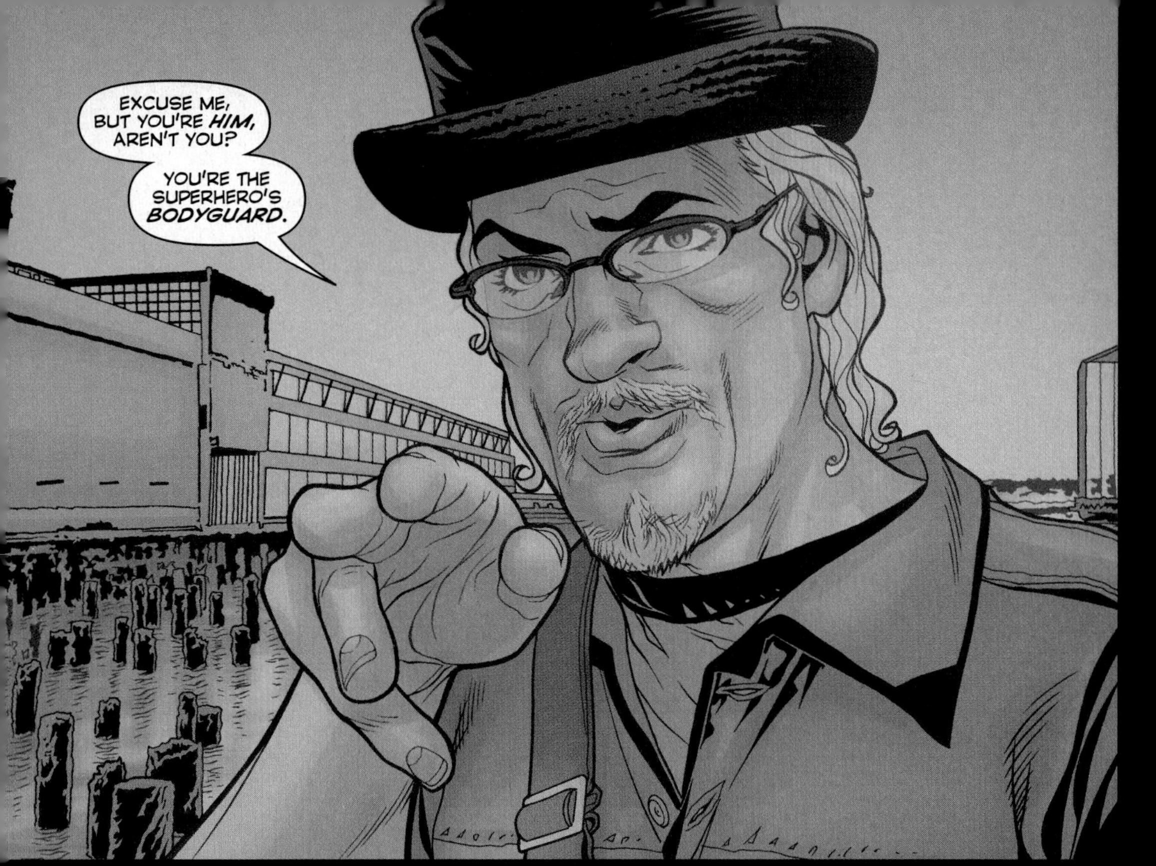
EXCUSE ME, BUT YOU'RE *HIM*, AREN'T YOU?
YOU'RE THE SUPERHERO'S *BODYGUARD*.

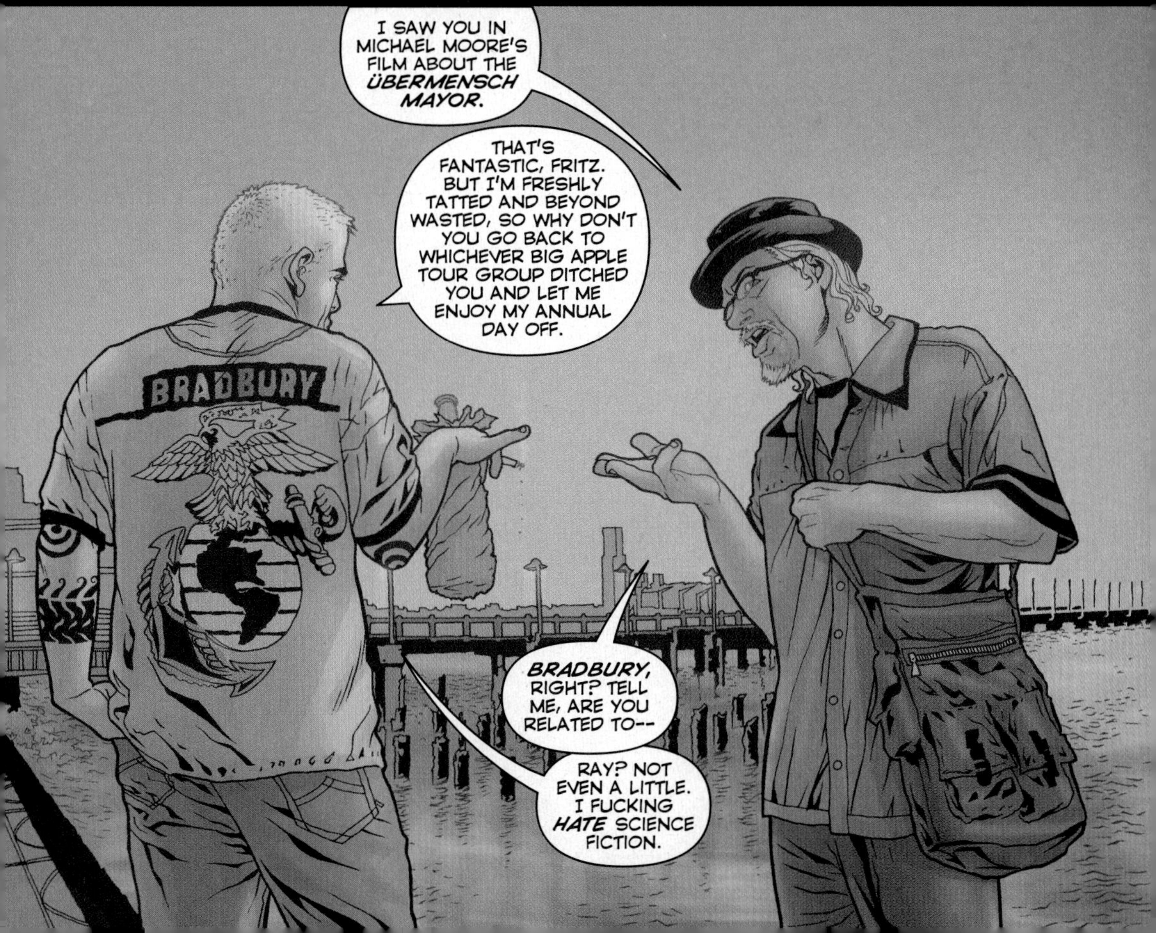
I SAW YOU IN MICHAEL MOORE'S FILM ABOUT THE *ÜBERMENSCH MAYOR*.
THAT'S FANTASTIC, FRITZ. BUT I'M FRESHLY TATTED AND BEYOND WASTED, SO WHY DON'T YOU GO BACK TO WHICHEVER BIG APPLE TOUR GROUP DITCHED YOU AND LET ME ENJOY MY ANNUAL DAY OFF.
BRADBURY
BRADBURY, RIGHT? TELL ME, ARE YOU RELATED TO--
RAY? NOT EVEN A LITTLE. I FUCKING *HATE* SCIENCE FICTION.

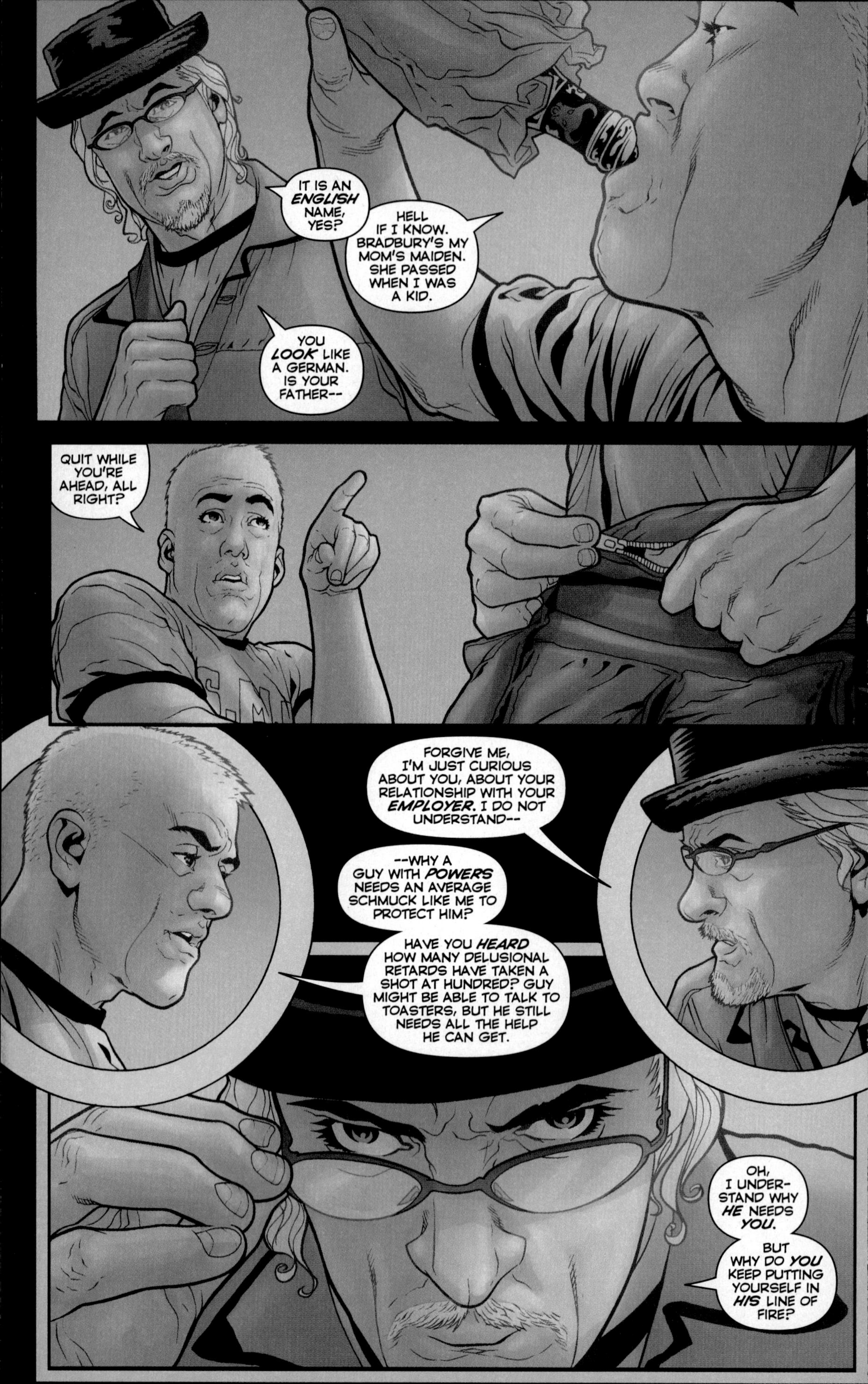
IT IS AN ENGLISH NAME, YES?
HELL IF I KNOW. BRADBURY'S MY MOM'S MAIDEN. SHE PASSED WHEN I WAS A KID.
YOU LOOK LIKE A GERMAN. IS YOUR FATHER--
QUIT WHILE YOU'RE AHEAD, ALL RIGHT?
FORGIVE ME, I'M JUST CURIOUS ABOUT YOU, ABOUT YOUR RELATIONSHIP WITH YOUR EMPLOYER. I DO NOT UNDERSTAND--
--WHY A GUY WITH POWERS NEEDS AN AVERAGE SCHMUCK LIKE ME TO PROTECT HIM?
HAVE YOU HEARD HOW MANY DELUSIONAL RETARDS HAVE TAKEN A SHOT AT HUNDRED? GUY MIGHT BE ABLE TO TALK TO TOASTERS, BUT HE STILL NEEDS ALL THE HELP HE CAN GET.
OH, I UNDERSTAND WHY HE NEEDS YOU.
BUT WHY DO YOU KEEP PUTTING YOURSELF IN HIS LINE OF FIRE?

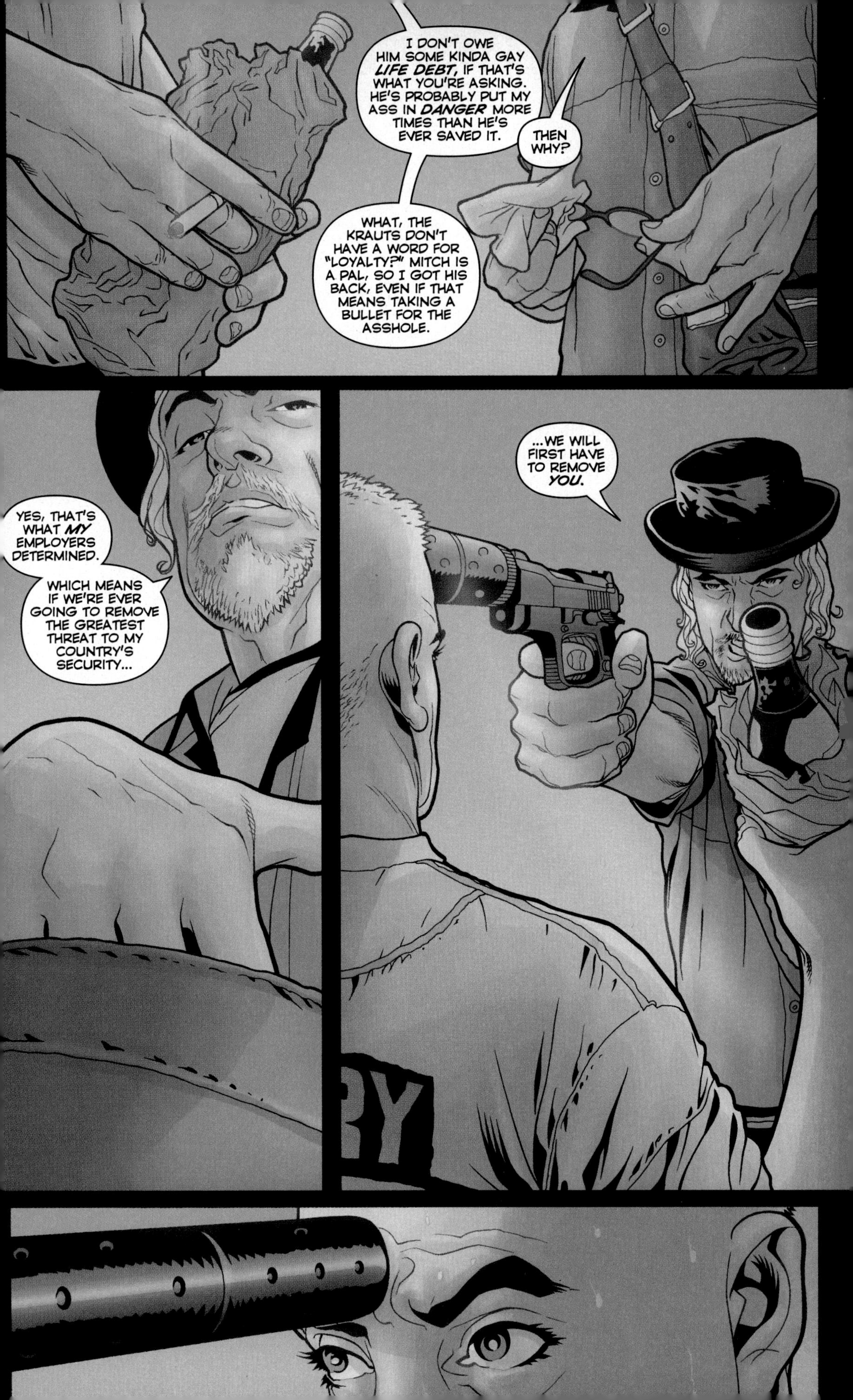

I DON'T OWE HIM SOME KINDA GAY *LIFE DEBT,* IF THAT'S WHAT YOU'RE ASKING. HE'S PROBABLY PUT MY ASS IN *DANGER* MORE TIMES THAN HE'S EVER SAVED IT.
THEN WHY?
WHAT, THE KRAUTS DON'T HAVE A WORD FOR "LOYALTY?" MITCH IS A PAL, SO I GOT HIS BACK, EVEN IF THAT MEANS TAKING A BULLET FOR THE ASSHOLE.
YES, THAT'S WHAT *MY* EMPLOYERS DETERMINED.
WHICH MEANS IF WE'RE EVER GOING TO REMOVE THE GREATEST THREAT TO MY COUNTRY'S SECURITY...
...WE WILL FIRST HAVE TO REMOVE *YOU.*

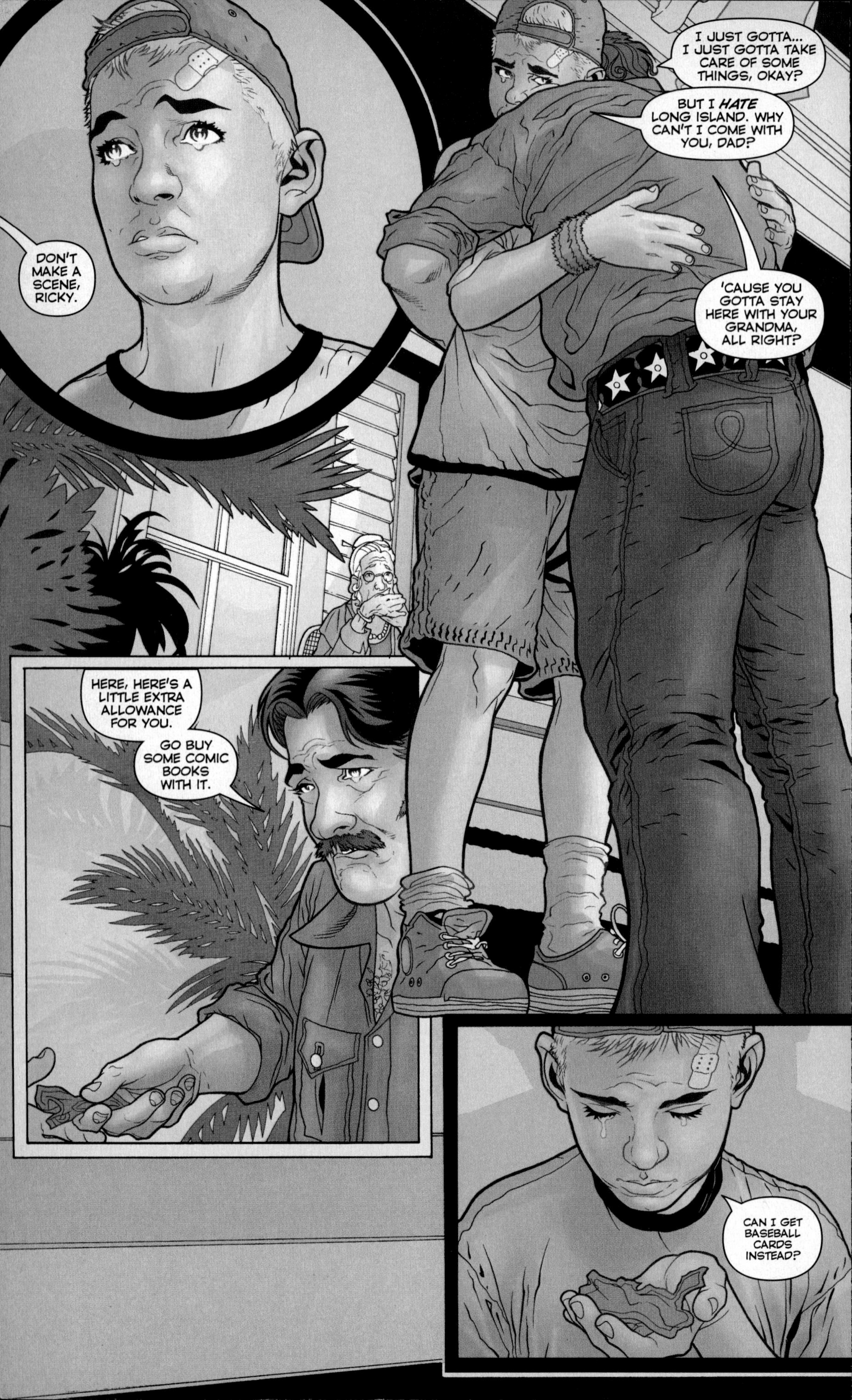
DON'T MAKE A SCENE, RICKY.
I JUST GOTTA... I JUST GOTTA TAKE CARE OF SOME THINGS, OKAY?
BUT I *HATE* LONG ISLAND. WHY CAN'T I COME WITH YOU, DAD?
'CAUSE YOU GOTTA STAY HERE WITH YOUR GRANDMA, ALL RIGHT?
HERE, HERE'S A LITTLE EXTRA ALLOWANCE FOR YOU.
GO BUY SOME COMIC BOOKS WITH IT.
CAN I GET BASEBALL CARDS INSTEAD?

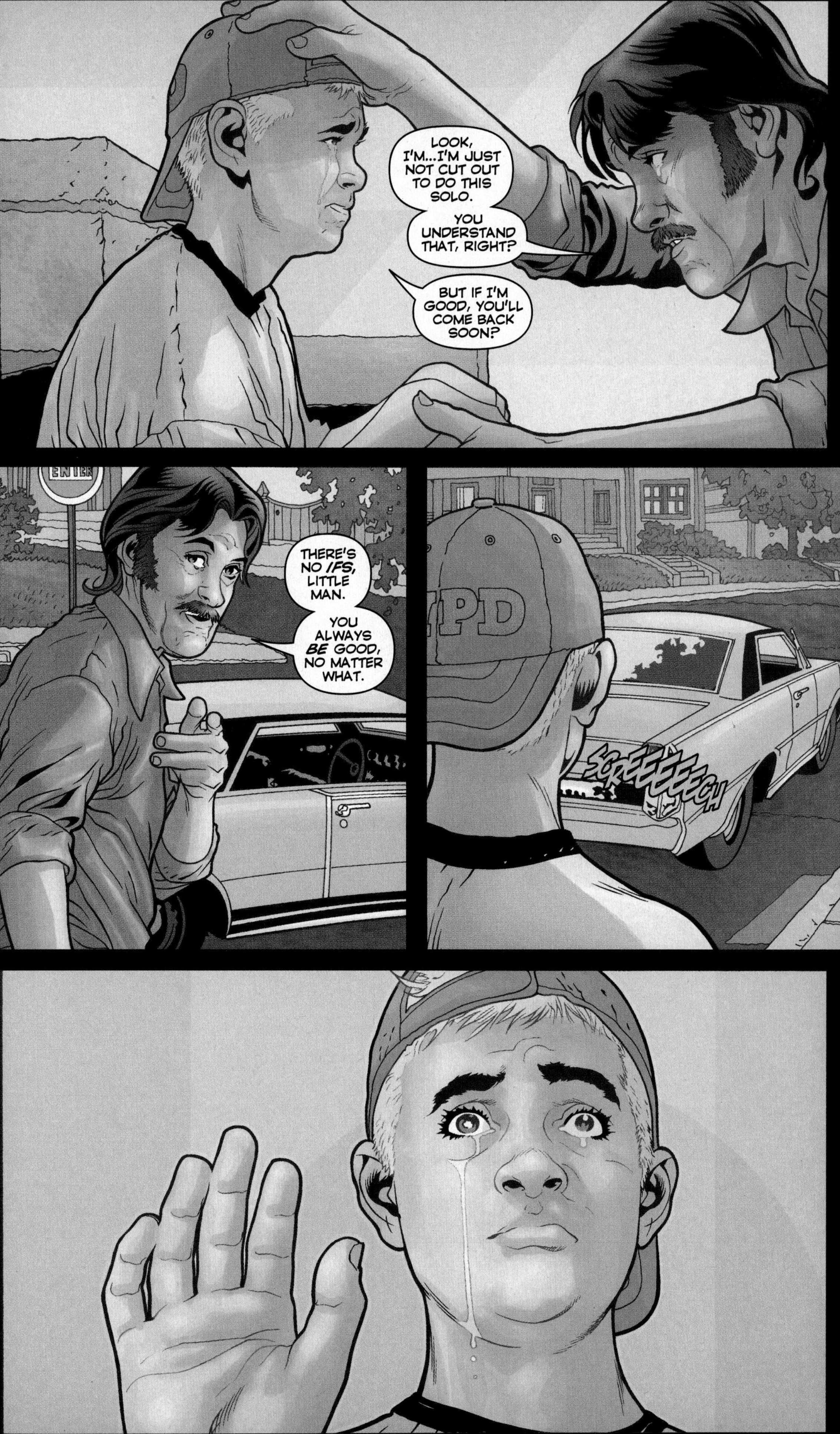
LOOK, I'M...I'M JUST NOT CUT OUT TO DO THIS SOLO.
YOU UNDERSTAND THAT, RIGHT?
BUT IF I'M GOOD, YOU'LL COME BACK SOON?
ENTER
THERE'S NO *IFS*, LITTLE MAN.
YOU ALWAYS *BE* GOOD, NO MATTER WHAT.
SCREEEEEECH

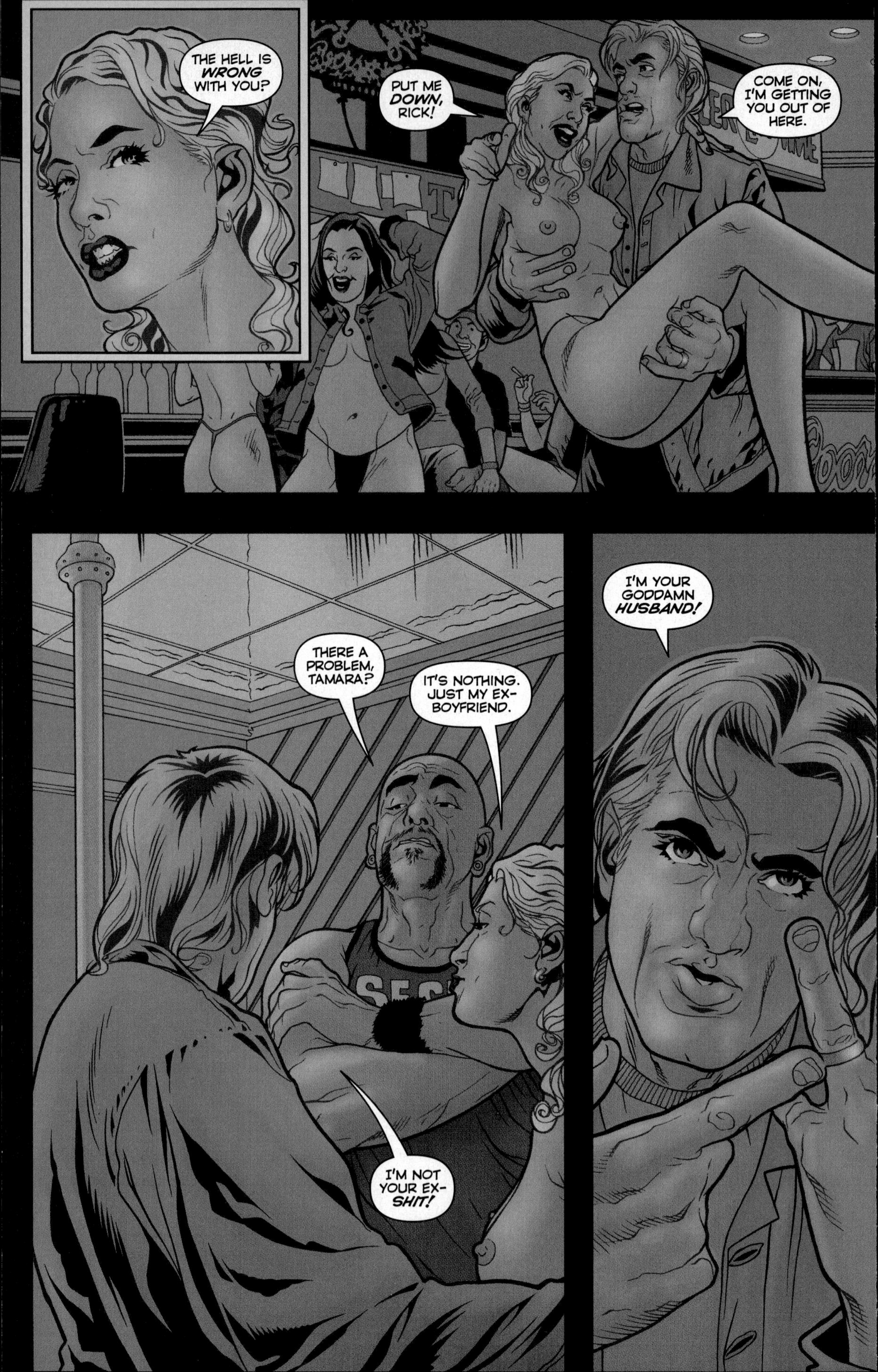
THE HELL IS WRONG WITH YOU?
PUT ME DOWN, RICK!
COME ON, I'M GETTING YOU OUT OF HERE.
THERE A PROBLEM, TAMARA?
IT'S NOTHING. JUST MY EX-BOYFRIEND.
I'M NOT YOUR EX-SHIT!
I'M YOUR GODDAMN HUSBAND!

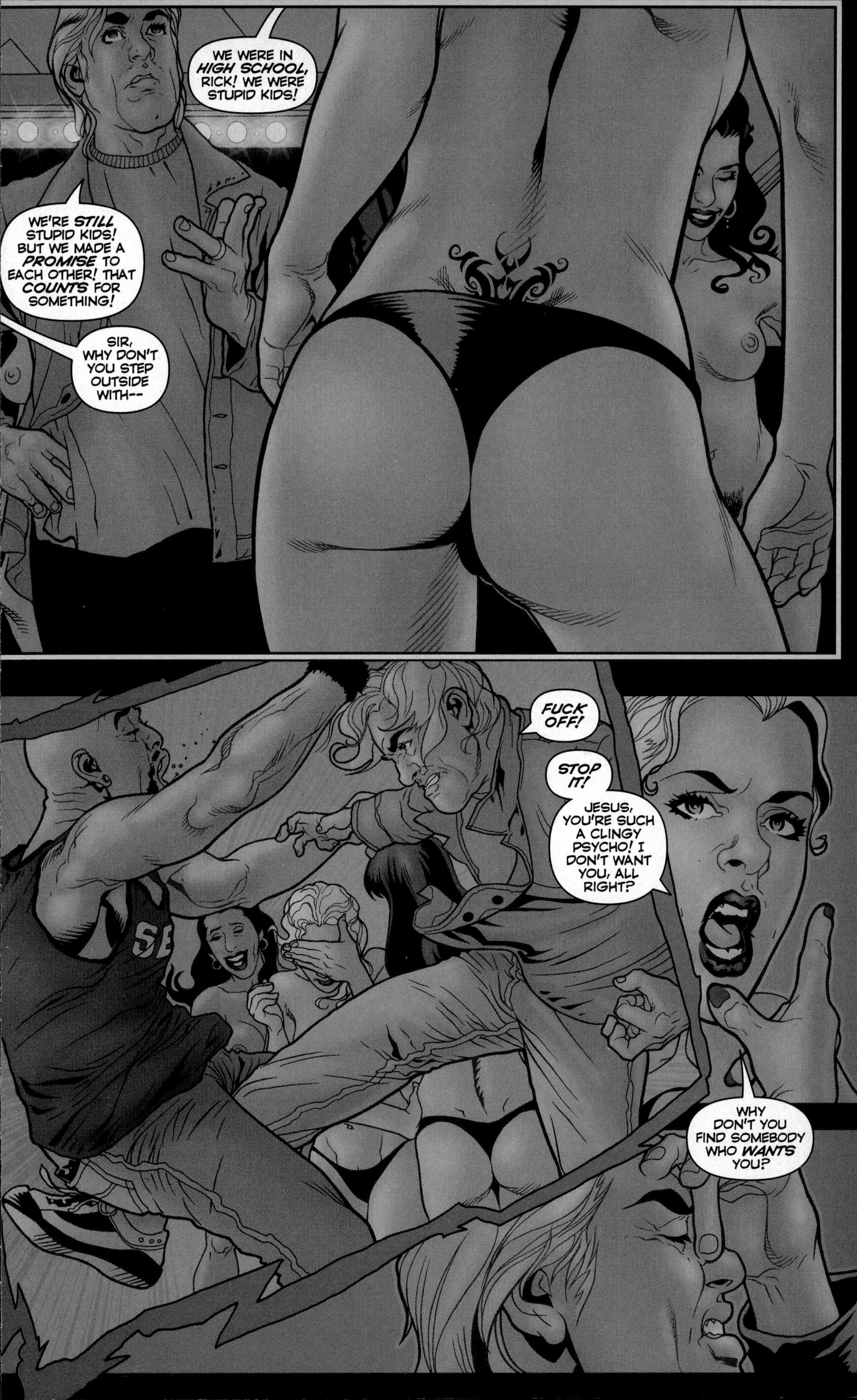
WE WERE IN HIGH SCHOOL, RICK! WE WERE STUPID KIDS!
WE'RE STILL STUPID KIDS! BUT WE MADE A PROMISE TO EACH OTHER! THAT COUNTS FOR SOMETHING!
SIR, WHY DON'T YOU STEP OUTSIDE WITH--
FUCK OFF!
STOP IT!
JESUS, YOU'RE SUCH A CLINGY PSYCHO! I DON'T WANT YOU, ALL RIGHT?
WHY DON'T YOU FIND SOMEBODY WHO WANTS YOU?

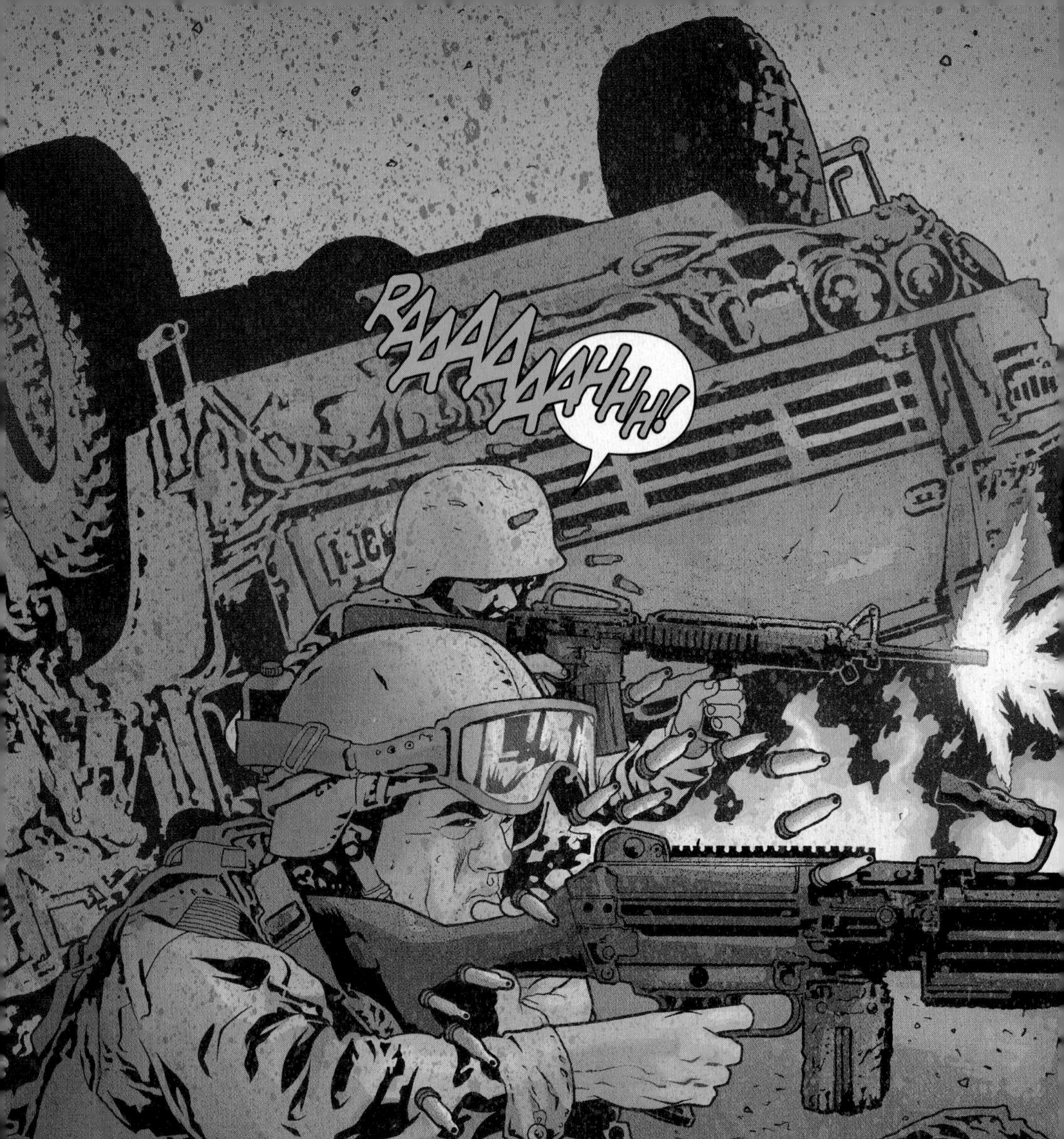
RAAAAAAHHH!

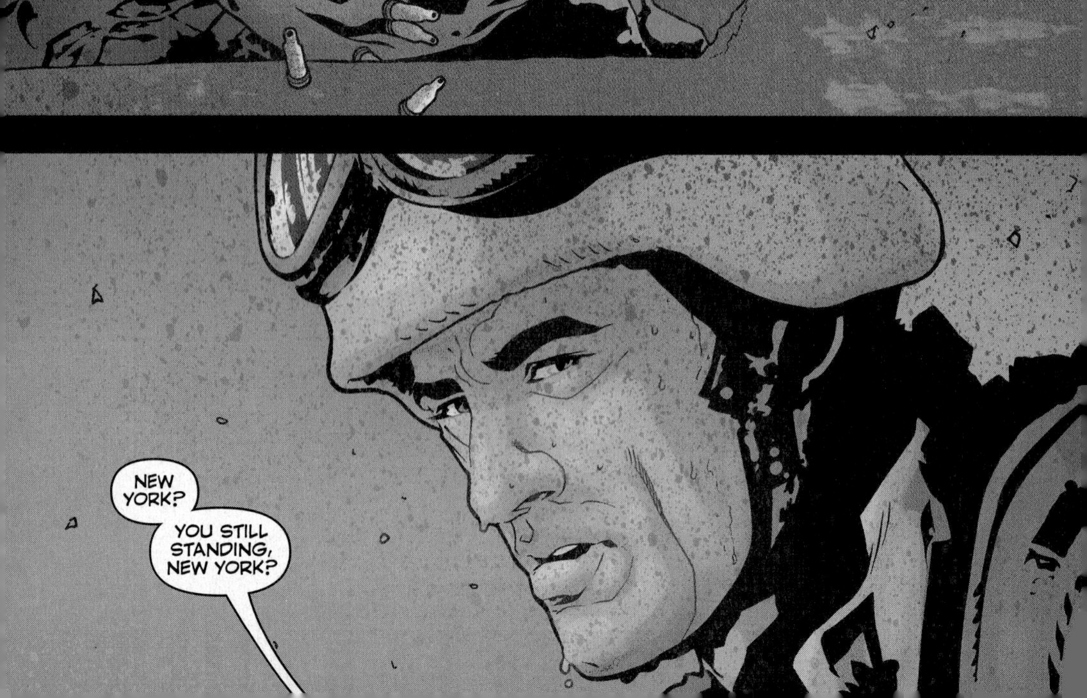
NEW YORK?
YOU STILL STANDING, NEW YORK?

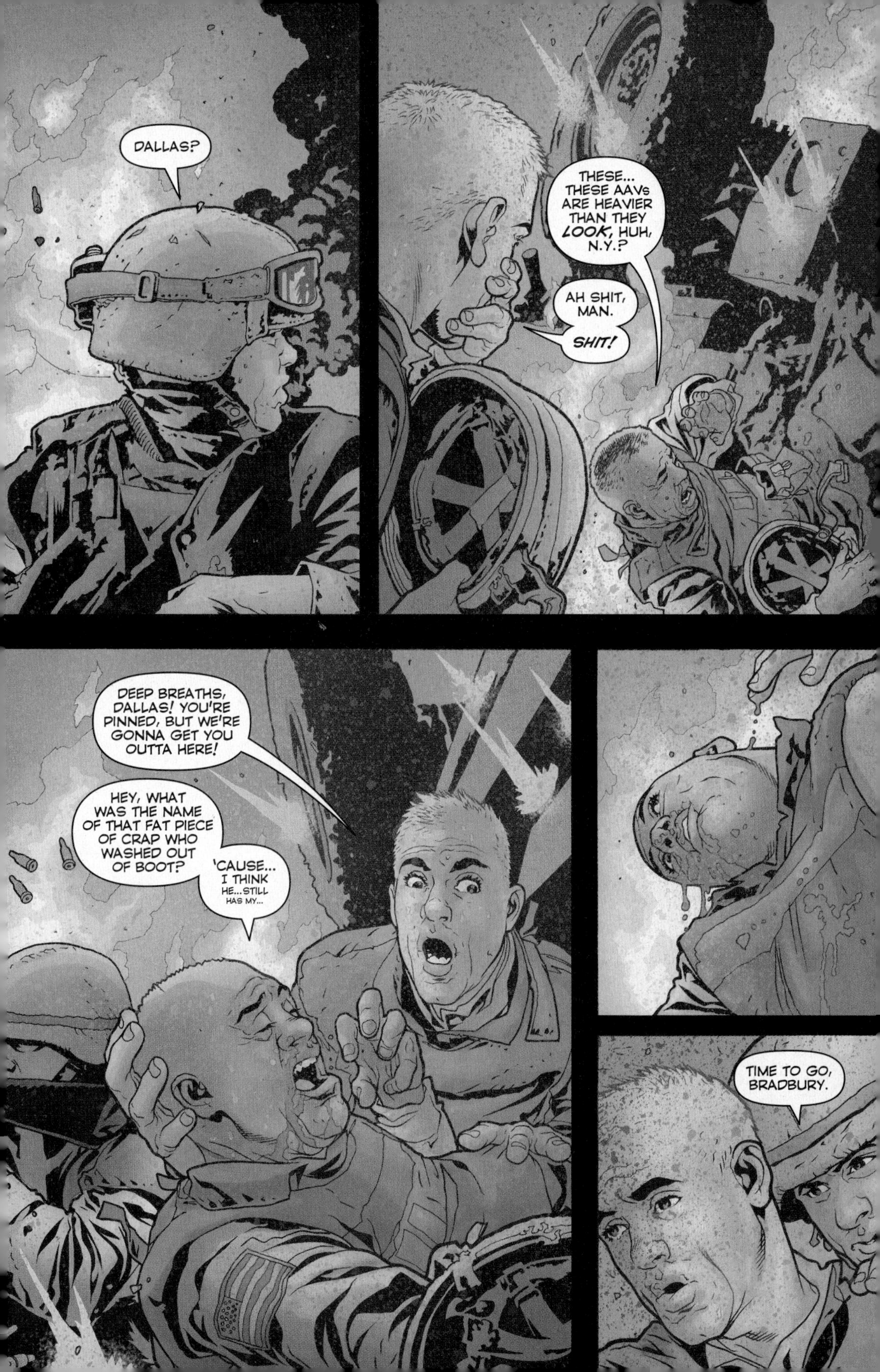
DALLAS?
THESE... THESE AAVs ARE HEAVIER THAN THEY LOOK, HUH, N.Y.?
AH SHIT, MAN.
SHIT!
DEEP BREATHS, DALLAS! YOU'RE PINNED, BUT WE'RE GONNA GET YOU OUTTA HERE!
HEY, WHAT WAS THE NAME OF THAT FAT PIECE OF CRAP WHO WASHED OUT OF BOOT?
'CAUSE... I THINK HE...STILL HAS MY...
TIME TO GO, BRADBURY.

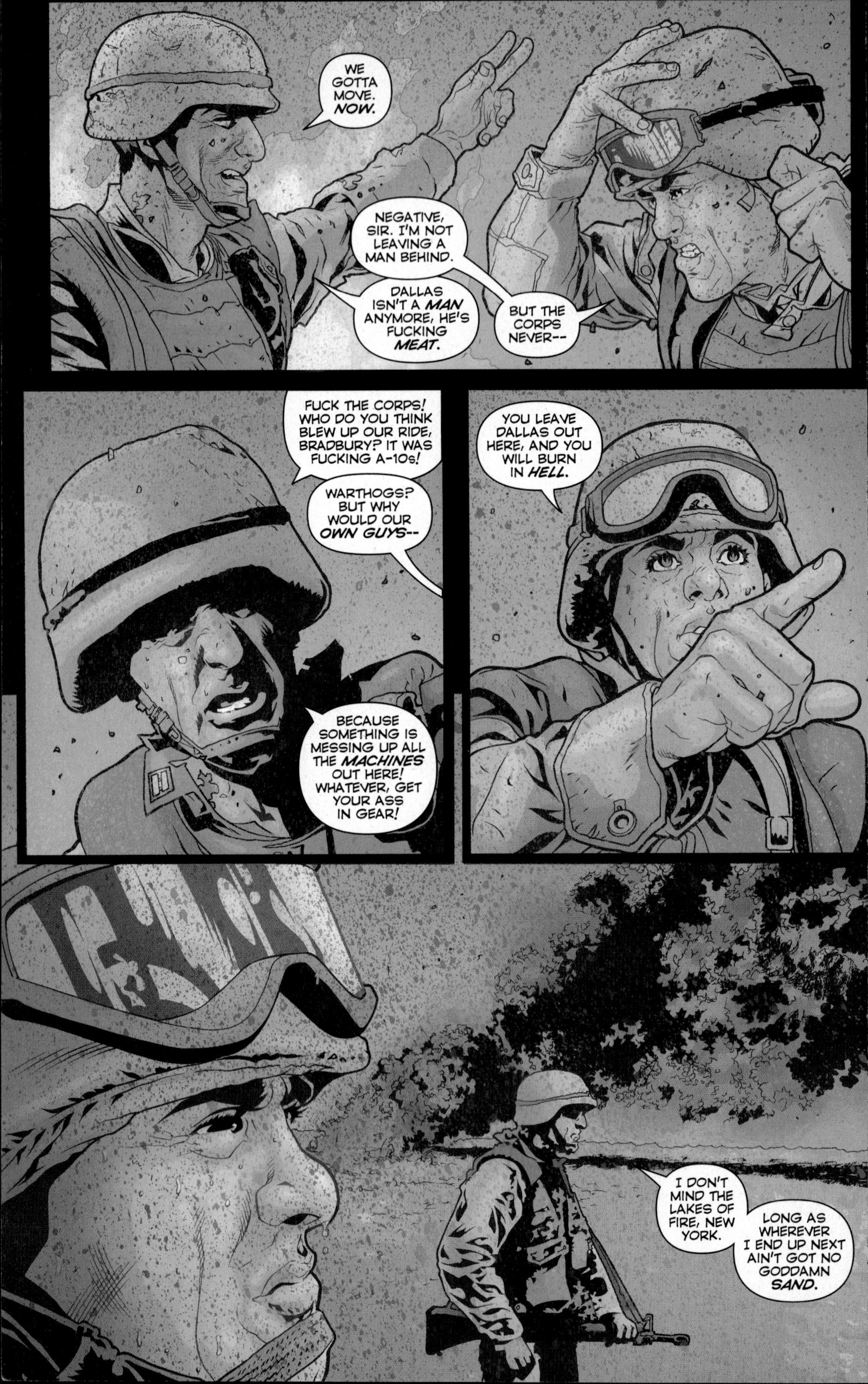
WE GOTTA MOVE. NOW.
NEGATIVE, SIR. I'M NOT LEAVING A MAN BEHIND.
DALLAS ISN'T A MAN ANYMORE, HE'S FUCKING MEAT.
BUT THE CORPS NEVER--
FUCK THE CORPS! WHO DO YOU THINK BLEW UP OUR RIDE, BRADBURY? IT WAS FUCKING A-10s!
WARTHOGS? BUT WHY WOULD OUR OWN GUYS--
BECAUSE SOMETHING IS MESSING UP ALL THE MACHINES OUT HERE! WHATEVER, GET YOUR ASS IN GEAR!
YOU LEAVE DALLAS OUT HERE, AND YOU WILL BURN IN HELL.
I DON'T MIND THE LAKES OF FIRE, NEW YORK.
LONG AS WHEREVER I END UP NEXT AIN'T GOT NO GODDAMN SAND.

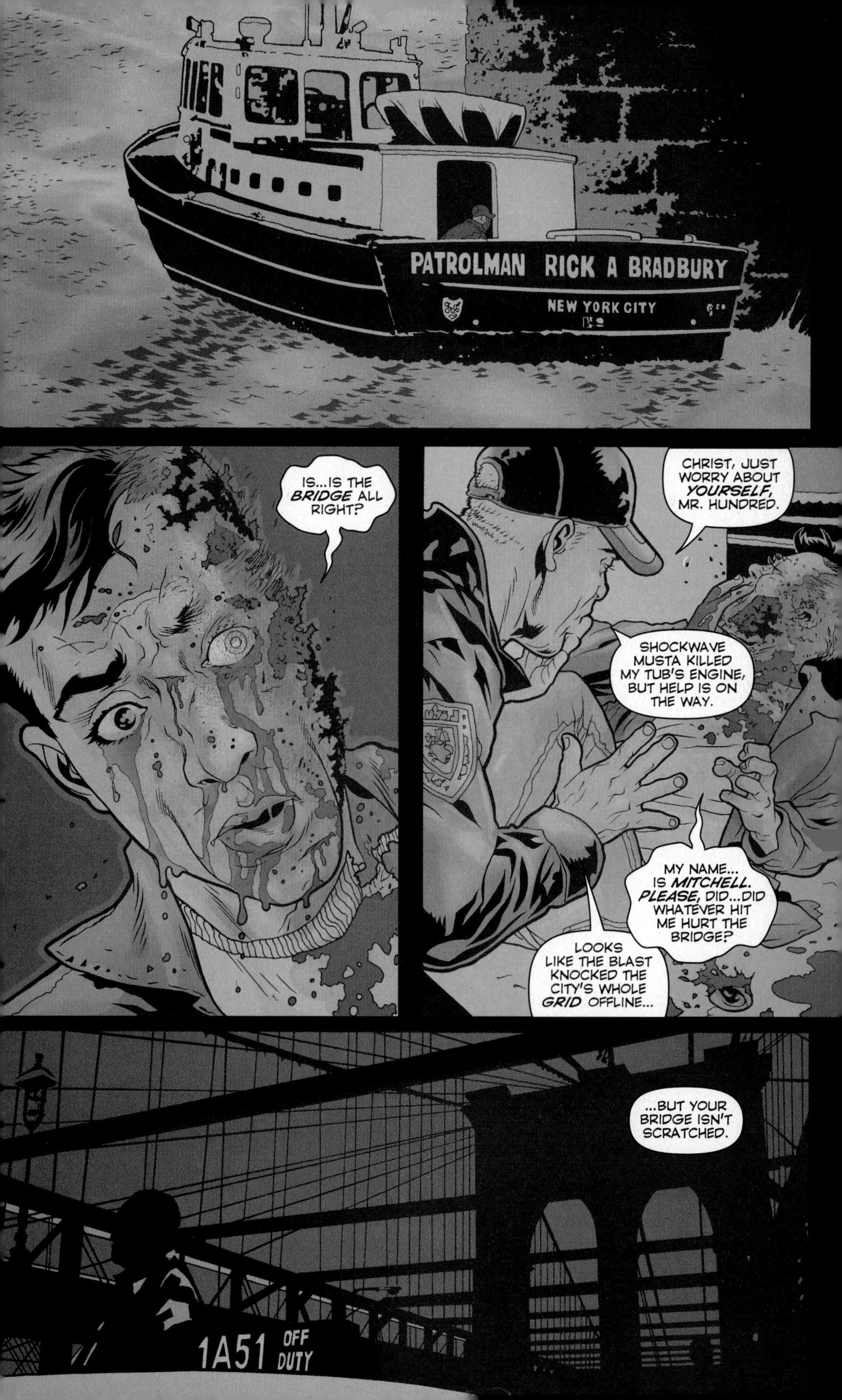

PATROLMAN RICK A BRADBURY
NEW YORK CITY
IS...IS THE *BRIDGE* ALL RIGHT?
CHRIST, JUST WORRY ABOUT *YOURSELF*, MR. HUNDRED.
SHOCKWAVE MUSTA KILLED MY TUB'S ENGINE, BUT HELP IS ON THE WAY.
MY NAME... IS *MITCHELL. PLEASE,* DID...DID WHATEVER HIT ME HURT THE BRIDGE?
LOOKS LIKE THE BLAST KNOCKED THE CITY'S WHOLE *GRID* OFFLINE...
...BUT YOUR BRIDGE ISN'T SCRATCHED.
1A51 OFF DUTY

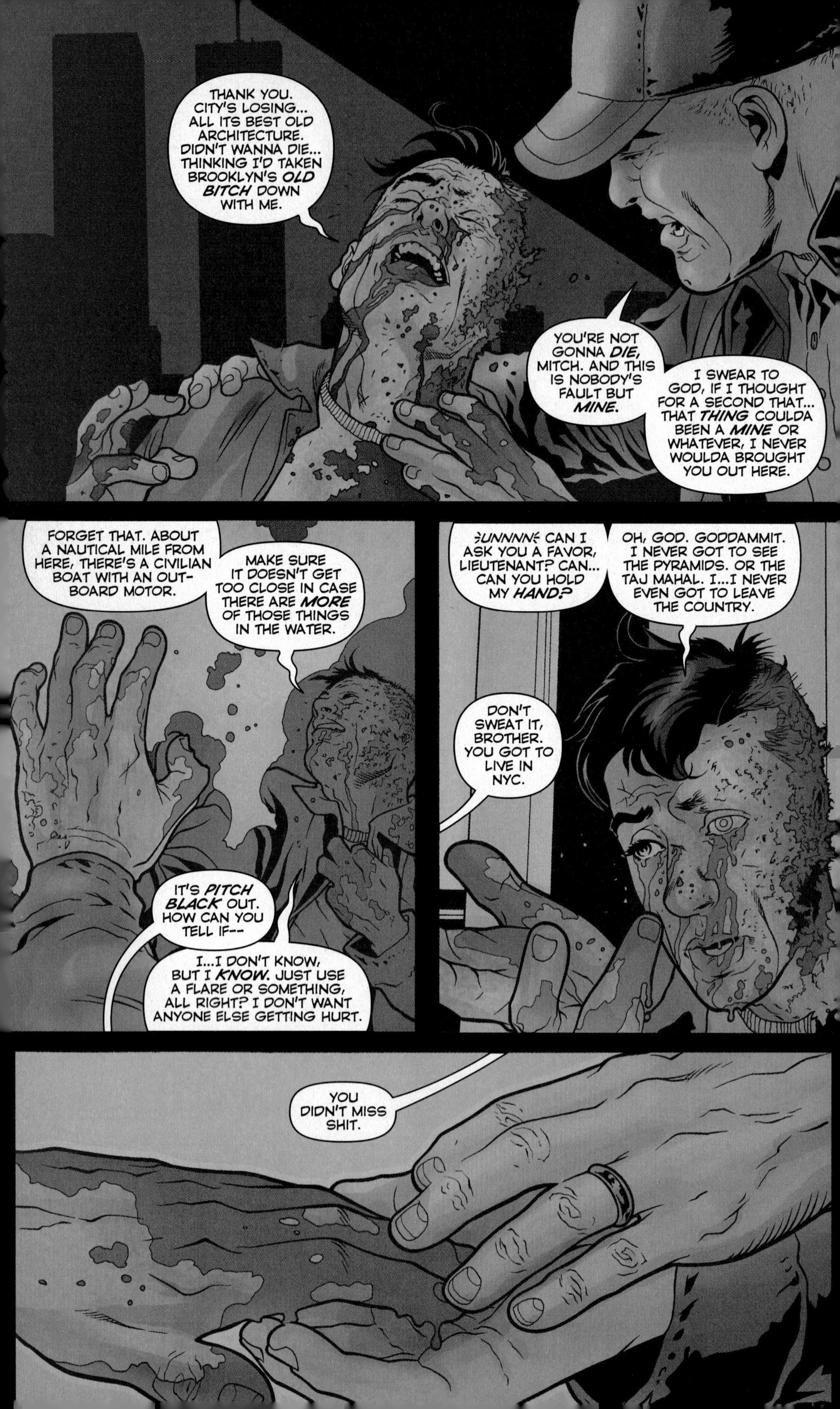
THANK YOU. CITY'S LOSING... ALL ITS BEST OLD ARCHITECTURE. DIDN'T WANNA DIE... THINKING I'D TAKEN BROOKLYN'S OLD BITCH DOWN WITH ME.
YOU'RE NOT GONNA DIE, MITCH. AND THIS IS NOBODY'S FAULT BUT MINE.
I SWEAR TO GOD, IF I THOUGHT FOR A SECOND THAT... THAT THING COULDA BEEN A MINE OR WHATEVER, I NEVER WOULDA BROUGHT YOU OUT HERE.
FORGET THAT. ABOUT A NAUTICAL MILE FROM HERE, THERE'S A CIVILIAN BOAT WITH AN OUT-BOARD MOTOR.
MAKE SURE IT DOESN'T GET TOO CLOSE IN CASE THERE ARE MORE OF THOSE THINGS IN THE WATER.
IT'S PITCH BLACK OUT. HOW CAN YOU TELL IF--
I...I DON'T KNOW, BUT I KNOW. JUST USE A FLARE OR SOMETHING, ALL RIGHT? I DON'T WANT ANYONE ELSE GETTING HURT.
UNNNN CAN I ASK YOU A FAVOR, LIEUTENANT? CAN... CAN YOU HOLD MY HAND?
OH, GOD. GODDAMMIT. I NEVER GOT TO SEE THE PYRAMIDS. OR THE TAJ MAHAL. I...I NEVER EVEN GOT TO LEAVE THE COUNTRY.
DON'T SWEAT IT, BROTHER. YOU GOT TO LIVE IN NYC.
YOU DIDN'T MISS SHIT.

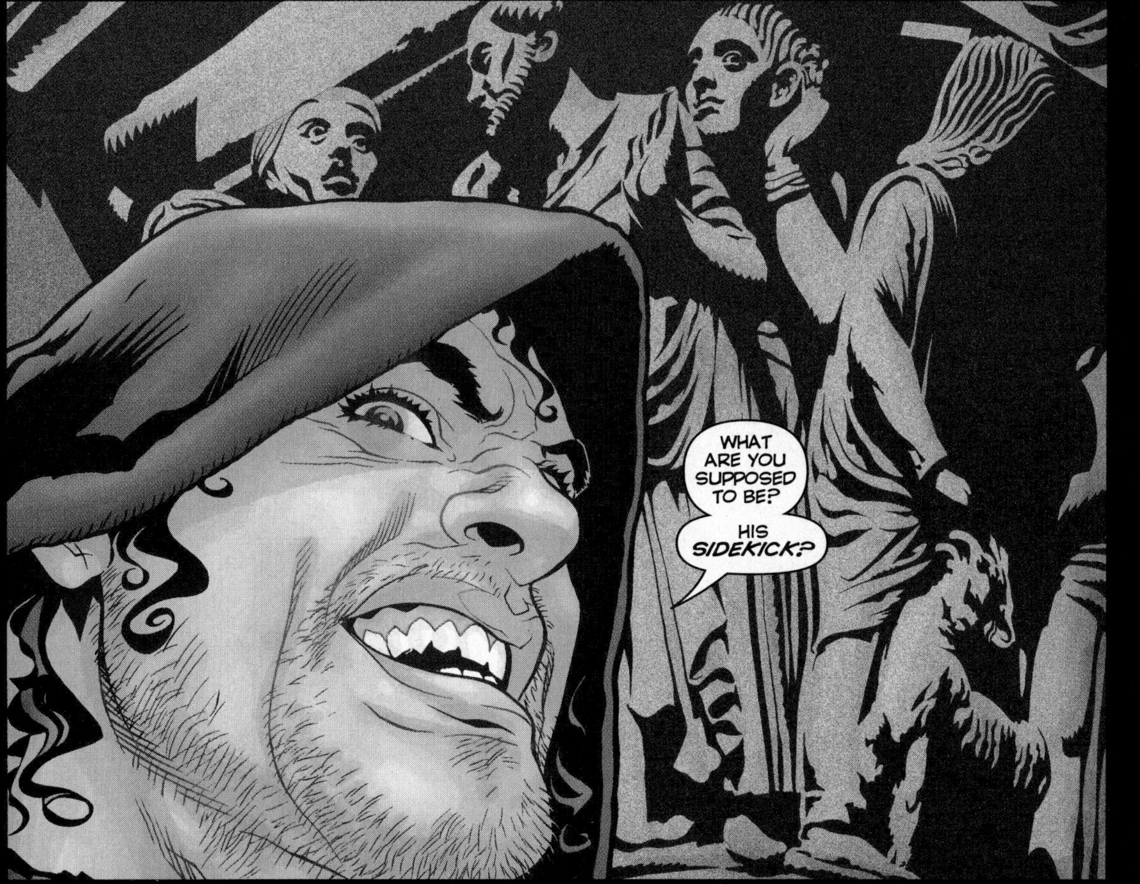
WHAT ARE YOU SUPPOSED TO BE?
HIS SIDEKICK?

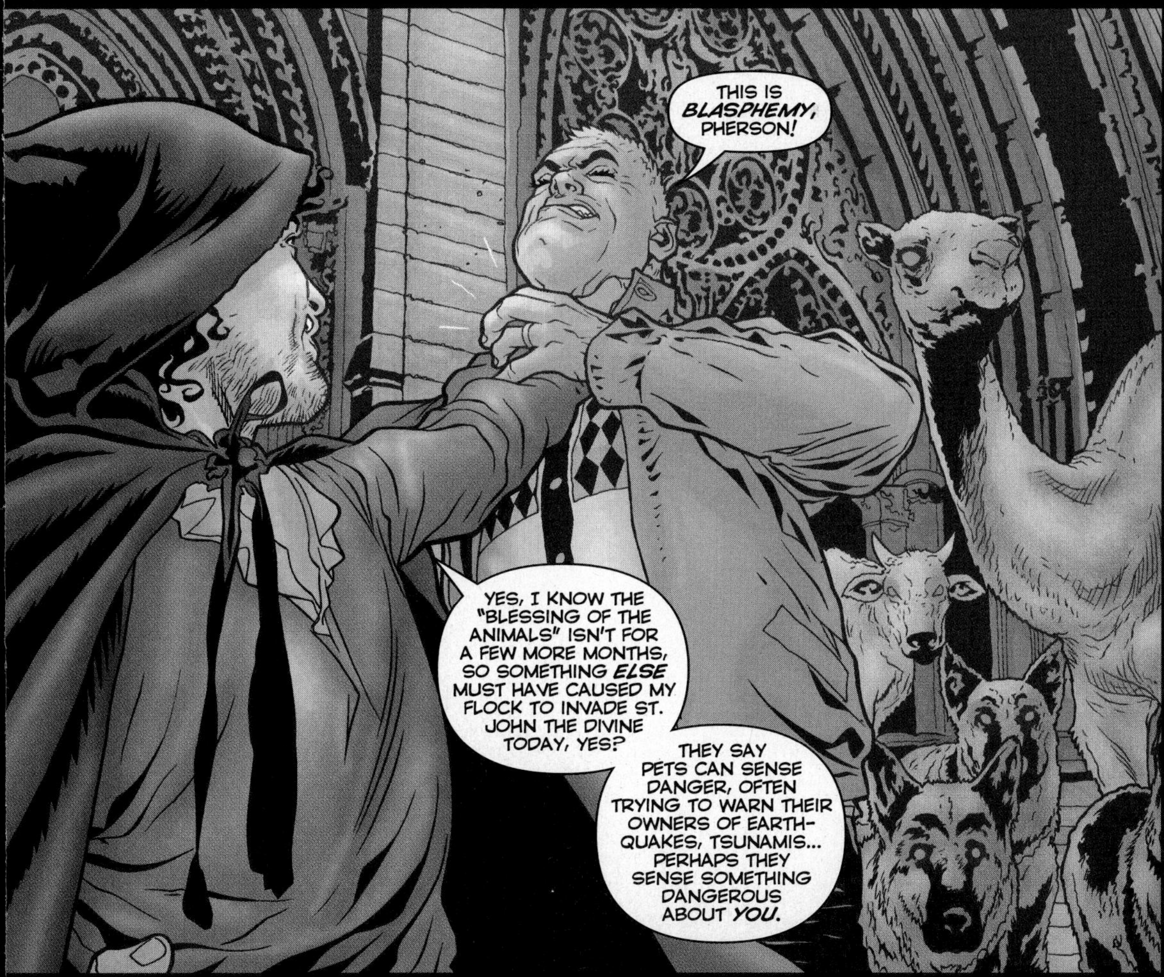
THIS IS BLASPHEMY, PHERSON!
YES, I KNOW THE "BLESSING OF THE ANIMALS" ISN'T FOR A FEW MORE MONTHS, SO SOMETHING ELSE MUST HAVE CAUSED MY FLOCK TO INVADE ST. JOHN THE DIVINE TODAY, YES?
THEY SAY PETS CAN SENSE DANGER, OFTEN TRYING TO WARN THEIR OWNERS OF EARTH-QUAKES, TSUNAMIS... PERHAPS THEY SENSE SOMETHING DANGEROUS ABOUT YOU.

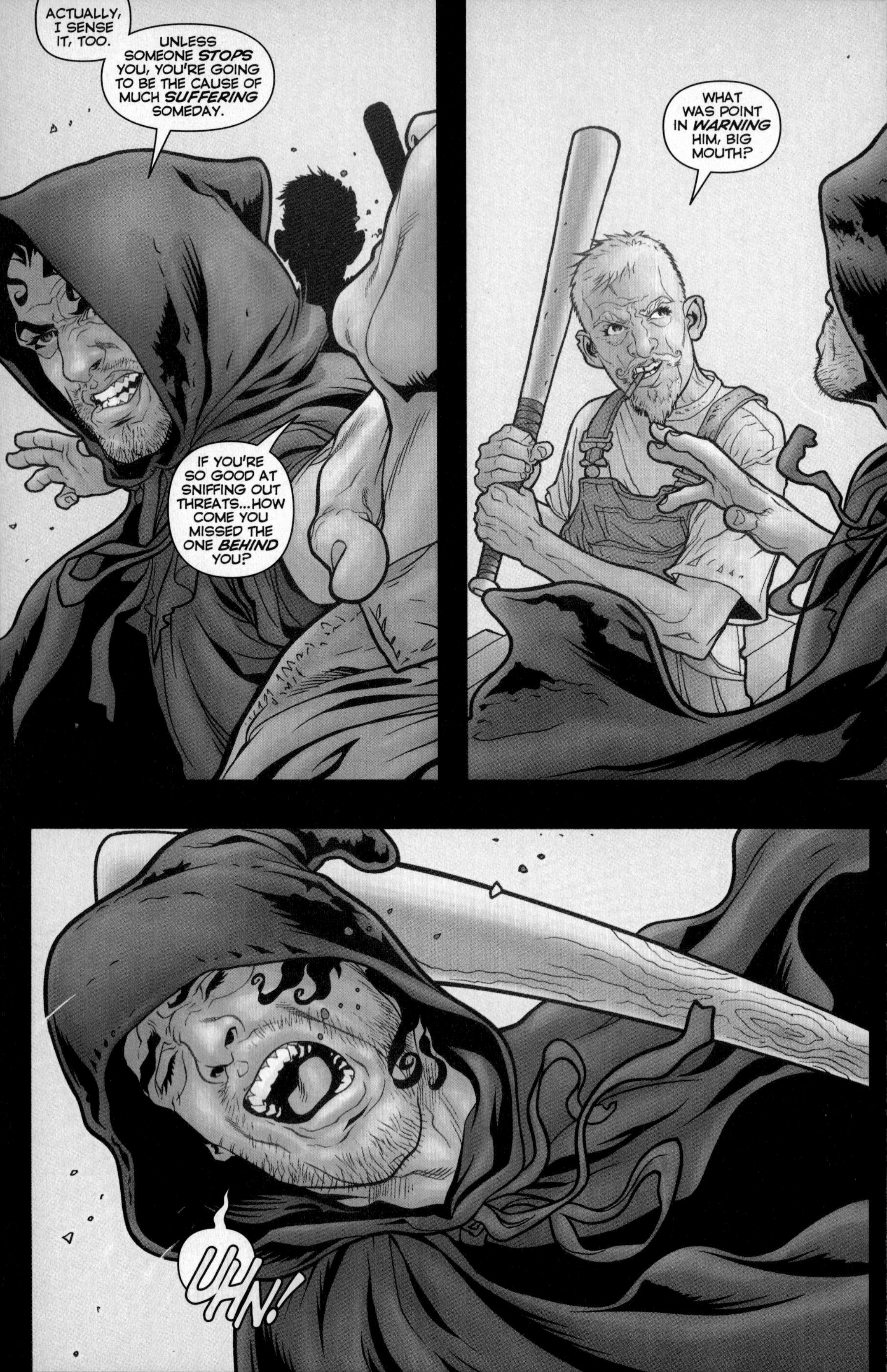
ACTUALLY, I SENSE IT, TOO.
UNLESS SOMEONE STOPS YOU, YOU'RE GOING TO BE THE CAUSE OF MUCH SUFFERING SOMEDAY.
IF YOU'RE SO GOOD AT SNIFFING OUT THREATS...HOW COME YOU MISSED THE ONE BEHIND YOU?
WHAT WAS POINT IN WARNING HIM, BIG MOUTH?
UHN!

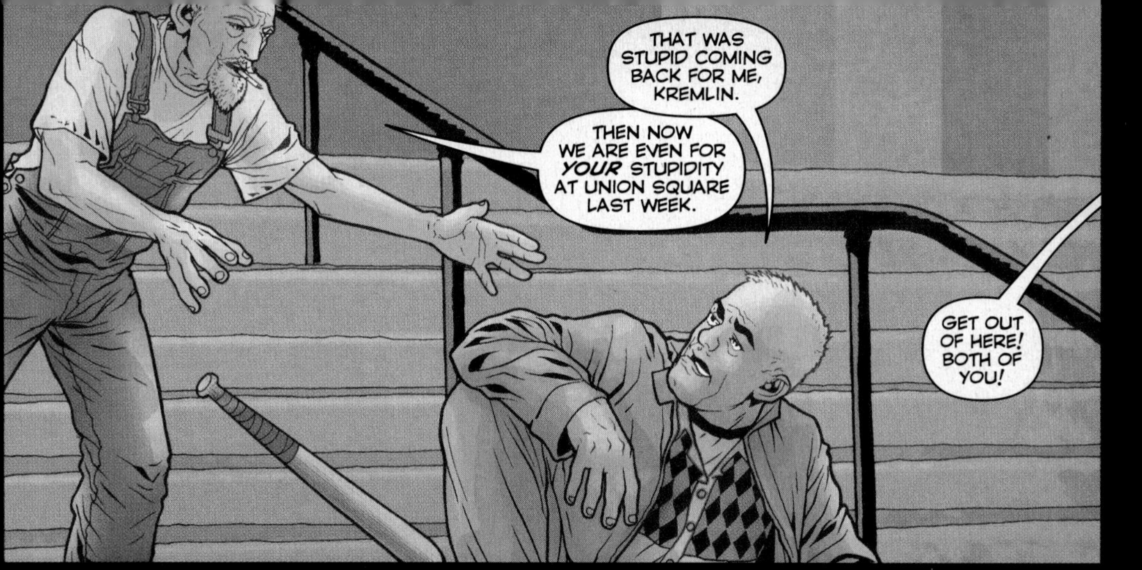
THAT WAS STUPID COMING BACK FOR ME, KREMLIN.
THEN NOW WE ARE EVEN FOR *YOUR* STUPIDITY AT UNION SQUARE LAST WEEK.
GET OUT OF HERE! BOTH OF YOU!

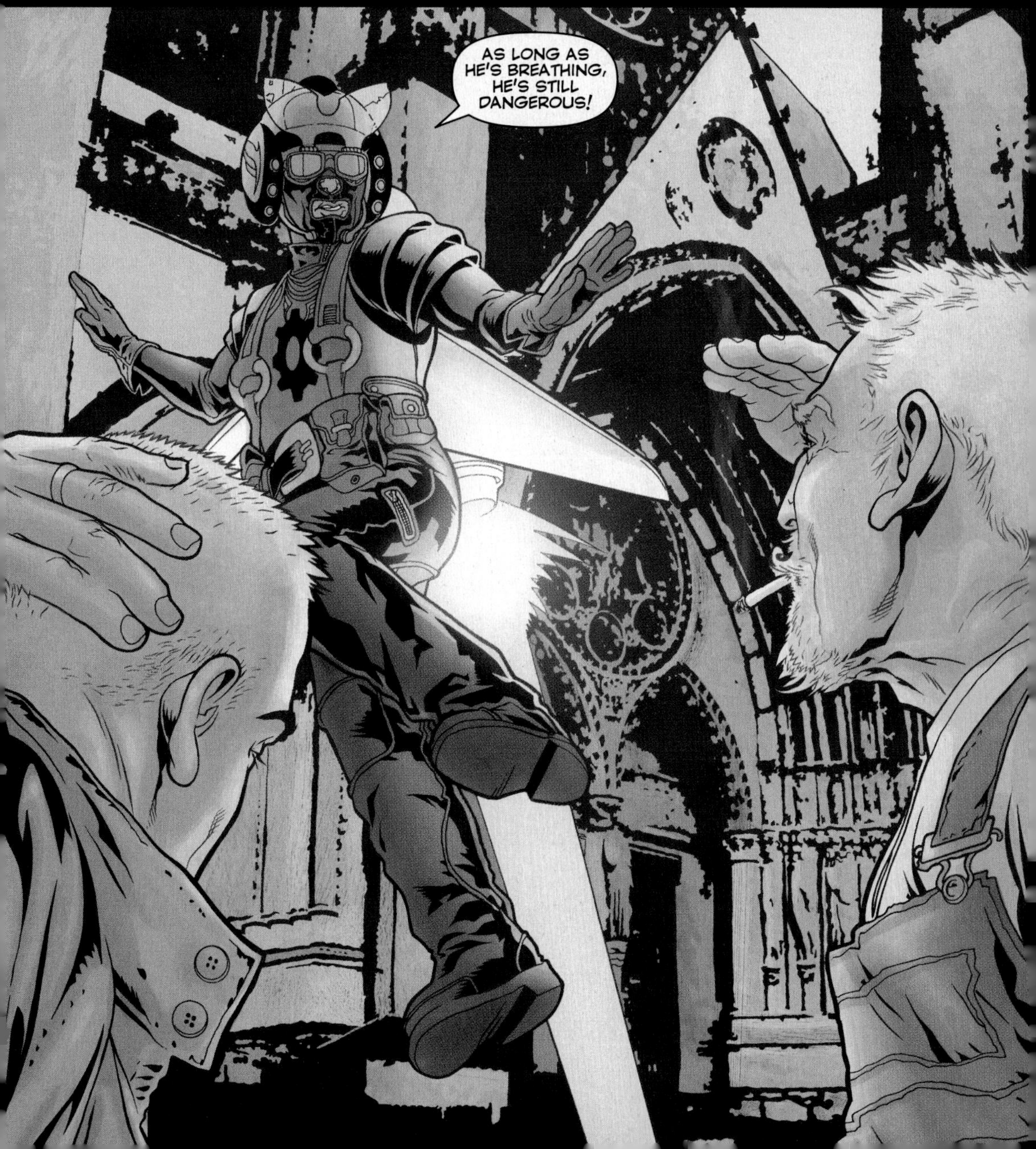
AS LONG AS HE'S BREATHING, HE'S STILL DANGEROUS!

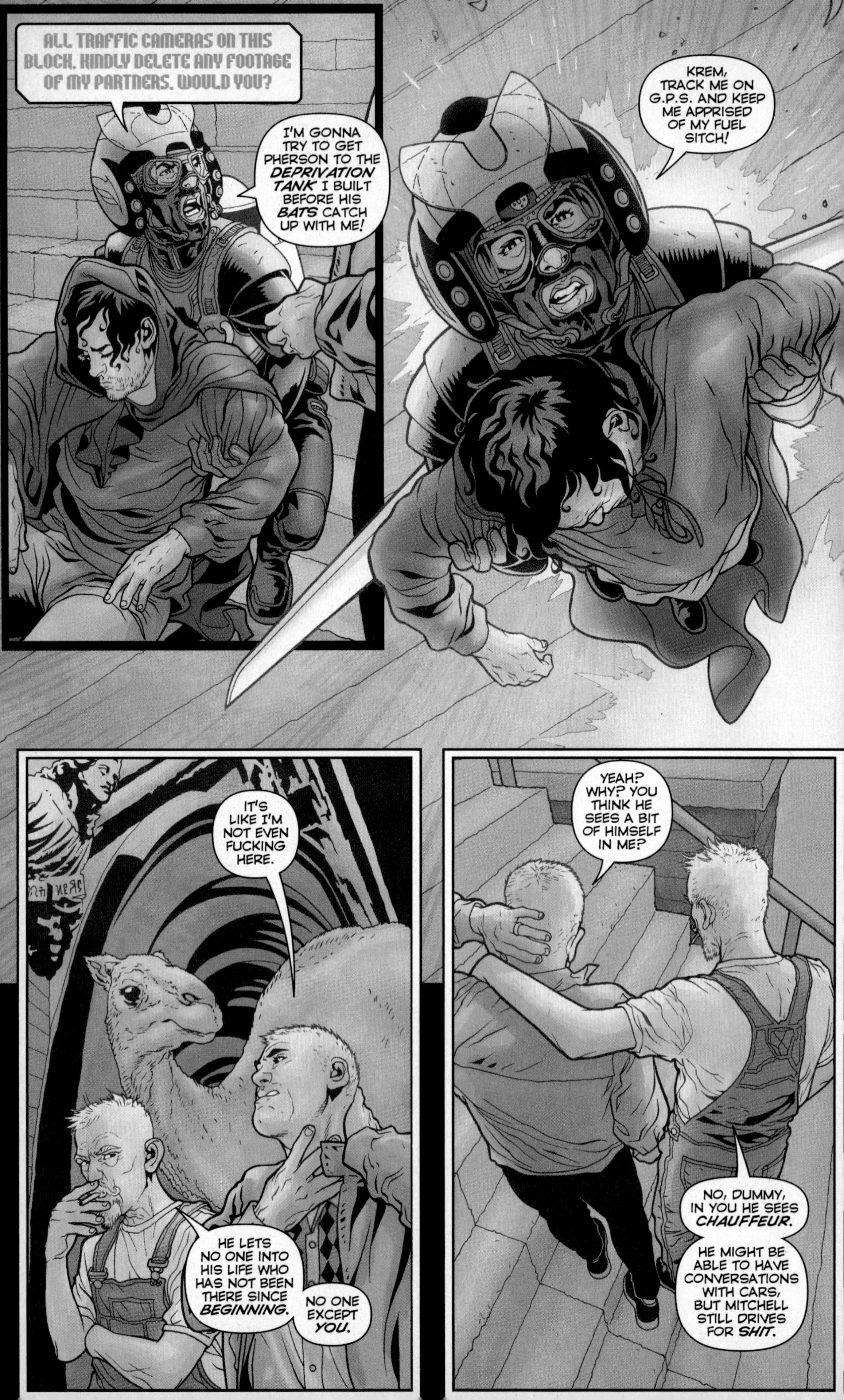
ALL TRAFFIC CAMERAS ON THIS BLOCK, KINDLY DELETE ANY FOOTAGE OF MY PARTNERS, WOULD YOU?
I'M GONNA TRY TO GET PHERSON TO THE *DEPRIVATION TANK* I BUILT BEFORE HIS *BATS* CATCH UP WITH ME!
KREM, TRACK ME ON G.P.S. AND KEEP ME APPRISED OF MY FUEL SITCH!
IT'S LIKE I'M NOT EVEN FUCKING HERE.
HE LETS NO ONE INTO HIS LIFE WHO HAS NOT BEEN THERE SINCE *BEGINNING*.
NO ONE EXCEPT *YOU*.
YEAH? WHY? YOU THINK HE SEES A BIT OF HIMSELF IN ME?
NO, DUMMY, IN YOU HE SEES *CHAUFFEUR*.
HE MIGHT BE ABLE TO HAVE CONVERSATIONS WITH CARS, BUT MITCHELL STILL DRIVES FOR *SHIT*.

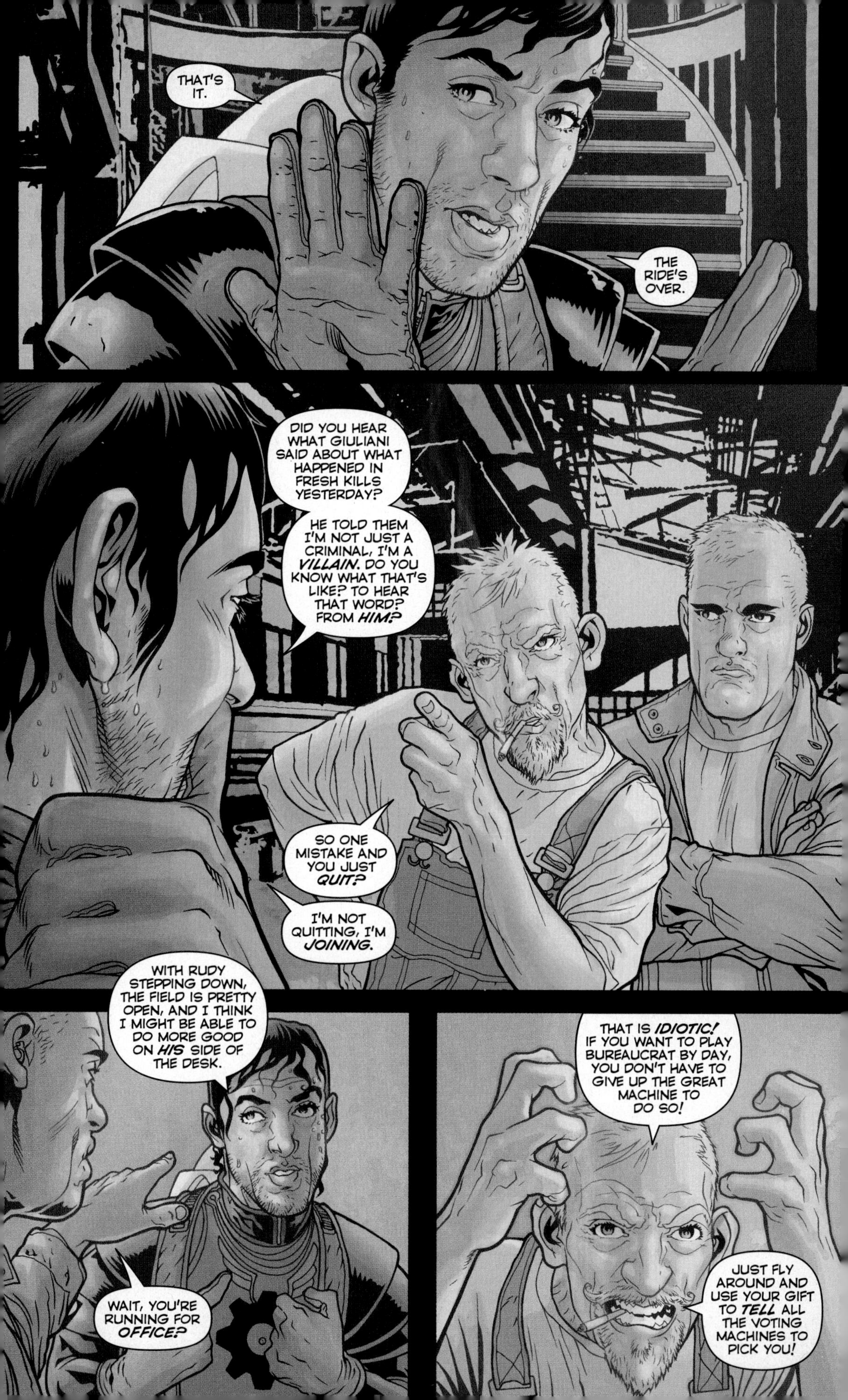
THAT'S IT.
THE RIDE'S OVER.
DID YOU HEAR WHAT GIULIANI SAID ABOUT WHAT HAPPENED IN FRESH KILLS YESTERDAY?
HE TOLD THEM I'M NOT JUST A CRIMINAL, I'M A *VILLAIN*. DO YOU KNOW WHAT THAT'S LIKE? TO HEAR THAT WORD? FROM *HIM*?
SO ONE MISTAKE AND YOU JUST *QUIT*?
I'M NOT QUITTING, I'M *JOINING*.
WITH RUDY STEPPING DOWN, THE FIELD IS PRETTY OPEN, AND I THINK I MIGHT BE ABLE TO DO MORE GOOD ON *HIS* SIDE OF THE DESK.
WAIT, YOU'RE RUNNING FOR *OFFICE*?
THAT IS *IDIOTIC*! IF YOU WANT TO PLAY BUREAUCRAT BY DAY, YOU DON'T HAVE TO GIVE UP THE GREAT MACHINE TO DO SO!
JUST FLY AROUND AND USE YOUR GIFT TO *TELL* ALL THE VOTING MACHINES TO PICK YOU!

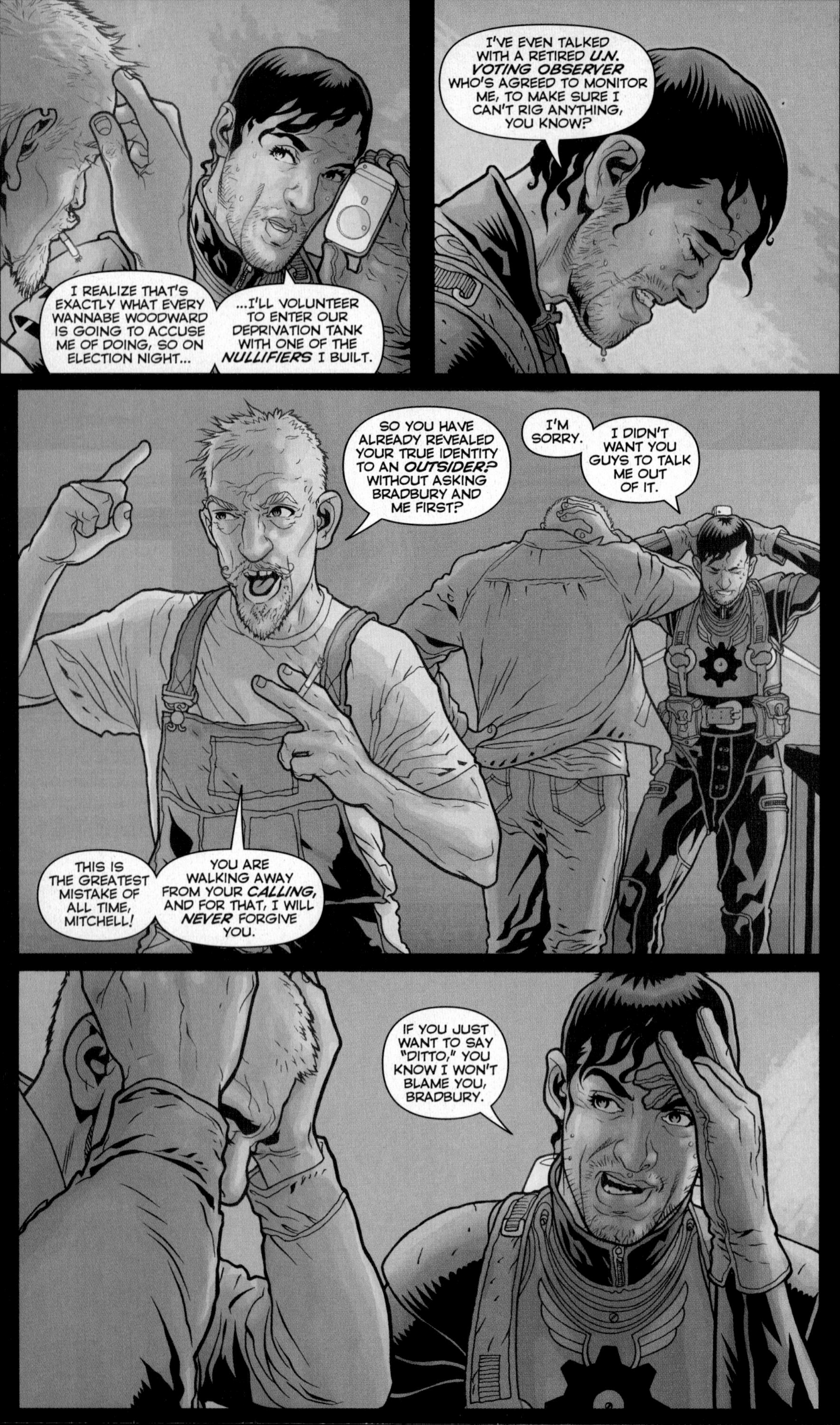
I REALIZE THAT'S EXACTLY WHAT EVERY WANNABE WOODWARD IS GOING TO ACCUSE ME OF DOING, SO ON ELECTION NIGHT...
...I'LL VOLUNTEER TO ENTER OUR DEPRIVATION TANK WITH ONE OF THE NULLIFIERS I BUILT.
I'VE EVEN TALKED WITH A RETIRED U.N. VOTING OBSERVER WHO'S AGREED TO MONITOR ME, TO MAKE SURE I CAN'T RIG ANYTHING, YOU KNOW?
SO YOU HAVE ALREADY REVEALED YOUR TRUE IDENTITY TO AN OUTSIDER? WITHOUT ASKING BRADBURY AND ME FIRST?
I'M SORRY.
I DIDN'T WANT YOU GUYS TO TALK ME OUT OF IT.
THIS IS THE GREATEST MISTAKE OF ALL TIME, MITCHELL!
YOU ARE WALKING AWAY FROM YOUR CALLING, AND FOR THAT, I WILL NEVER FORGIVE YOU.
IF YOU JUST WANT TO SAY "DITTO," YOU KNOW I WON'T BLAME YOU, BRADBURY.

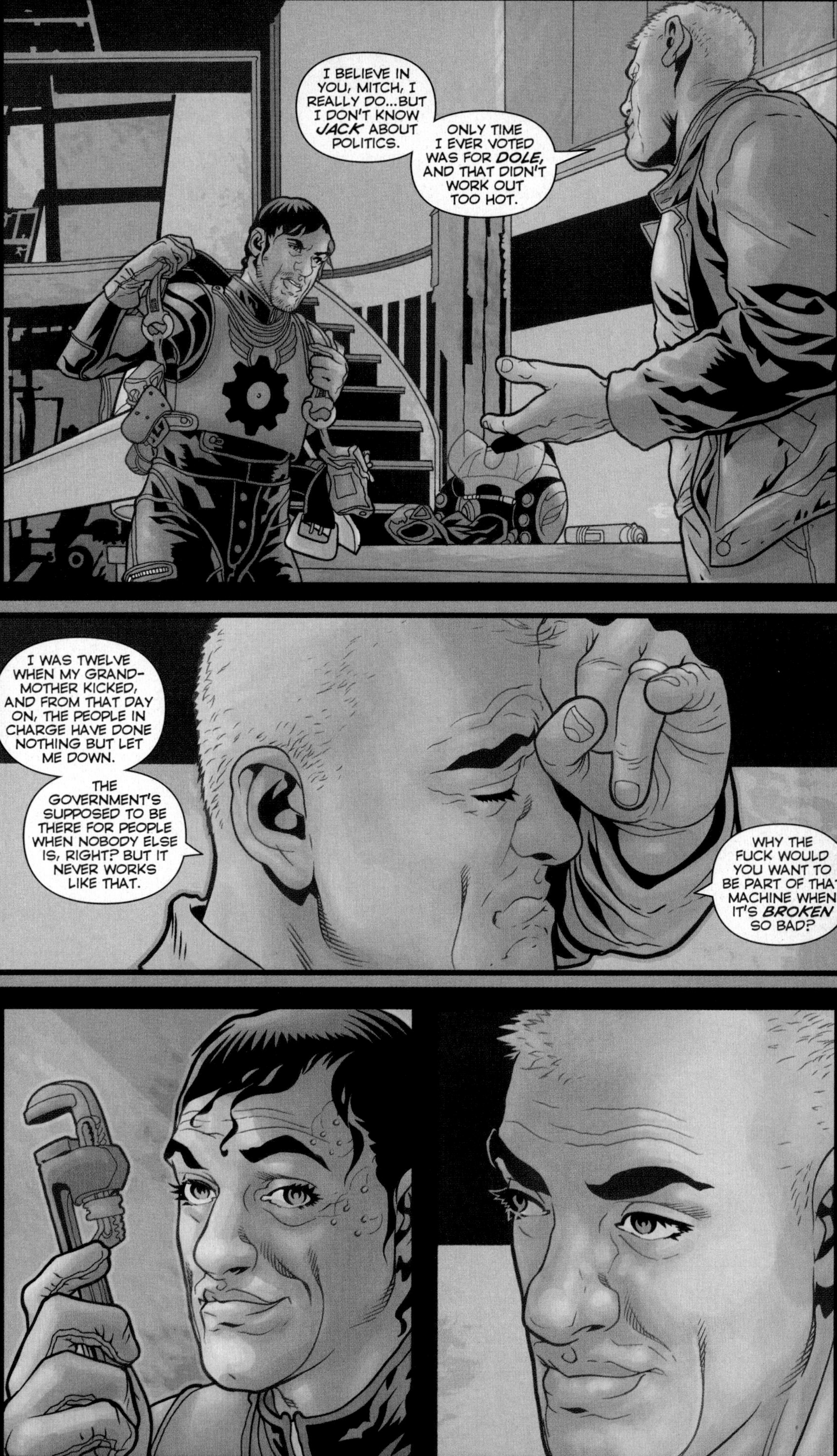
I BELIEVE IN YOU, MITCH, I REALLY DO...BUT I DON'T KNOW *JACK* ABOUT POLITICS.
ONLY TIME I EVER VOTED WAS FOR *DOLE*, AND THAT DIDN'T WORK OUT TOO HOT.
I WAS TWELVE WHEN MY GRAND-MOTHER KICKED, AND FROM THAT DAY ON, THE PEOPLE IN CHARGE HAVE DONE NOTHING BUT LET ME DOWN.
THE GOVERNMENT'S SUPPOSED TO BE THERE FOR PEOPLE WHEN NOBODY ELSE IS, RIGHT? BUT IT NEVER WORKS LIKE THAT.
WHY THE FUCK WOULD YOU WANT TO BE PART OF THAT MACHINE WHEN IT'S *BROKEN* SO BAD?

DON'T DO IT, MAN.

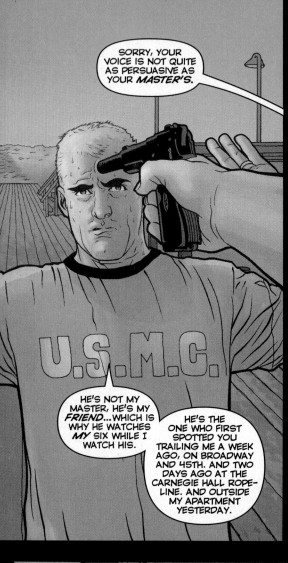

SORRY, YOUR VOICE IS NOT QUITE AS PERSUASIVE AS YOUR *MASTER'S*.

HE'S NOT MY MASTER, HE'S MY *FRIEND*...WHICH IS WHY HE WATCHES *MY* SIX WHILE I WATCH HIS.

HE'S THE ONE WHO FIRST SPOTTED YOU TRAILING ME A WEEK AGO, ON BROADWAY AND 45TH. AND TWO DAYS AGO AT THE CARNEGIE HALL ROPE-LINE. AND OUTSIDE MY APARTMENT YESTERDAY.

WHICH IS WHY HE CALLED HIS BUDDIES IN THE CIA, FBI, NSA, NYPD, AND MORE ACRONYMS THAN A BOWL OF FUCKING *ALPHABET SOUP*...

...AND HAD A DOZEN OF THEIR BEST SNIPERS HELP ME SET UP THIS LITTLE *TRAP*.

...

BULLSHIT.

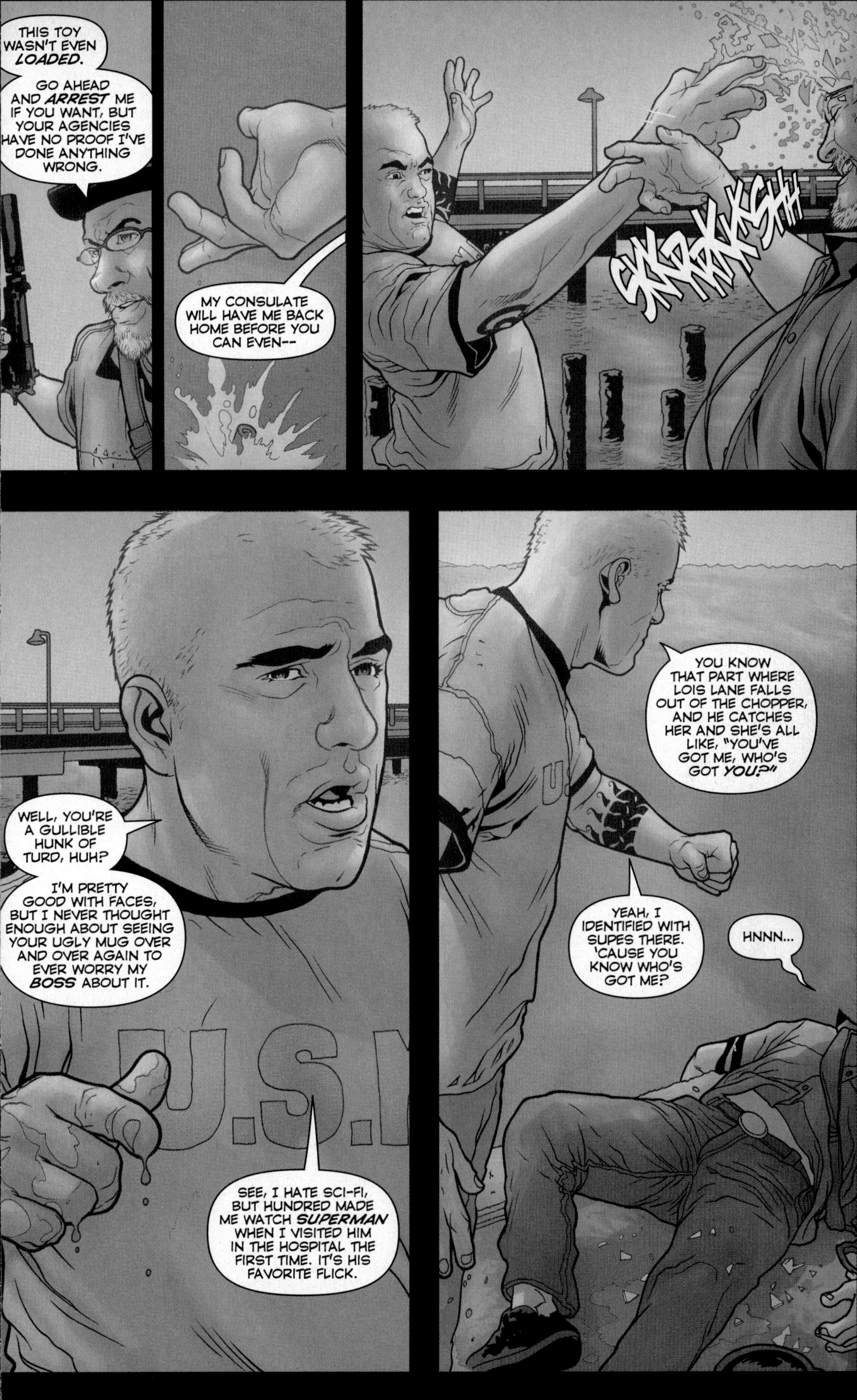
THIS TOY WASN'T EVEN LOADED.
GO AHEAD AND ARREST ME IF YOU WANT, BUT YOUR AGENCIES HAVE NO PROOF I'VE DONE ANYTHING WRONG.
MY CONSULATE WILL HAVE ME BACK HOME BEFORE YOU CAN EVEN--
SKRRKKSHH
WELL, YOU'RE A GULLIBLE HUNK OF TURD, HUH?
I'M PRETTY GOOD WITH FACES, BUT I NEVER THOUGHT ENOUGH ABOUT SEEING YOUR UGLY MUG OVER AND OVER AGAIN TO EVER WORRY MY BOSS ABOUT IT.
SEE, I HATE SCI-FI, BUT HUNDRED MADE ME WATCH SUPERMAN WHEN I VISITED HIM IN THE HOSPITAL THE FIRST TIME. IT'S HIS FAVORITE FLICK.
YOU KNOW THAT PART WHERE LOIS LANE FALLS OUT OF THE CHOPPER, AND HE CATCHES HER AND SHE'S ALL LIKE, "YOU'VE GOT ME, WHO'S GOT YOU?"
YEAH, I IDENTIFIED WITH SUPES THERE. 'CAUSE YOU KNOW WHO'S GOT ME?
HNNN...

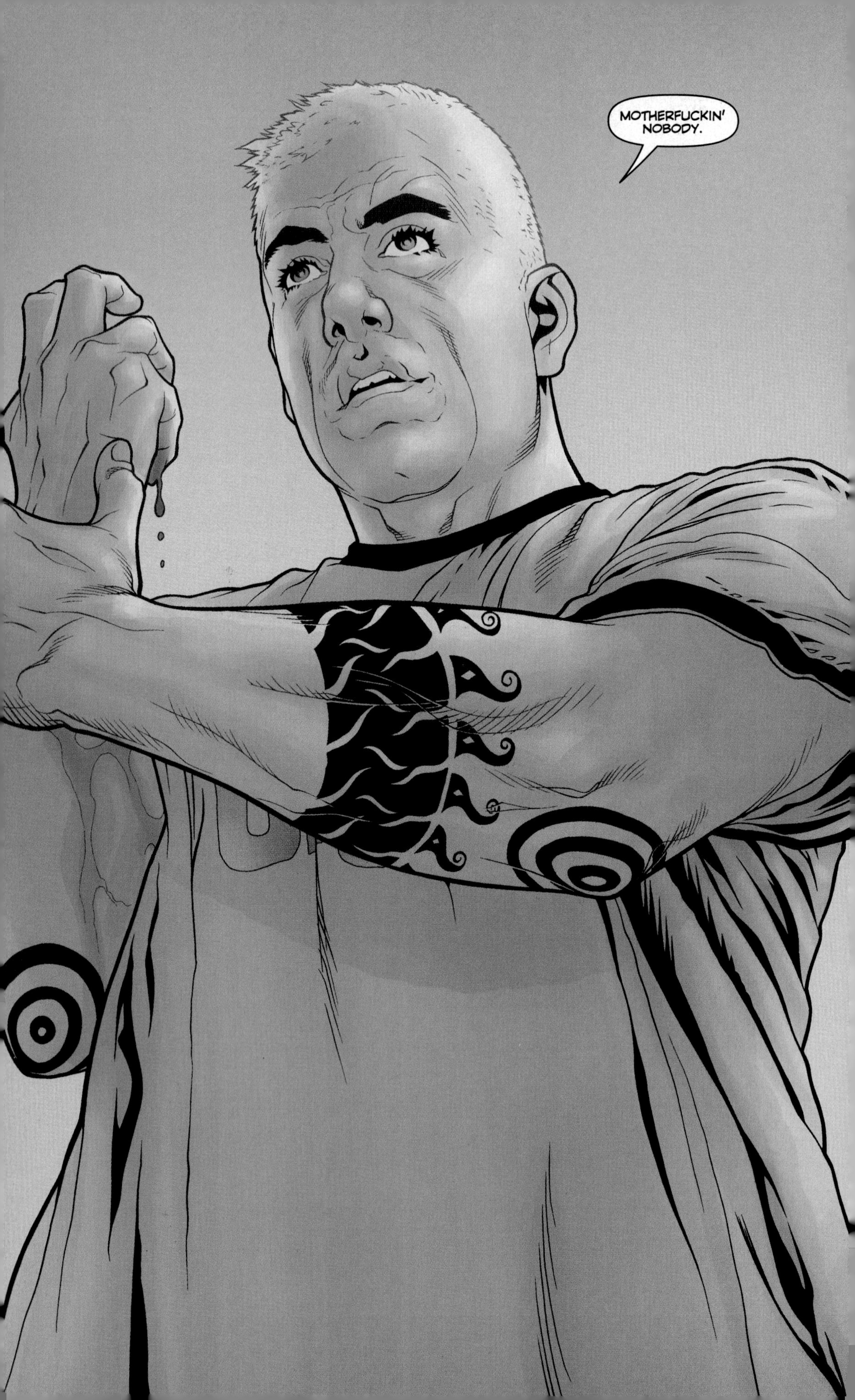
MOTHERFUCKIN' NOBODY.